SCHAUM'S OUTLINE OF

COMPUTER ARCHITECTURE

NICHOLAS CARTER, Ph.D.

Assistant Professor
Electrical and Computer Engineering Department
University of Illinois

Schaum's Outline Series

McGraw-Hill

New York   Chicago   San Francisco   Lisbon   London
Madrid   Mexico City   Milan   New Delhi   San Juan
Seoul   Singapore   Sydney   Toronto

NICHOLAS P. CARTER is an Assistant Professor in the Electrical and Computer Engineering Department at the University of Illinois at Urbana-Champaign. He holds a Ph.D. in Electrical Engineering and Computer Science from the Massachusetts Institute of Technology. His bachelor's and master's degrees are also from that institution. Dr. Carter's research interests are in computer architecture, in particular the interaction of fabrication technology and computer architecture as well as the design of computer systems using non-traditional fabrication technologies. He has received a number of awards, including an AASERT fellowship, and has been named a Collins Scholar by the University of Illinois.

Schaum's Outline of Theory and Problems of
COMPUTER ARCHITECTURE

Copyright © 2002 by The McGraw-Hill Companies, Inc. All rights reserved. Printed in the United States of America. Except as permitted under the United States Copyright Act of 1976, no part of this publication may be reproduced or distributed in any form or by any means, or stored in a data base or retrieval system, without the prior written permission of the publisher.

Product or brand names used in this book may be trade names or trademarks. Where we believe that there may be proprietary claims to such trade names or trademarks, the name has been used with an initial capital or it has been capitalized in the style used by the name claimant. Regardless of the capitalization used, all such names have been used in an editorial manner without any intent to convey endorsement of or other affiliation with the name claimant. Neither the author nor the publisher intends to express any judgment as to the validity or legal status of any such proprietary claims.

9 10 DIG/DIG 10

ISBN 0-07-136207-X

Sponsoring Editor: Barbara Gilson
Production Supervisor: Elizabeth J. Shannon
Editing Supervisor: Maureen B. Walker
Compositor: Techset Composition Limited

Library of Congress Cataloging-in-Publication Data

Carter, Nicholas (Nicholas P.)
    Schaum's outline of computer architecture / Nicholas Carter.
        p. cm. – (Schaum's outline series)
    ISBN 0-07-136207-X (pbk.)
    1. Computer architecture. I. Title

QA76.9.A73 C38 2001
004.2′2–dc21   2001052142

McGraw-Hill

A Division of The McGraw-Hill Companies

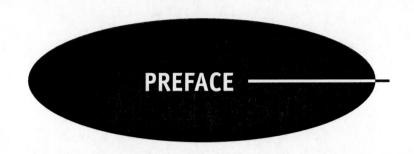

PREFACE

One of the most interesting aspects of computer architecture is the rate at which the field changes. Innovation occurs on an almost-daily basis, offering opportunities for individuals to contribute to the field. However, this rate of progress is one of the greatest challenges to teaching computer architecture and organization. Unlike many other fields, courses in computer architecture and organization must change on a term-by-term basis to incorporate new developments in the field without overloading students with material. Writing textbooks for the field is similarly difficult, as the author must find a balance between cutting-edge material and historical perspective.

This book includes a selection of topics intended to make it useful to readers with a wide range of previous exposure to the field. Chapters 1 through 5 cover many of the basic concepts in computer organization, including how performance is measured, how computers represent numerical data and programs, different programming models for computers, and the basics of processor design. Chapters 6 and 7 cover pipelining and instruction-level parallelism, two technologies that are extremely important to the performance of modern processors. Chapters 8, 9, and 10 cover memory system design, including memory hierarchies, caches, and virtual memory. Chapter 11 describes I/O systems, while Chapter 12 provides an introduction to multiprocessor systems—computers that combine multiple processors to deliver improved performance.

It is my hope that readers will find this book useful in their study of the field. I have tried to make my explanations of each topic as clear as possible and to avoid getting bogged down in detail. Compressing the field of computer architecture and organization into a book this size was a challenge, and I look forward to any comments that readers may have about the selection of material, the exercises, or anything else related to this work.

In conclusion, I would like to thank all those who have made this effort possible: my parents, my friends, my colleagues at the University of Illinois, and all of the teachers who contributed to my own education. In addition, I would like to thank the staff at McGraw-Hill for encouraging this work and for their tolerance of schedule delays.

NICHOLAS P. CARTER

CONTENTS

CHAPTER 1

Introduction

1.1 Purpose of This Book

This book is intended for use as a companion text for advanced undergraduate-level or introductory graduate-level courses in computer architecture. Its primary intended audience is students and faculty involved in computer architecture courses who are interested in additional explanations, practice problems, and examples to use in increasing their understanding of the material or in preparing assignments.

1.2 Background Assumed

This book assumes that the reader has a background similar to that of college sophomores or juniors in electrical engineering or computer science programs who have not yet had a course on computer organization or computer architecture. Basic familiarity with computer operation and terminology is assumed, as is some familiarity with programming in high-level languages.

1.3 Material Covered

This book covers a slightly wider range of topics than most one-term computer architecture courses in order to increase its utility. Readers may find the additional material useful as review or as an introduction to more advanced topics. The book begins with a discussion of data representation and computer arithmetic, followed by chapters on computer organization and programming models. Chapter 5 begins a three-chapter discussion of processor design, including pipelining and instruction-level parallelism. This is followed by three chapters on memory systems, including coverage of virtual memory and caches. The final two chapters discuss I/O and provide an introduction to multiprocessors.

1.4   Chapter Objectives

The goal of this chapter is to prepare the reader for the material in later chapters by discussing the basic technologies that drive computer performance and the techniques used to measure and discuss performance. After reading this chapter and completing the exercises, a student should

1. Understand and be able to discuss the historical rates of improvement in transistor density, circuit performance, and overall system performance
2. Understand common methods of evaluating computer performance
3. Be able to calculate how changes to one part of a computer system will affect overall performance

1.5   Technological Trends

Since the early 1980s, computer performance has been driven by improvements in the capabilities of the integrated circuits used to implement microprocessors, memory chips, and other computer components. Over time, integrated circuits improve in *density* (how many transistors and wires can be placed in a fixed area on a silicon chip), *speed* (how quickly basic logic gates and memory devices operate), and *area* (the physical size of the largest integrated circuit that can be fabricated).

The tremendous growth in computer performance over the last two decades has been driven by the fact that chip speed and density improve *geometrically* rather than linearly, meaning that the increase in performance from one year to the next has been a relatively constant fraction of the previous year's performance, rather than a constant absolute value. On average, the number of transistors that can be fabricated on a silicon chip increases by about 50 percent per year, and transistor speed increases such that the delay of a basic logic gate (AND, OR, etc.) decreases by 13 percent per year. The observation that computer performance improves geometrically, not linearly, is often referred to as *Moore's Law*.

> **EXAMPLE**
> The amount of data that can be stored on a dynamic RAM (DRAM) memory chip has quadrupled every three years since the late 1970s, an annual growth rate of 60 percent.

From the late 1970s until the late 1980s, microprocessor performance was mainly driven by improvements in fabrication technology and improved at a rate of 35 percent per year. Since then, the rate of improvement has actually increased, to over 50 percent per year, although the rate of progress in semiconductor fabrication has remained relatively constant. The increase in the rate of performance improvement has been due to improvements in computer architecture and organization—computer architects have been able to take advantage of the increasing density of integrated circuits to add features to microprocessors and memory systems that improve performance over and above the improvements in speed of the underlying transistors.

1.6   Measuring Performance

In this chapter, we have discussed how computer performance has improved over time, without giving a formal definition of what performance is. In part, this is because *performance* is a very vague term when used in the context of computer systems. Generally, performance describes how quickly a given system can execute a program or programs. Systems that execute programs in less time are said to have higher performance.

The best measure of computer performance is the execution time of the program or programs that the user wants to execute, but it is generally impractical to test all of the programs that will be run on a given system before deciding which computer to purchase or when making design decisions. Instead, computer architects have come up with a variety of metrics to describe computer performance, some of which will be discussed in this chapter. Architects have also devised a number of metrics for the performance of individual computer subsystems, which will be discussed in the chapters that cover those subsystems.

Keep in mind that many factors other than performance may influence design or purchase decisions. Ease of programming is an important consideration, because the time and expense required to develop needed programs may be more significant than the difference in execution times of the programs once they have been developed. Also important is the issue of compatibility; most programs are sold as binary images that will only run on a particular family of processors. If the program you need won't run on a given system, it doesn't matter how quickly the system executes other programs.

1.6.1 MIPS

An early measure of computer performance was the rate at which a given machine executed instructions. This is calculated by dividing the number of instructions executed in running a program by the time required to run the program and is typically expressed in *millions of instructions per second* (MIPS). MIPS has fallen out of use as a measure of performance, mainly because it does not account for the fact that different systems often require different numbers of instructions to implement a given program. A computer's MIPS rating does not tell you anything about how many instructions it requires to perform a given task, making it less useful than other metrics for comparing the performance of different systems.

1.6.2 CPI/IPC

Another metric used to describe computer performance is the number of clock cycles required to execute each instruction, known as *cycles per instruction*, or CPI. The CPI of a given program on a given system is calculated by dividing the number of clock cycles required to execute the program by the number of instructions executed in running the program. For systems that can execute more than one instruction per cycle, the number of *instructions executed per cycle*, or IPC, is often used instead of CPI. IPC is calculated by dividing the number of instructions executed in running a program by the number of clock cycles required to execute the program, and is the reciprocal of CPI. These two metrics give the same information, and the choice of which one to use is generally made based on which of the values is greater than the number 1. When using IPC and CPI to compare systems, it is important to remember that high IPC values indicate that the reference program took fewer cycles to execute than low IPC values, while high CPI values indicate that more cycles were required than low CPI values. Thus, a large IPC tends to indicate good performance, while a large CPI indicates poor performance.

EXAMPLE

A given program consists of a 100-instruction loop that is executed 42 times. If it takes 16,000 cycles to execute the program on a given system, what are that system's CPI and IPC values for the program?

Solution

The 100-instruction loop is executed 42 times, so the total number of instructions executed is $100 \times 42 = 4200$. It takes 16,000 cycles to execute the program, so the CPI is $16,000/4200 = 3.81$. To compute the IPC, we divide 4200 instructions by 16,000 cycles, getting an IPC of 0.26.

In general, IPC and CPI are even less useful measures of actual system performance than MIPS, because they do not contain any information about a system's clock rate or how many instructions the system requires to perform a task. If you know a system's MIPS rating on a given program, you can multiply it by the number of instructions executed in running the program to determine how long the program took to complete. If you know a system's CPI on a given program, you can multiply it by the number of instructions in the program to get the number of cycles it took to complete the program, but you have to know the number of cycles per second (the system's clock rate) to convert that into the amount of time required to execute the program.

As a result, CPI and IPC are rarely used to compare actual computer systems. However, they are very common metrics in computer architecture research, because most computer architecture research is done in simulation, using programs that simulate a particular architecture to estimate how many cycles a given program will take to execute on that architecture. These simulators are generally unable to predict the cycle time of the systems that they simulate, so CPI/IPC is often the best available estimate of performance.

1.6.3 BENCHMARK SUITES

Both MIPS and CPI/IPC have significant limitations as measures of computer performance, as we have discussed. *Benchmark suites* are a third measure of computer performance and were developed to address the limitations of MIPS and CPI/IPC.

A benchmark suite consists of a set of programs that are believed to be typical of the programs that will be run on the system. A system's score on the benchmark suite is based on how long it takes the system to execute all of the programs in the suite. Many different benchmark suites exist that generate estimates of a system's performance on different types of applications.

One of the best-known benchmark suites is the SPEC suite, produced by the Standard Performance Evaluation Corporation. The current version of the SPEC suite as of the publication of this book is the SPEC CPU2000 benchmark, the third major revision since the first SPEC benchmark suite was published in 1989.

Benchmark suites provide a number of advantages over MIPS and CPI/IPC. First, their performance results are based on total execution times, not rate of instruction execution. Second, they average a system's performance across multiple programs to generate an estimate of its average speed. This makes a system's overall rating on a benchmark suite a better indicator of its overall performance than its MIPS rating on any one program. Also, many benchmarks require manufacturers to publish their systems' results on the individual programs within the benchmark, as well as the system's overall score on the benchmark suite, making it possible to do a direct comparison of individual benchmark results if you know that a system will be used for a particular application.

1.6.4 GEOMETRIC VERSUS ARITHMETIC MEAN

Many benchmark suites use the *geometric* rather than the *arithmetic* mean to average the results of the programs contained in the benchmark suite, because a single extreme value has less of an impact on the geometric mean of a series than on the arithmetic mean. Using the geometric mean makes it harder for a system to achieve a high score on the benchmark suite by achieving good performance on just one of the programs in the suite, making the system's overall score a better indicator of its performance on most programs.

The geometric mean of n values is calculated by multiplying the n values together and taking the nth root of the product. The arithmetic mean, or average, of a set of values is calculated by adding all of the values together and dividing by the number of values.

EXAMPLE
What are the arithmetic and geometric means of the values 4, 2, 4, 82?

Solution

The arithmetic mean of this series is

$$\frac{4 + 2 + 4 + 82}{4} = 23$$

The geometric mean is

$$\sqrt[4]{4 \times 2 \times 4 \times 82} = 7.16$$

Note that the inclusion of one extreme value in the series had a much greater effect on the arithmetic mean than on the geometric mean.

1.7 Speedup

Computer architects often use the term *speedup* to describe how the performance of an architecture changes as different improvements are made to the architecture. Speedup is simply the ratio of the execution times before and after a change is made, so:

$$Speedup = \frac{Execution\ time_{before}}{Execution\ time_{after}}$$

For example, if a program takes 25 seconds to run on one version of an architecture and 15 seconds to run on a new version, the overall speedup is 25 seconds/15 seconds = 1.67.

1.8 Amdahl's Law

The most important rule for designing high-performance computer systems is *make the common case fast*. Qualitatively, this means that the impact of a given performance improvement on overall performance is dependent on both how much the improvement improves performance when it is in use and how often the improvement is in use. Quantitatively, this rule has been expressed as *Amdahl's Law*, which states

$$Execution\ Time_{new} = Execution\ Time_{old} \times \left[Frac_{unused} + \frac{Frac_{used}}{Speedup_{used}} \right]$$

In this equation, $Frac_{unused}$ is the fraction of time (not instructions) that the improvement is not in use, $Frac_{used}$ is the fraction of time that the improvement is in use, and $Speedup_{used}$ is the speedup that occurs when the improvement is used (this would be the overall speedup if the improvement were in use at all times). Note that $Frac_{used}$ and $Frac_{unused}$ are computed using the execution time *before* the modification is applied. Computing these values using the execution time after the modification is applied will give incorrect results.

Amdahl's Law can be rewritten using the definition of speedup to give

$$\text{Speedup} = \frac{\text{Execution Time}_{old}}{\text{Execution Time}_{new}} = \frac{1}{\text{Frac}_{unused} + \dfrac{\text{Frac}_{used}}{\text{Speedup}_{used}}}$$

EXAMPLE

Suppose that a given architecture does not have hardware support for multiplication, so multiplications have to be done through repeated addition (this was the case on some early microprocessors). If it takes 200 cycles to perform a multiplication in software, and 4 cycles to perform a multiplication in hardware, what is the overall speedup from hardware support for multiplication if a program spends 10 percent of its time doing multiplications? What about a program that spends 40 percent of its time doing multiplications?

In both cases, the speedup when the multiplication hardware is used is $200/4 = 50$ (ratio of time to do a multiplication without the hardware to time with the hardware). In the case where the program spends 10 percent of its time doing multiplications, $\text{Frac}_{unused} = 0.9$, and $\text{Frac}_{used} = 0.1$. Plugging these values into Amdhal's Law, we get Speedup $= 1/[.9 + (.1/50)] = 1.11$. If the program spends 40 percent of its time doing multiplications before the addition of hardware multiplication, then $\text{Frac}_{unused} = 0.6$, $\text{Frac}_{used} = 0.4$, and we get Speedup $= 1/[.6 + (.4/50)] = 1.64$.

This example illustrates the impact that the fraction of time an improvement is used has on overall performance. As Speedup_{used} goes to infinity, overall speedup converges to $1/\text{Frac}_{unused}$, because the improvement can't do anything about the execution time of the fraction of the program that does not use the improvement.

1.9 Summary

This chapter has been intended to provide a context for the rest of the book by explaining some of the technology forces that drive computer performance and providing a framework for discussing and evaluating system performance that will be used throughout the book.

The important concepts for the reader to understand after studying this chapter are as follows:

1. Computer technology is driven by improvements in semiconductor fabrication technology, and these improvements proceed at a geometric, rather than a linear, pace.
2. There are many ways to measure computer performance, and the most effective measures of overall performance are based on the performance of a system on a wide variety of applications.
3. It is important to understand how a given performance metric is generated

in order to understand how useful it is in predicting system performance on a given application.

4. The impact of a change to an architecture on overall performance is dependent not only on how much that change improves performance when it is used, but on how often the change is useful. A consequence of this is that the overall performance impact of an improvement is limited by the fraction of time that the improvement is not in use, regardless of how much speedup the improvement gives when it is useful.

 ## Solved Problems

Technology Trends (I)

1.1.   As an illustration of just how fast computer technology is improving, let's consider what would have happened if automobiles had improved equally quickly. Assume that an average car in 1977 had a top speed of 100 miles per hour (mi/h, an approximation) and an average fuel economy of 15 miles per gallon (mi/g). If both top speed and efficiency improved at 35 percent per year from 1977 to 1987, and by 50 percent per year from 1987 to 2000, tracking computer performance, what would the average top speed and fuel economy of a car be in 1987? In 2000?

Solution

In 1987:

The span 1977 to 1987 is 10 years, so both traits would have improved by a factor of $(1.35)^{10} = 20.1$, giving a top speed of 2010 mi/h and a fuel economy of 301.5 mi/g.

In 2000:

Thirteen more years elapse, this time at a 50 percent per year improvement rate, for a total factor of $(1.5)^{13} = 194.6$ over the 1987 values. This gives a top speed of 391,146 mi/h and a fuel economy of 58,672 mi/g. This is fast enough to cover the distance from the earth to the moon in under 40 min, and to make the round trip on less than 10 gal of gasoline.

Technology Trends (II)

1.2.   Since 1987, computer performance has been increasing at about 50 percent per year, with improvements in fabrication technology accounting for about 35 percent per year and improvements in architecture accounting for about 15 percent per year.

1. If the performance of the best available computer on 1/01/1988 was defined to be 1, what would be the expected performance of the best available computer on 1/01/2001?

2. Suppose that there had been no improvements in computer architecture since 1987, making fabrication technology the only source of performance improvements. What would the expected performance of the best available computer on 1/01/2001 be?

3. Now suppose that there had been no improvements in fabrication technology, making improvements in architecture the only source of performance improvements. What would the expected performance of the fastest computer on 1/01/2001 be then?

Solution

1. Performance improves at 50 percent per year, and 1/01/1988 to 1/01/2001 is 13 years, so the expected performance of the 1/01/2001 machine is $1 \times (1.5)^{13} = 194.6$.

2. Here, performance only improves at 35 percent per year, so the expected performance is 49.5.

3. Performance improvement is 15 percent per year, giving an expected performance of 6.2.

Speedup (I)

1.3.   If the 1998 version of a computer executes a program in 200 s and the version of the computer made in the year 2000 executes the same program in 150 s, what is the speedup that the manufacturer has achieved over the two-year period?

Solution

$$\text{Speedup} = \frac{\text{Execution time}_{before}}{\text{Execution time}_{after}}$$

Given this, the speedup is $200\,s/150\,s = 1.33$. Clearly, this manufacturer is falling well short of the industrywide performance growth rate.

Speedup (II)

1.4.   To achieve a speedup of 3 on a program that originally took 78 s to execute, what must the execution time of the program be reduced to?

Solution

Here, we have values for speedup and Execution time$_{before}$. Substituting these into the formula for speedup and solving for Execution time$_{after}$ tells us that the execution time must be reduced to 26 s to achieve a speedup of 3.

Measuring Performance (I)

1.5.   1.   Why are benchmark programs and benchmark suites used to measure computer performance?

2.   Why are there multiple benchmarks that are used by computer architects, instead of one "best" benchmark?

Solution

1.   Computer systems are often used to run a wide range of programs, some of which may not exist at the time the system is purchased or built. Thus, it is generally not possible to measure a system's performance on the set of programs that will be run on the machine. Instead, benchmark programs and suites are used to measure the performance of a system on one or

more applications that are believed to be representative of the set of programs that will be run on the machine.

2. Multiple benchmark programs/suites exist because computers are used for a wide range of applications, the performance of which can depend on very different aspects of the computer system. For example, the performance of database and transaction-processing applications tends to depend strongly on the performance of a computer's input/output subsystem. In contrast, scientific computing applications depend mainly on the performance of a system's processor and memory system. Like applications, benchmark suites vary in terms of the amount of stress they place on each of the computer's subsystems, and it is important to use a benchmark that stresses the same subsystems as the intended applications; using a processor-intensive benchmark to evaluate computers intended for transaction processing would not give a good estimate of the rate at which these systems could process transactions.

Measuring Performance (II)

1.6. When running a particular program, computer A achieves 100 MIPS and computer B achieves 75 MIPS. However, computer A takes 60 s to execute the program, while computer B takes only 45 s. How is this possible?

Solution

MIPS measures the rate at which a processor executes instructions, but different processor architectures require different numbers of instructions to perform a given computation. If computer A had to execute significantly more instructions than computer B to complete the program, it would be possible for computer A to take longer to run the program than processor B despite the fact that computer A executes more instructions per second.

Measuring Performance (III)

1.7. Computer C achieves a score of 42 on a benchmark suite (higher scores are better), while computer D's score is 35 on the same benchmark. When running your program, you find that computer C takes 20 percent longer to run the program than computer D. How is this possible?

Solution

The most likely explanation is that your program is highly dependent on an aspect of the system that is not stressed by the benchmark suite. For example, your program might perform a large number of floating-point calculations, while the benchmark suite emphasized integer performance, or vice versa.

CPI

1.8. When run on a given system, a program takes 1,000,000 cycles. If the system achieves a CPI of 40, how many instructions were executed in running the program?

Solution

CPI = #Cycles/#Instructions. Therefore, #Instructions = #Cycles/CPI. 1,000,000 cycles/40 CPI = 25,000. So, 25,000 instructions were executed in running the program.

IPC

1.9. What is the IPC of a program that executes 35,000 instructions and requires 17,000 cycles to complete?

Solution

IPC = #Instructions/#Cycles, so the IPC of this program is 35,000 instructions/17,000 cycles = 2.06.

Geometric versus Arithmetic Mean

1.10. Given the following set of individual benchmark scores for each of the programs in the integer portion of the SPEC2000 benchmark, compute the arithmetic and geometric means of each set. Note that these scores do not represent an actual set of measurements taken on a machine. They were selected to illustrate the impact that using a different method to calculate the mean value has on benchmark scores.

Benchmark	Score Before Improvement	Score After Improvement
1.64.gzip	10	12
175.vpr	14	16
176.gcc	23	28
181.mcf	36	40
186.crafty	9	12
197.parser	12	120
252.eon	25	28
253.perlbmk	18	21
254.gap	30	28
255.vortex	17	21
256.bzip2	7	10
300.twolf	38	42

Solution

There are 12 benchmarks in the suite, so the arithmetic mean is computed by adding together all of the values in each set and dividing by 12, while the geometric mean is calculated by taking the 12th root of the product of all of the values in a set. This gives the following values:

Before improvement: Arithmetic Mean = 19.92. Geometric Mean = 17.39
After improvement: Arithmetic Mean = 31.5. Geometric Mean = 24.42

What we see from this is that the arithmetic mean is much more sensitive to large changes in one of the values in the set than the geometric mean. Most of the individual benchmarks see relatively small changes as we add the improvement to the architecture, but 197.parser improves by a factor of 10. This causes the arithmetic mean to increase by almost 60 percent, while the geometric mean increases by only 40 percent. This reduced sensitivity to individual values is why benchmarking experts prefer the geometric mean for averaging the results of multiple benchmarks, since one very good or very bad result in the set of benchmarks has less of an impact on the overall score.

Amdahl's Law (I)

1.11. Suppose a computer spends 90 percent of its time handling a particular type of computation when running a given program, and its manufacturers make a change that improves its performance on that type of computation by a factor of 10.

1. If the program originally took 100 s to execute, what will its execution time be after the change?
2. What is the speedup from the old system to the new system?
3. What fraction of its execution time does the new system spend executing the type of computation that was improved?

Solution

1. This is a direct application of Amdahl's Law:

$$\text{Execution Time}_{new} = \text{Execution Time}_{old} \times \left[\text{Frac}_{unused} + \frac{\text{Frac}_{used}}{\text{Speedup}_{used}} \right]$$

Execution Time$_{old}$ = 100 s, Frac$_{used}$ = 0.9, Frac$_{unused}$ = 0.1, and Speedup$_{used}$ = 10. This gives an Execution Time$_{new}$ of 19 s.

2. Using the definition of speedup, we get a speedup of 5.3. Alternately, we could substitute the values from part 1 into the speedup version of Amdahl's Law to get the same result.

3. Amdahl's Law doesn't give us a direct way to answer this question. The original system spent 90 percent of its time executing the type of computation that was improved, so it spent 90 s of a 100-s program executing that type of computation. Since the computation was improved by a factor of 10, the improved system spends 90/10 = 9 s executing that type of computation. Because 9 s is 47 percent of 19 s, the new execution time, the new system spends 47 percent of its time executing the type of computation that was improved.

   Alternately, we could have calculated the time that the original system spent executing computations that weren't improved (10 s). Since these computations weren't changed when the improvement was made, the amount of time spent executing them in the new system is the same as the old system. This could then be used to compute the percent of time spent on computations that weren't improved, and the percent of time spent on computations that were improved generated by subtracting that from 100.

Amdahl's Law (II)

1.12. A computer spends 30 percent of its time accessing memory, 20 percent performing multiplications, and 50 percent executing other instructions. As a computer architect, you have to choose between improving either the memory, multiplication hardware, or execution of nonmultiplication instructions. There is only space on the chip for one improvement, and each of the improvements will improve its associated part of the computation by a factor of 2.

1. Without performing any calculations, which improvement would you expect to give the largest performance increase, and why?
2. What speedup would making each of the three changes give?

Solution

1. Improving the execution of nonmultiplication instructions should give the greatest benefit. Each benefit increases the performance of its affected area by the same amount, and the system spends more time executing nonmultiplication instructions than either of the other categories. Since Amdahl's Law says that the overall impact of an improvement goes up as the fraction of time the improvement is used goes up, improving nonmultiplication instructions should give the greatest improvement.

2. Substituting the percentage of time used and improvement when used values into the speedup form of Amdahl's Law shows that improving the memory system gives a speedup of 1.18, improving multiplication gives a speedup of 1.11, and improving the nonmultiplication instructions gives a speedup of 1.33, confirming the intuition from part 1.

Comparing Different Changes to an Architecture

1.13. Which improvement gives a greater reduction in execution time: one that is used 20 percent of the time but improves performance by a factor of 2 when used, or one that is used 70 percent of the time but only improves performance by a factor of 1.3 when used?

Solution

Applying Amdahl's Law, we get the following equation for the first improvement:

$$\text{Execution Time}_{new} = \text{Execution Time}_{old} \times \left[.8 + \frac{.2}{2} \right]$$

So the execution time with the first improvement is 90 percent of the execution time without the improvement. Plugging the values for the second improvement into Amdahl's Law shows that the execution time with the second improvement is 84 percent of the execution time without the improvement. Thus, the second improvement will have a greater impact on overall execution time despite the fact that it gives less of an improvement when it is in use.

Converting Individual Improvements to Overall Performance Impact

1.14. A computer architect is designing the memory system for the next version of a processor. If the current version of the processor spends 40 percent of its time processing memory references, by how much must the architect speed up the memory system to achieve an overall speedup of 1.2? A speedup of 1.6?

Solution

To solve this, we apply Amdahl's Law for speedups, with Speedup_{used} as the unknown, rather than overall Speedup. Frac_{used} is 0.4, since the original system spends 40 percent of its time handling memory references, so Frac_{unused} is 0.6. For the 20 percent increase in overall performance, this gives:

$$\text{Speedup} = 1.2 = \frac{1}{.6 + \dfrac{.4}{\text{Speedup}_{used}}}$$

Solving for Speedup$_{used}$, we get

$$\text{Speedup}_{used} = \frac{.4}{\dfrac{1}{1.2} - .6} = 1.71$$

To find the value of Speedup$_{used}$ required to give a speedup of 1.6, the only value that changes in the above equation is Speedup. Solving again, we get Speedup$_{used} = 16$. Here we again see the diminishing returns that come from repeatedly improving only one aspect of a system's performance. To increase the overall speedup from 1.2 to 1.6, we have to increase Speedup$_{used}$ by almost a factor of 10, because the 60 percent of the time that the memory system is not in use begins to dominate the overall performance as we improve the memory system performance.

Improving Instructions

1.15. Consider an architecture that has four types of instructions: additions, multiplications, memory operations, and branches. The following table gives the number of instructions that belong to each type in the program you care about, the number of cycles it takes to execute each instruction by type, and the speedup in execution of the instruction type from a proposed improvement (each improvement only affects one instruction type). Rank the improvements for each of the instruction types in terms of their impact on overall performance.

Instruction Type	Number	Execution Time	Speedup to Type
Addition	10 million	2 cycles	2.0
Multiplication	30 million	20 cycles	1.3
Memory	35 million	10 cycles	3.0
Branch	15 million	4 cycles	4.0

Solution

To solve this problem, we must first compute the number of cycles spent executing each instruction type before the improvements are applied and the fraction of the total cycles spent executing each instruction type (Frac$_{used}$ for each of the improvements). This will allow us to use Amdahl's Law to compute the overall speedup for each of the proposed improvements. Multiplying the number of instructions in each type by the execution time per instruction gives the number of cycles spent executing each instruction type, and adding these values together gives the total number of cycles to execute the program. This gives the values in the following table: (Total execution time is 1030 million cycles).

Instruction Type	Number	Execution Time	Speedup to Type	Number of Cycles	Fraction of Cycles
Addition	10 million	2 cycles	2.0	20 million	2%
Multiplication	30 million	20 cycles	1.3	600 million	58%
Memory	35 million	10 cycles	3.0	350 million	34%
Branch	15 million	4 cycles	4.0	60 million	6%

We can then plug these values into Amdahl's Law, using the fraction of cycles as Frac$_{used}$, to get the overall speedup from each of the improvements.

Thus, improving memory operations gives the best overall speedup, followed by improving multiplications, improving branches, and improving additions:

Instruction Type	Number	Execution Time	Speedup to Type	Number of Cycles	Fraction of Cycles	Overall Speedup
Addition	10 million	2 cycles	2.0	20 million	2%	1.01
Multiplication	30 million	20 cycles	1.3	600 million	58%	1.15
Memory	35 million	10 cycles	3.0	350 million	34%	1.29
Branch	15 million	4 cycles	4.0	60 million	6%	1.05

CHAPTER 2

Data Representations and Computer Arithmetic

2.1 Objectives

This chapter covers the most common methods that computer systems use to represent data and how arithmetic operations are performed on these representations. It begins with a discussion of how bits (binary digits) are represented by electrical signals and proceeds to discuss how integers and floating-point numbers are represented as sequences of bits.

After reading this chapter, you should

1. Have an understanding of how computers represent data internally, at both the bit-pattern and the electrical-signal level
2. Be able to translate integer and floating-point numbers to and from their binary representations
3. Be able to perform basic mathematical operations (addition, subtraction, and multiplication) on integers and floating-point numbers

2.2 From Electrons to Bits

Modern computers are *digital* systems, meaning that they interpret electrical signals as having a set of discrete values, rather than as analog quantities. While this increases the number of signals required to convey a given amount of information, it

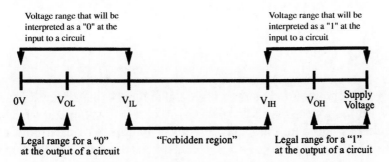

Fig. 2-1.   Mapping voltages to bits.

makes storing information much easier and makes digital systems less subject to electrical noise than analog systems.

A digital system's *signaling convention* determines how analog electrical signals are interpreted as digital values. Figure 2-1 illustrates the most common signaling convention in modern computers. Each signal carries one of two values, depending on the voltage level of the signal. Low voltages are interpreted as a 0 and high voltages as a 1.

The digital signaling convention divides the range of possible voltages into several regions. The region from 0V to V_{IL} is the range of voltages that are guaranteed to be interpreted as a 0 at the input to a circuit, while the region from V_{IH} to the supply voltage is guaranteed to be interpreted as a 1 at a circuit's input. The region between V_{IL} and V_{IH} is known as the "forbidden region," because it is not possible to predict whether a circuit will interpret a voltage in that range as a 0 or as a 1.

V_{OL} is the highest voltage that a circuit is allowed to produce when generating a 0, and V_{OH} is the lowest voltage that a circuit is allowed to produce when generating a 1. It is important that V_{OH} and V_{OL} be closer to the extremes of the voltage range than V_{IH} and V_{IL}, because the gaps between V_{OL} and V_{IL} and between V_{IH} and V_{OH} determine the *noise margins* of the digital system. The noise margin of a digital system is the amount by which the output signal of a circuit can change before it is possible that it will be interpreted as the opposite value by another circuit. The wider the noise margin, the better the system is able to tolerate the effects of coupling between electrical signals, resistive losses in wires, and other effects that can cause signals to change between the point where they are generated and the point where they are used.

Systems that map each electrical signal onto two values are known as *binary systems*, and the information carried by each signal is called a *bit* (short for BInary digiT). Systems with more values per signal are possible, but the additional complexity of designing circuits to interpret these signaling conventions and the reduction in noise margins that occurs when the voltage range is divided into more than two values make such systems difficult to build. For this reason, almost all digital systems are binary.

2.3   Binary Representation of Positive Integers

Positive integers are represented using a place-value binary (base-2) system, similar to the place-value system used in decimal (base-10) arithmetic. In base-10 arithmetic, numbers are represented as the sum of multiples of each power of 10, so the number $1543 = (1 \times 10^3) + (5 \times 10^2) + (4 \times 10^1) + (3 \times 10^0)$. For binary numbers, the base of the number is 2, so each position in the number represents an increasing power of 2, rather than an increasing power of 10. For example, the number $0b100111 = (1 \times 2^5) + (0 \times 2^4) + (0 \times 2^3) + (1 \times 2^2) + (1 \times 2^1) + (1 \times 2^0) = 39$. Binary quantities are usually preceded by the prefix "0b" to identify them as binary, rather than decimal numbers. Just as an n-digit decimal number can represent values from 0 to $10^n - 1$, an n-bit unsigned binary number can represent values from 0 to $2^n - 1$.

A disadvantage of binary numbers as compared to decimal numbers is that they require significantly more digits to represent a given integer, which can make them cumbersome to work with. To address this, *hexadecimal* notation, in which each digit has 16 possible values, is often used to represent binary numbers. In hexadecimal notation, the numbers 0 through 9 have the same value that they do in decimal notation, and the letters A through F (or a through f—case is irrelevant in hexadecimal) are used to represent the numbers 10 through 15, as shown in Fig. 2-2. To differentiate hexadecimal numbers from binary or decimal numbers, the prefix

Decimal Number	Binary Representation	Hexadecimal Representation
0	0b0000	0x0
1	0b0001	0x1
2	0b0010	0x2
3	0b0011	0x3
4	0b0100	0x4
5	0b0101	0x5
6	0b0110	0x6
7	0b0111	0x7
8	0b1000	0x8
9	0b1001	0x9
10	0b1010	0xA
11	0b1011	0xB
12	0b1100	0xC
13	0b1101	0xD
14	0b1110	0xE
15	0b1111	0xF

Fig. 2-2.   Hexadecimal notation.

"0x" is usually placed to the left of the number. Place-value notation with a base of 16 is used when representing values larger than 15 in hexadecimal notation.

EXAMPLE
What are the binary and hexadecimal representations of the decimal number 47?

Solution

To convert decimal numbers to binary, we express them as a sum of values that are powers of two:

$$47 = 32 + 8 + 4 + 2 + 1 = 2^5 + 2^3 + 2^2 + 2^1 + 2^0$$

Therefore, the binary representations of 47 is 0b101111.

To convert decimal numbers to hexadecimal, we can either express the number as the sum of powers of 16 or group the bits in the binary representation into sets of 4 bits and look each set up in Fig. 2-2. Converting directly, $47 = 2 \text{x} 16 + 15 = \text{0x}2F$. Grouping bits, we get $47 = \text{0b}101111 = \text{0b}0010\ 1111$. $\text{0b}0010 = \text{0x}2$, $\text{0b}1111 = \text{0x}F$, so $47 = \text{0x}2F$.

2.4   Arithmetic Operations on Positive Integers

Arithmetic in base-2 (binary) can be done using the same techniques that humans use for base-10 (decimal) arithmetic, except for the restricted set of values that can be represented by each digit. This is often the easiest way for humans to solve math problems involving binary numbers, but in some cases these techniques cannot be implemented easily in circuits, leading computer designers to choose other implementations of these operations. As we will see in the following sections, addition and multiplication are implemented using circuits that are analogous to the techniques used by humans in doing arithmetic. Division is implemented using computer-specific methods, and subtraction is implemented differently on different systems depending on the representation they use for negative integers.

EXAMPLE
Compute the sum of 9 and 5 using binary numbers in 4-bit binary format.

Solution

The 4-bit binary representations of 9 and 5 are 0b1001 and 0b0101, respectively. Adding the low bits, we get 0b1 + 0b1 = 0b10, which is a 0 in the low bit of the result, and a carry of 1 into the next bit position. Computing the next bit of the sum, we get 0b1 (carry) + 0b0 + 0b0 = 0b1. Repeating for all bits, we get the final result of 0b1110. Figure 2-3 illustrates this process.

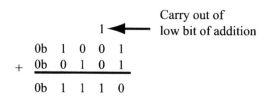

Fig. 2-3. Binary addition example.

2.4.1 ADDITION/SUBTRACTION

The hardware that computers use to implement addition is very similar to the method outlined above. Modules, known as *full adders*, compute each bit of the output based on the corresponding bits of the input and the carry generated by the next-lower bit of the computation. Figure 2-4 shows an 8-bit adder circuit.

For the type of adder described above, the speed of the circuit is determined by the time it takes for the carry signals to propagate through all of the full adders. Essentially, each full adder can't perform its part of the computation until all the full adders to the right of it have completed their parts, so the computation time grows linearly with the number of bits in the inputs. Designers have developed circuits that speed this up somewhat by doing as much of the work of the full adder as possible before the carry input is available to reduce the delay once the carry becomes available, or by taking several input bits into account when generating carries, but the basic technique remains the same.

Subtraction can be handled by similar methods, using modules that compute 1 bit of the difference between two numbers. However, the most common format for negative integers, two's-complement notation, allows subtraction to be performed by negating the second input and adding, making it possible to use the same hardware for addition and subtraction. Two's-complement notation is discussed in Section 2.5.2.

2.4.2 MULTIPLICATION

Unsigned integer multiplication is handled in a similar manner to the way humans multiply multidigit decimal numbers. The first input to the multiplication is multiplied by each bit of the second input separately, and the results added. In binary multiplication, this is simplified by the fact that the result of multiplying a

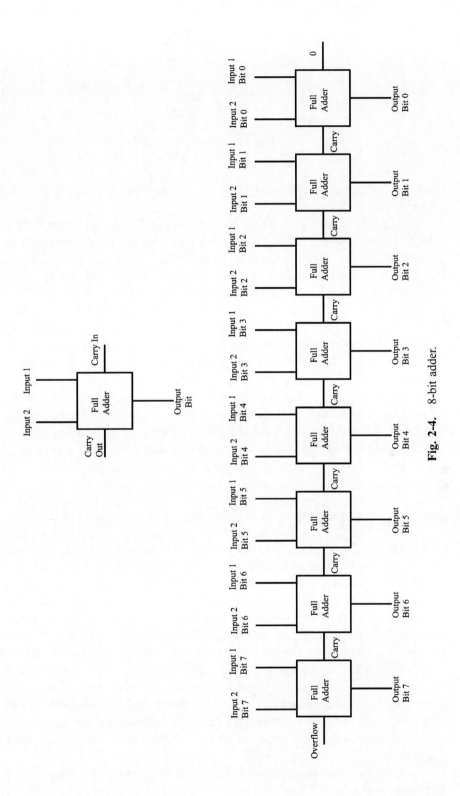

Fig. 2-4. 8-bit adder.

$$
\begin{array}{r}
\text{0b1011} \\
\times\ \underline{\text{0b0101}} \\
1011 \\
0000 \\
1011 \\
+\ \underline{0000} \\
\hline
\text{0b110111}
\end{array}
$$

Fig. 2-5.   Multiplication example.

number by a bit is either the original number or 0, making the hardware less complex.

Figure 2-5 shows an example of multiplying 11 (0b1011) by 5 (0b0101). First, 0b1011 is multiplied by each bit of 0b0101 to get the partial products shown in the figure. Then, the partial products are added to get the final result. Note that each successive partial product is shifted to the left one position to account for the differing place values of the bits in the second input.

One problem with integer multiplication is that the product of two n-bit numbers can require as many as $2n$ bits to represent. For example, the product of the two 4-bit numbers in Fig. 2-5 requires 6 bits to represent. Many arithmetic operations can generate results that cannot be represented in the same number of bits as their inputs. This is known as *overflow* or *underflow*, and is discussed in Section 2.4.4. In the case of multiplication, the number of bits of overflow is so large that hardware designers take special measures to deal with it. In some cases, designers provide separate operations to compute the high and low n bits of the result of an n-bit by n-bit multiplication. In others, the system discards the high n bits, or places them in a special output register where the programmer can access them if necessary.

2.4.3 DIVISION

Division can be implemented on computer systems by repeatedly subtracting the divisor from the dividend and counting the number of times that the divisor can be subtracted from the dividend before the dividend becomes smaller than the divisor. For example, 15 can be divided by 5 by subtracting 5 repeatedly from 15, getting 10, 5, and 0 as intermediate results. The quotient, 3, is the number of subtractions that had to be performed before the intermediate result became less than the dividend.

While it would be possible to build hardware to implement division through repeated subtraction, it would be impractical because of the number of subtractions required. For example, 2^{31} (one of the larger numbers representable in 32-bit unsigned integers) divided by 2 is 2^{30}, meaning that 2^{30} subtractions would have to be done to perform this division by repeated subtraction. On a system operating at 1 GHz, this would take approximately 1 s, far longer than any other arithmetic operation.

Instead, designers use table lookup-based methods to implement division. Using pregenerated tables, these techniques generate 2 to 4 bits of the quotient in each cycle. This allows 32-bit or 64-bit integer divisions to be done in a reasonal number of cycles, although division is typically the slowest of the basic mathematical operations on a computer.

2.4.4 OVERFLOW/UNDERFLOW

The bit width of a computer limits the maximum and minimum numbers it can represent as integers. For unsigned integers, an n-bit number can represent values from 0 to $2^n - 1$. However, arithmetic operations on numbers that can be represented in a given number of bits can generate results that cannot be represented in the same format. For example, adding two n-bit integers can generate a result of up to $2(2^n - 1)$, which cannot be represented in n bits, and it is possible to generate negative results by subtracting two positive integers, which also cannot be represented by an n-bit unsigned number.

When an operation generates a result that cannot be expressed in the format of its input operands, an *overflow* or *underflow* is said to have occurred. Overflows occur when the result of an operation is too large to represent in the input format, and underflows occur when the result is too small to represent in the format. Different systems handle overflows and underflows in different ways. Some signal an error when they occur. Others replace the result with the closest value that can be represented in the format. For floating-point numbers, the IEEE standard specifies a set of special representations that indicate that overflow or underflow has occurred. These representations are called not-a-numbers (NaNs) and are discussed in Section 2.6.1.

2.5   Negative Integers

To represent negative integers as sequences of bits, the place-value notation used for positive integers must be extended to indicate whether a number is positive or negative. We will cover two schemes for doing this: sign-magnitude representations and two's-complement notation.

2.5.1 SIGN-MAGNITUDE REPRESENTATION

In sign-magnitude representations, the high bit (also known as the sign bit) of a binary number indicates whether the number is positive or negative, and the remainder of the number indicates the absolute value (or magnitude) of the number, using the same format as unsigned binary representation. N-bit sign-magnitude numbers can represent quantities from $-(2^{(N-1)} - 1)$ to $+(2^{(N-1)} - 1)$. Note that there are two representations of 0 in sign-magnitude notation: $+0$ and -0. $+0$ has a value of 0 in the magnitude field and a positive sign bit. -0 has a value of 0 in the magnitude field and a negative sign bit.

EXAMPLE

The 16-bit unsigned binary representation of 152 is 0b0000 0000 1001 1000. In a 16-bit sign-magnitude system, −152 would be represented as 0b1000 0000 1001 1000. Here, the leftmost bit of the number is the sign bit, and the rest of the number gives the magnitude.

Sign-magnitude representations have the advantage that taking the negative of a number is very easy—just invert the sign bit. Determining whether a number is positive or negative is also easy, as it only requires examining the sign bit. Sign-magnitude representation makes it easy to perform multiplication and division on signed numbers, but hard to perform addition and subtraction. For multiplication and division, the hardware can simply perform unsigned operations on the magnitude portion of the inputs and examine the sign bits of the inputs to determine the sign bit of the result.

EXAMPLE

Multiply the numbers +7 and −5, using 6-bit signed-magnitude integers.

Solution

The binary representation of +7 is 000111, and −5 is 100101. To multiply them, we multiply their magnitude portions as unsigned integers, giving 0100011 (35). We then examine the sign bits of the numbers being multiplied and determine that one of them is negative. Therefore, the result of the multiplication must be negative, giving 1100011 (−35).

Addition and subtraction of sign-magnitude numbers requires relatively complex hardware because adding (or subtracting) the binary representation of a positive number and the binary representation of a negative number does not give the correct result. The hardware must take the value of the sign bit into account when computing each bit of the output, and different hardware is required to perform addition and subtraction. This hardware complexity is the reason why very few current systems use sign-magnitude notation for integers.

EXAMPLE

What is the result if you try to directly add the 8-bit sign-magnitude representations of +10 and −4?

Solution

The 8-bit sign-magnitude representations of +10 and −4 are 0b00001010 and 0b10000100. Adding these binary numbers together gives 0b10001110, which sign-magnitude systems interpret as −14, not 6 (the correct result of the computation).

2.5.2 TWO'S-COMPLEMENT NOTATION

In two's-complement notation, a negative number is represented by inverting each bit of the unsigned representation of the number and adding 1 to the result (discarding any overflow bits that do not fit in the width of the representation). The name "two's complement" comes from the fact that the unsigned sum of an n-bit two's-complement number and its negative is 2^n.

EXAMPLE

What is the 8-bit two's-complement representation of -12, and what is the unsigned result of adding the representations of $+12$ and -12?

Solution

The 8-bit representation of $+12$ is 0b00001100, so the 8-bit two's-complement representation of -12 is 0b11110100. (Negating each bit in the positive representation gives 0b11110011, and adding 1 gives the final result of 0b11110100.) This process is illustrated in Fig. 2-6.

```
Original value:   0b00001100   (12)
Negate each bit:  0b11110011
     Add 1:       0b11110100   (Two's-complement
                                representation of -12)
```

Fig. 2-6.   Two-complement negation.

Adding the representations of $+12$ and -12 gives 0b00001100 + 0b11110100, which is 0b100000000. Treating this as a 9-bit unsigned number, we interpret it as 256. $256 = 2^8$. Treating the result as an 8-bit two's-complement number, we drop the 1 that overflowed out of the 8-bit computation to get the 8-bit result 0b00000000 $= 0$, which is the result we'd expect from adding $+12$ and -12.

Two's-complement numbers have a number of useful properties, which explain why they are used in almost all modern computers:

1. The sign of a number can be determined by examining the high bit of the representation. Negative numbers have 1s in their high bit; positive numbers have 0s.
2. Negating a number twice gives the original number, so no special hardware is required to negate negative numbers.
3. Two's-complement notation has only one representation for zero, eliminating the need for hardware to detect $+0$ and -0.
4. Most importantly, adding the representations of a positive and a negative two's-complement number (discarding overflows) gives the two's-complement representation of the correct result. In addition to eliminating the need for special hardware to handle addition of negative numbers, subtraction can be recast as addition by computing the two's-complement

negation of the subtrahend and adding that to the two's-complement representation of the minuend (e.g., $14 - 7$ becomes $14 + (-7)$), further reducing hardware costs.

While sign-magnitude representations share the first two advantages of two's-complement numbers, the other two give two's-complement notation a significant advantage over sign-magnitude notation. One somewhat unusual characteristic of two's-complement notation is that an n-bit two's-complement number can represent values from $-(2^{(n-1)})$ to $+(2^{(n-1)} - 1)$. This asymmetry comes from the fact that there is only one representation for zero, allowing an odd number of nonzero quantities to be represented.

EXAMPLE
What is the result of negating the 4-bit two's-complement representation of $+5$ twice?

Solution

$+5 = $ 0b0101. The two's-complement negation of this is 0b1011 (-5). Negating that quantity gives 0b0101, the original number.

EXAMPLE
Add the quantities $+3$ and -4 in 4-bit two's-complement notation.

Solution

The 4-bit two's-complement representations of $+3$ and -4 are 0b0011 and 0b1100. Adding these together gives 0b1111, which is the two's-complement representation of -1.

EXAMPLE
Compute $-3 - 4$ in 4-bit two's-complement notation.

Solution

To perform subtraction, we negate the second operand and add. Thus, the actual computation we want to perform is $-3 + (-4)$. The two's-complement representations of -3 and -4 are 0b1101 and 0b1100. Adding these quantities, we get 0b11001 (a 5-bit result, counting the overflow). Discarding the fifth bit, which doesn't fit in the representation, gives 0b1001, the two's-complement representation of -7.

Multiplication of two's-complement numbers is more complicated, because performing a straightforward unsigned multiplication of the two's-complement representations of the inputs does not give the correct result. Multipliers could be designed to convert both of their inputs to positive quantities and use the sign bits of the original inputs to determine the sign of the result, but this increases the time required to perform a multiplication. Instead, a technique called *booth encoding*, which is beyond the scope of this book, is used to quickly convert two's-complement numbers into a format that is easily multiplied.

As we have seen, both sign-magnitude and two's-complement numbers have their pros and cons. Two's-complement numbers allow simple implementations of addition and subtraction, while sign-magnitude numbers facilitate multiplication and division. Because addition and subtraction are much more common in computer programs than multiplication and division, virtually all computer manufacturers have chosen two's-complement representations for integers, allowing them to "make the common case fast."

2.5.3 SIGN EXTENSION

In computer arithmetic, it is sometimes necessary to convert numbers represented in a given number of bits to a representation that uses a larger number of bits. For example, a program might need to add an 8-bit input to a 32-bit quantity. To get the correct result, the 8-bit input must be converted to a 32-bit quantity before it can be added to the 32-bit integer, which is known as *sign extension*.

Converting unsigned numbers to wider representations simply requires filling in the bits to the left of those in the original representation with zeroes. For example, the 8-bit unsigned quantity 0b10110110 becomes the 16-bit unsigned quantity 0b0000000010110110. To sign-extend a sign-magnitude number, move the sign bit (the most significant bit) of the old representation into the sign bit of the new representation, and fill in all of the additional bits in the new representation (including the bit position of the old sign bit) with zeroes.

> **EXAMPLE**
> What is the 16-bit sign-magnitude representation of the 8-bit sign-magnitude quantity 0b10000111 (−7)?

Solution

To sign-extend the number, we move the old sign bit to the most significant bit of the new representation and fill in all other bit positions with zeroes. This gives 0b1000000000000111 as the 16-bit sign-magnitude representation of −7.

Sign-extending two's-complement numbers is slightly more complicated. To sign-extend a two's-complement number, *copy* the high bit of the old representation into each additional bit of the new representation. Thus, sign-extended positive numbers will have zeroes in all of the bits added in going to the wider representation, and sign-extended negative numbers will have ones in all of these bit positions.

EXAMPLE
What is the 16-bit sign-extension of the 8-bit two's-complement quantity 0b10010010 (−110)?

Solution

To sign-extend this number, we copy the high bit into all of the new bit positions introduced by widening the representation. This gives 0b1111111110010010. Negating this, we get 0b0000000001101110 (+110), confirming that sign-extending two's-complement numbers gives the correct result.

2.6 Floating-Point Numbers

Floating-point numbers are used to represent quantities that cannot be represented by integers, either because they contain fractional values or because they lie outside the range representable within the system's bit width. Virtually all modern computers use the floating-point representation specified in IEEE standard 754, in which numbers are represented by a mantissa and an exponent. Similar to scientific notation, the value of a floating-point number is *mantissa* $\times 2^{exponent}$.

This representation allows a wide range of values to be represented in a relatively small number of bits, including both fractional values and values whose magnitude is much too large to represent in an integer with the same number of bits. However, it creates the problem that many of the values in the range of the floating-point representation cannot be represented exactly, just as many of the real numbers cannot be represented by a decimal number with a fixed number of significant digits. When a computation creates a value that cannot be represented exactly by the floating-point format, the hardware must round the result to a value that can be represented exactly. In the IEEE 754 standard, the default way of rounding (called the *rounding mode*) is round-to-nearest. In round-to-nearest, values are rounded to the closest representable number, and results that lie exactly halfway between two representable numbers are rounded such that the least-significant digit of their result is even. The standard specifies several other rounding modes that can be selected by programs, including round toward 0, round toward +infinity, and round toward −infinity.

EXAMPLE
The rounding modes in the IEEE standard can be applied to decimal numbers as well as floating-point binary representations. How would the following decimal numbers be rounded to two significant digits, using round-to-nearest mode?
a. 1.345
b. 78.953
c. 12.5
d. 13.5

Solution

a. 1.345 is closer to 1.3 than 1.4, so it will be rounded to 1.3. Another way to look at this is that the third-most-significant digit is less than 5, so it rounds to 0 when we round to two significant digits.

b. In 78.953, the third-most-significant digit is 9, which rounds up to 10, so 78.953 will round to 79.

c. In 12.5, the third-most-significant digit is 5, so we round in the direction that makes the least-significant digit of the result even. In this case, that means rounding down to a result of 12.

d. Here, we have to round up to 14 because the third-most-significant digit is 5, and we have to round up to make the result even.

The IEEE 754 standard specifies a number of bit widths for floating-point numbers. The two most commonly used widths are single-precision and double-precision, which are illustrated in Fig. 2-7. Single-precision numbers are 32 bits long and contain 8 bits of exponent, 23 bits of fraction, and 1 sign bit, which contains the sign of the fraction field. Double-precision numbers have 11 bits of exponent, 52 bits of fraction, and 1 sign bit.

Sign	Exponent	Fraction	
1	8	23	Single Precision (32 bits)

Sign	Exponent	Fraction	
1	11	52	Double Precision (64 bits)

Fig. 2-7.   IEEE 754 Floating-point formats.

Both the exponent and the fraction field of an IEEE 754 floating-point number are encoded differently than the integer representations we have discussed in this chapter. The fraction field is a sign-magnitude number that represents the fractional portion of a binary number whose integer portion is assumed to be 1. Thus, the mantissa of an IEEE 754 floating number is $+/-$ 1. *fraction*, depending on the value of the sign bit. Using an assumed "leading 1" in this way increases the number of significant digits that can be represented by a floating-point number of a given width.

EXAMPLE

What is the fraction field of the single-precision floating point representation of 6.25?

Solution

Fractional binary numbers use the same place-value representation as decimal numbers, with a base of 2, so the binary number 0b11.111 = $2^1 + 2^0 + 2^{-1} + 2^{-2} + 2^{-3} = 3.875$. Using this format, a decimal fraction can be converted to a binary fraction directly, so $6.25 = 2^2 + 2^1 + 2^{-2} = 0b110.01$.

To find the fraction field, we shift the binary representation of the number down so that the value to the left of the binary[1] point is 1, so 0b110.01 becomes $0b1.1001 \times 2^2$. In the normalized fraction representation used in floating-point numbers, the leading 1 is assumed, and only the values to the right of the binary point (1001 in this case) are represented. Extending the value to the 23-bit fraction format of single-precision floating-point, we get 1001 0000 0000 0000 0000 000 as the fraction field. Note that, when we extend fractional values to a wider representation, we add zeroes to the *right* of the last one, as opposed to sign-extending unsigned integers, where the zeroes are added to the left of the most-significant one.

The exponent field of a floating-point number uses a biased integer representation, in which a fixed bias is added to a value to determine its representation. For single-precision floating-point numbers, the bias is 127 (bias = 1023 for double-precision numbers), so the value of the exponent field can be found by subtracting 127 from the unsigned binary number contained in the field.

EXAMPLE

How would the numbers −45 and 123 be represented in the 8-bit biased notation used in the exponents of single-precision numbers?

Solution

The bias value for this format is 127, so we add 127 to each number to get the biased representation. $-45 + 127 = 82 = 0b01010010$. $123 + 127 = 250 = 0b11111010$.

EXAMPLE

What is the value of the exponent represented by an exponent field of 0b11100010 in a single-precision floating-point number?

Solution

$0b11100010 = 226$. $226 - 127 = 99$, so the exponent field has a value of 99.

Biased representations are somewhat unusual, but they have one significant advantage: They allow floating-point comparisons to be done using the same comparison hardware as unsigned integer comparisons, since larger values of a biased encoding correspond to larger values of the encoded number. Given the

---

[1] The binary point is the equivalent of the decimal point in a binary representation.

formats for the fraction and exponent field, the value of a floating-point number is then $(-1$ if sign bit 1, 1 if sign bit $0) \times (1.fraction) \times 2^{(exponent-\text{bias})}$.

EXAMPLE
What is the value of the single-precision floating-point number represented by the bit string 0b0100 0000 0110 0000 0000 0000 0000 0000?

Solution

Dividing this number into the fields specified in Fig. 2-7, we get a sign bit of 0, an exponent field of 0b10000000 $= 128$, and a fraction field of 0b1100000000000000000000. Subtracting the bias of 127 from the exponent field gives an exponent of 1. The mantissa is $1.11_2 = 1.75$ once we include the implied 1 to the left of the binary point in the fraction field, so the value of the floating-point number is $1 \times 1.75 \times 2^1 = 3.5$.

2.6.1   NaNs AND DENORMALIZED NUMBERS

The IEEE floating-point standard specifies several bit patterns that represent values that it is not possible to represent exactly in the base floating-point format: zero, denormalized numbers, and NaNs (not-a-numbers). The assumed 1 in the mantissa of floating-point numbers allows an additional bit of precision in the representation but prevents the value 0 from being represented exactly, since a fraction field of 0 represents the mantissa 1.0. Since representing 0 exactly is very important for numerical computations, the IEEE standard specifies that, when the exponent field of a floating-point number is 0, the leading bit of the mantissa is assumed to be 0. Thus, a floating-point number with a fraction field of 0 and an exponent field of 0 represents 0 exactly. This convention also allows numbers that lie closer to 0 than $1.0 \times 2^{(1\text{-bias})}$ to be represented, although they have fewer bits of precision than numbers that can be represented with an assumed 1 before the fraction field.

Floating-point numbers (except for 0) that have an exponent field of 0 are known as *denormalized* numbers because of the assumed 0 in the integer portion of their mantissa. This is in contrast to numbers with other values of the exponent field, which have an assumed 1 in the integer portion of their mantissa and are known as *normalized* numbers. All denormalized numbers are assumed to have an exponent field of (1-bias), instead of the (0-bias) that would be generated by just subtracting the bias from the value of their exponent. This provides a smaller gap between the smallest-magnitude normalized number and the largest-magnitude denormalized number that can be represented by a format.

The other type of special value in the floating-point standard is NaNs. NaN stands for "not a number," and NaNs are used to signal error conditions such as overflows, underflows, division by 0, and so on. When one of these error conditions occur in an operation, the hardware generates a NaN as its result rather than signaling an exception. Subsequent operations that receive a NaN as one of their inputs copy that NaN to their outputs rather than performing their normal computation. NaNs are indicated by all 1s in the exponent field of a floating-point number, unless the fraction field of the number is 0, in which case the number represents infinity. The existence of NaNs makes it easier to write programs that run on multiple different computers, because programmers can check the results of each computation for errors within the program, rather than relying on the system's exception-handling functions, which vary significantly between different computers. Figure 2-8 summarizes the interpretation of different values of the exponent and fraction fields of a floating-point number.

Exponent Field	Fraction Field	Represents
0	0	0
0	not 0	$+/- (0.\text{fraction}) \times 2^{(1-bias)}$ [depending on sign bit]
Not 0, not all 1s	any	$+/- (1.\text{fraction}) \times 2^{(exponent-bias)}$ [depending on sign bit]
All 1s	0	$+/-$ infinity [depending on sign bit]
All 1s	not 0	NaN

Fig. 2-8.   Interpretation of IEEE floating-point numbers.

2.6.2 ARITHMETIC ON FLOATING-POINT NUMBERS

Given the similarities between the IEEE floating-point representation and scientific notation, it is not surprising that the techniques used for floating-point arithmetic on computers are very similar to the techniques used to do arithmetic on decimal numbers that are expressed in scientific notation. A good example of this is floating-point multiplication.

To multiply two numbers using scientific notation, the mantissas of the numbers are multiplied and the exponents added. If the result of multiplying the mantissas is greater than 10, the product of the mantissas is shifted so that there is exactly one nonzero digit to the left of the decimal point, and the sum of the exponents is incremented as necessary to keep the value of the product the same. For example, to multiply 5×10^3 by 2×10^6, we multiply the mantissas ($5 \times 2 = 10$) and add the exponents ($3 + 6 = 9$) to get an initial result of 10×10^9. Since the mantissa of this number is greater than 10, we shift it down one position and add 1 to the exponent to get the final result of 1×10^{10}.

Computers multiply floating-point numbers using a very similar process, as illustrated in Fig. 2-9. The first step is to multiply the mantissas of the two numbers, using techniques analogous to those used to multiply decimal numbers, and to add their exponents. IEEE floating-point numbers use a biased representation for exponents, so adding the exponent fields of two floating-point numbers is slightly more complicated than adding two integers. To compute the sum of the exponents, the exponent fields of the two floating-point numbers are treated as integers and

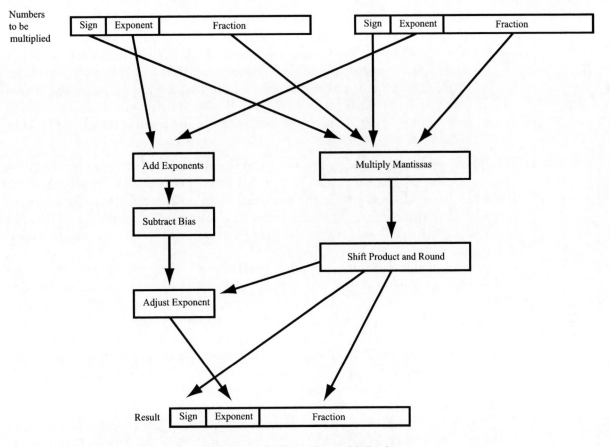

Fig. 2-9.　Floating-point multiplication.

added, and the bias value is subtracted from the result. This gives the correct biased representation for the sum of the two exponents.

Once the mantissas have been multiplied, the result may need to be shifted so that only 1 bit remains to the left of the binary point (i.e., so that it fits the form $1.xxxxx_2$), and the sum of the exponents incremented so that the value of the mantissa $\times 2^{\text{exponent}}$ remains the same. The product of the mantissas may also have to be rounded to fit within the number of bits allocated to the fraction field, since the product of two n-bit mantissas may require up to $2n$ bits to represent exactly. Once the mantissa has been shifted and rounded, the final product is assembled out of the product of the mantissas and the sum of the exponents.

EXAMPLE
Using single-precision floating-point numbers, multiply 2.5 by 0.75.

Solution

$2.5 = 0$b0100 0000 0010 0000 0000 0000 0000 0000 (exponent field of 0b10000000, fraction field of 0b010 0000 0000 0000 0000 0000, mantissa of

1.010 0000 0000 0000 0000 0000$_2$). $0.75 = $ 0b0011 1111 0100 0000 0000 0000 0000 0000 (exponent field of 0b01111110, fraction field of 0b100 0000 0000 0000 0000 0000, mantissa of 1.100 0000 0000 0000 0000 0000$_2$). Adding the exponent fields directly and subtracting the bias gives a result of 0b01111111, the biased representation of 0. Multiplying the mantissas gives a result of 1.111 0000 0000 0000 0000 0000$_2$, which converts into a fraction field of 0b111 0000 0000 0000 0000 0000, so the result is 0b0011 1111 1111 0000 0000 0000 0000 0000 $= 1.111_2 \times 2^0 = 1.875$.

Floating-point division is very similar to multiplication. The hardware computes the quotient of the mantissas and the difference between the exponents of the numbers being divided, adding the bias value to the difference between the exponent fields of the two numbers to get the correct biased representation of the result. The quotient of the mantissas is then shifted and rounded to fit within the fraction field of the result.

Floating-point addition requires a different set of computations, which are illustrated in Fig. 2-10. As with adding numbers in scientific notation, the first step is to shift one of the inputs until both inputs have the same exponent. In adding floating-point numbers, the number with the smaller exponent is right-shifted. For example, in adding $1.01_2 \times 2^3$ and $1.001_2 \times 2^0$, the smaller value is shifted to become $0.001001_2 \times 2^3$. Shifting the number with the smaller exponent allows the use of techniques that retain just enough information about the less-significant bits of the smaller number to perform rounding, reducing the number of bits that actually have to be added.

Once the inputs have been shifted, their mantissas are added, and the result shifted if necessary. Finally, the result is rounded to fit in the fraction field, and the computation is complete. Floating-point subtraction uses the same process, except that the difference between, rather than the sum of, the shifted mantissas is computed.

EXAMPLE
Using single-precision floating-point numbers, compute the sum of 0.25 and 1.5.

Solution

$0.25 = $ 0b0011 1110 1000 0000 0000 0000 0000 0000 (1.0×2^{-2}). $1.5 = $ 0b0011 1111 1100 0000 0000 0000 0000 0000 (1.5×2^0).

To add these numbers, we shift the one with the smaller exponent (0.25) to the right until both exponents are the same (two places in this case). This gives mantissas of 1.100 0000 0000 0000 0000 0000 and 0.010 000 0000 0000 0000 0000 for the two numbers (including the assumed 1s in the values to be shifted.) Adding these two mantissas gives a result of 1.110 0000 0000 0000 0000 0000 $\times 2^0$ (the exponent of the input with the larger exponent) $= 1.75$. The single-precision representation of the full result is 0b0011 1111 1110 0000 0000 0000 0000 0000.

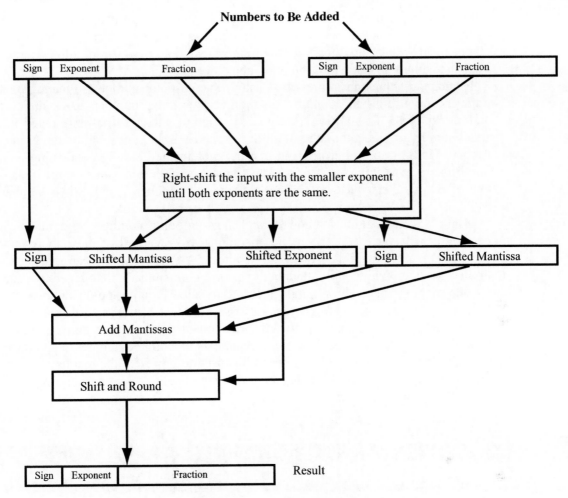

Fig. 2-10.   Floating-point addition.

2.7   Summary

This chapter has described techniques that computer systems use to represent and manipulate data. In general, computers use two levels of abstraction in representing data, one layered on top of the other. The lower-level abstraction is the digital signaling convention that maps the numbers 0 and 1 onto an analog electrical signal. A variety of signaling conventions are used, but the most common one defines a logical 0 as a range of voltages near the ground voltage of the system, and a logical 1 as a range of voltages near the supply voltage of the system (V_{dd}). Different ranges are defined for the voltage levels that may be generated by a circuit and the input values that are guaranteed to be interpreted as a 0 or 1 by another circuit, to protect the circuit against electrical noise.

The second-level abstraction defines how groups of bits are used to represent integer and noninteger numbers. Positive integer numbers are represented using a place-value system analogous to the decimal system. Sign-magnitude or two's-complement representations are used to represent negative integers, with two's-complement being the more common representation because it allows simple implementations of both addition and subtraction.

Noninteger values are represented using floating-point numbers. Floating-point numbers are similar to scientific notation, representing numbers as a mantissa and an exponent. This allows a very wide range of values to be represented in a small number of bits, although not all of the values in the range can be represented exactly. Multiplication and division can be implemented simply on floating-point numbers, while addition and subtraction are more complicated, since the mantissa of one of the numbers must be shifted to make the exponents of the two numbers equal.

Using a combination of integer and floating-point numbers, programs can perform a wide variety of arithmetic operations. However, all of these representations have their limitations. The range of integers that a computer can represent is limited by its bit width, and attempts to perform computations that generate results outside of this range will generate incorrect results. Floating-point numbers also have a limited range, although the mantissa-exponent representation makes this range much larger. A more significant limitation of floating-point numbers comes from the fact that they can only represent numbers to a limited number of significant digits, because of the limited number of bits used to represent the mantissa of each number. Computations that require more accuracy than the floating-point representation allows will not operate correctly.

Solved Problems

Signaling Conventions (I)

2.1. Suppose a digital system has $V_{DD} = 3.3$ V, $V_{IL} = 1.2$ V, $V_{OL} = 0.7$ V, $V_{IH} = 2.1$ V, $V_{OH} = 3.0$ V.
What is the noise margin of this signaling convention?

Solution

The noise margin is the lesser of the differences between the valid output and input levels for a 0 or 1. For this signaling convention $|V_{OL} - V_{IL}| = 0.5$ V, and $|V_{OH} - V_{IH}| = 0.9$ V. Therefore, the noise margin for this signaling convention is 0.5 V, indicating that the value of any valid output signal from a logic gate can change by up to 0.5 V due to noise in the system without becoming an invalid value.

Signaling Conventions (II)

2.2. Suppose you were told that a given signaling convention had $V_{DD} = 3.3$ V, $V_{IL} = 1.0$ V, $V_{OL} = 1.2$ V, $V_{IH} = 2.1$ V, $V_{OH} = 3.0$ V.
Why would this signaling convention be a bad idea?

Solution

In this signaling convention, $V_{IH} > V_{OL} > V_{IL}$. This means that a logic gate is allowed to generate an output value that lies in the forbidden region between V_{IH} and V_{IL}. Such an output value is not guaranteed to be interpreted as either a 0 or a 1 by any gate that receives it as an input. Another way of expressing this is to say that this signaling convention allows a gate that is trying to output a 0 to generate an output voltage that will not be interpreted as a 0 by the input of another gate, even if there is no noise in the system.

Binary Representation of Positive Integers (I)

2.3. Show how the following integers would be represented by a system that uses 8-bit unsigned integers.
  a. 37
  b. 89
  c. 4
  d. 126
  e. 298

Solution

  a. $37 = 32 + 4 + 1 = 2^5 + 2^2 + 2^0$. Therefore, the 8-bit unsigned binary representation of 37 is 0b00100101.
  b. $89 = 64 + 16 + 8 + 1 = 2^6 + 2^4 + 2^3 + 2^0 = 0b01011001$
  c. $4 = 2^2 = 0b00000100$
  d. $126 = 64 + 32 + 16 + 8 + 4 + 2 = 2^6 + 2^5 + 2^4 + 2^3 + 2^2 + 2^1 = 0b01111110$
  e. This is a trick question. The maximum value that can be represented by an 8-bit unsigned number is $2^8 - 1 = 255$. 298 is greater than 255, so it cannot be represented by an 8-bit unsigned binary number.

Binary Representation of Positive Integers (II)

2.4. What is the decimal value of the following unsigned binary integers?
  a. 0b1100
  b. 0b100100
  c. 0b11111111

Solution

  a. $0b1100 = 2^3 + 2^2 = 8 + 4 = 12$
  b. $0b100100 = 2^5 + 2^2 = 32 + 4 = 36$
  c. $0b11111111 = 2^7 + 2^6 + 2^5 + 2^4 + 2^3 + 2^2 + 2^1 + 2^0 = 128 + 64 + 32 + 16 + 8 + 4 + 2 + 1 = 255$

Hexadecimal Notation (I)

2.5. What are the hexadecimal representations of the following integers?
  a. 67
  b. 142
  c. 1348

Solution

a. $67 = (4 \times 16) + 3 = 0x43$
b. $142 = (8 \times 16) + 14 = 0x8e$
c. $1348 = (5 \times 16 \times 16) + (4 \times 16) + 4 = 0x544$

Hexadecimal Notation (II)

2.6. What are the decimal values of the following hexadecimal numbers?
  a. 0x1b
  b. 0xa7
  c. 0x8ce

Solution

a. $0x1b = (1 \times 16) + 11 = 27$
b. $0xa7 = (10 \times 16) + 7 = 167$
c. $0x8ce = (8 \times 16 \times 16) + (12 \times 16) + 14 = 2254$

Addition of Unsigned Integers

2.7. Compute the sums of the following pairs of unsigned integers:
  a. 0b11000100 + 0b00110110
  b. 0b00001110 + 0b10101010
  c. 0b11001100 + 0b00110011
  d. 0b01111111 + 0b00000001

Solution

(Note that all of these problems can be checked by converting the inputs and outputs into decimal.)
  a. 0b11111010
  b. 0b10111000
  c. 0b11111111
  d. 0b10000000

Multiplication of Unsigned Integers

2.8. Compute the product of the following pairs of unsigned integers. Generate the full 8-bit result.
  a. 0b1001 × 0b0110
  b. 0b1111 × 0b1111
  c. 0b0101 × 0b1010

Solution

a. $0b1001 \times 0b0110 = (0b1001 \times 0b100) + (0b1001 \times 0b10) = 0b100100 + 0b10010 = 0b00110110$
b. 0b11100001
c. 0b00110010

Number of Bits Required

2.9. How many bits are required to represent the following decimal numbers as unsigned binary integers?
  a. 12
  b. 147
  c. 384
  d. 1497

Solution

a. 12 is greater than $2^3 - 1$, and less than $2^4 - 1$, so 12 cannot be represented in a 3-bit unsigned integer, but can be represented in a 4-bit binary integer. Therefore, 4 bits are required.
b. $2^7 - 1 < 147 < 2^8 - 1$, so 8 bits are required.
c. $2^8 - 1 < 384 < 2^9 - 1$, so 9 bits are required.
d. $2^{10} - 1 < 1497 < 2^{11} - 1$, so 11 bits are required.

Ranges of Binary Representations

2.10. What are the largest and smallest integers representable in 4-, 8-, and 16-bit values using
  a. Unsigned binary representation
  b. Sign-magnitude binary representation
  c. Two's-complement representation

Also, why are your answers to b and c different?

Solution

a. In any unsigned representation, 0 is the smallest representable value. The largest value representable in an n-bit unsigned binary integer is $2^n - 1$, giving maximum representable values of 15, 255, and 65,535 for 4-, 8-, and 16-bit unsigned integers.
b. Sign-magnitude representations use 1 bit to record the sign of a number, allowing them to represent values from $-(2^{n-1} - 1)$ to $2^{n-1} - 1$. This gives a range of -7 to $+7$ for 4-bit quantities, -127 to $+127$ for 8-bit quantities, and $-32,767$ to $+32,767$ for 16-bit quantities.
c. n-bit two's-complement integers can represent values from $-(2^{n-1})$ to $2^{n-1} - 1$. Therefore, 4-bit two's-complement integers can represent values from -8 to $+7$, 8-bit numbers can represent values from -128 to $+127$, and 16-bit numbers can represent values from $-32,768$ to $+32,767$.

Sign-magnitude representations have two representations for zero, while two's-complement representations have only one. This gives two's-complement representations the ability to represent one more value than sign-magnitude representations with the same number of bits.

Sign-Magnitude Representation

2.11. Convert the following decimal numbers to 8-bit sign-magnitude representation:
  a. 23
  b. −23
  c. −48
  d. −65

Solution

a. In sign-magnitude representation, positive integers are represented in the same way as they are in unsigned binary representation, except that the high bit of the representation is reserved for the sign bit. Therefore, the 8-bit sign-magnitude representation of 23 is 0b00010111.

b. To get the sign-magnitude representation of −23, we simply set the sign bit of the representation of +23 to 1, giving 0b10010111.

c. 0b10110000

d. 0b11000001

Two's-Complement Notation

2.12. Give the 8-bit two's-complement representation of the quantities from Problem 2.11.

Solution

a. Like sign-magnitude representation, the two's-complement representation of a positive number is the same as the unsigned representation of that number, giving 0b00010111 as the 8-bit two's-complement representation of 23.

b. To negate a number in two's-complement representation, we invert all of the bits of its representation and add 1 to the result, giving 0b11101001 as the 8-bit two's-complement representation of −23.

c. 0b11010000

d. 0b10111111

Sign-Extension

2.13. Give the 8-bit representation of the numbers 12 and −18 in sign-magnitude and two's-complement notation, and show how these representations are sign-extended to give 16-bit representations in each notation.

Solution

The 8-bit sign-magnitude representations of 12 and −18 are 0b00001100 and 0b10010010, respectively. To sign-extend a sign-magnitude number, the sign bit is copied into the most significant bit of the new representation and the sign bit of the old representation is cleared, giving 16-bit sign-magnitude representations of 0b0000000000001100 for 12 and 0b1000000000010010 for −18.

The 8-bit two's-complement representations of 12 and −18 are 0b00001100 and 0b11101110. Two's-complement numbers are sign-extended by copying the high bit of the number into the additional bits of the new representation, giving 16-bit representations of 0b0000000000001100 and 0b1111111111101110, respectively.

Math on Two's-Complement Integers

2.14. Using 8-bit two's-complement integers, perform the following computations:

a. $-34 + (-12)$

b. $17 - 15$

c. $-22 - 7$

d. $18 - (-5)$

Solution

a. In two's-complement notation, $-34 = 0b11011110$ and $-12 = 0b11110100$. Adding these, we get $0b11010010$ (remember that the 9th bit is dropped when two 8-bit two's-complement numbers are added). This is -46, the correct answer.

b. Here, we can take advantage of the fact that we're using two's-complement notation to transform $17 - 15$ into $17 + (-15)$, or $0b00010001 + 0b11110001 = 0b00000010 = 2$.

c. Again, transform this to $-22 + (-7)$ to get the result of $0b11100011 = -29$.

d. This transforms into $18 + 5 = 0b00010111 = 23$.

Comparing Integer Representations

2.15. Which of the two integer representations described in this chapter (sign-magnitude and two's-complement) would be better suited to the following situations:

a. When it is critical that the hardware to negate a number be as simple as possible.

b. When most of the mathematical operations performed will be additions and subtractions.

c. When most of the mathematical operations performed will be multiplications and divisions.

d. When it is essential that it be as easy as possible to detect whether a number is positive or negative.

Solution

a. In this case, sign-magnitude representation would be better, because negating a number simply requires inverting the sign bit.

b. Two's-complement numbers allow simpler hardware for addition and subtraction than sign-magnitude numbers. With two's-complement numbers, no additional hardware is required to add positive and negative numbers—treating the numbers as unsigned quantities and adding them gives the correct two's-complement result. Subtraction can be implemented by negating the second operand and then adding.

In contrast, sign-magnitude representations require different hardware to perform subtractions or to add positive and negative numbers, making this representation more expensive if most of the computations to be performed are additions and/or subtractions.

c. Sign-magnitude representation is better in this case, because multiplication and division can be implemented by treating the magnitude portions of the numbers as unsigned integers and then determining the sign of the result by examining the sign bits of the two values.

d. In this case, the two representations are very close. In general, the sign of a number in either representation can be determined by examining the high bit of the number—if the high bit is 1, the number is negative. The exception to this is when the value of the number is 0. Sign-magnitude representations have two representations of zero, one with the sign bit 1, and one with it equal to 0, while there is only one representation of zero in two's-complement notation.

In summary, the two representations are equivalent if it is unimportant whether zero values detect as positive or negative. If it is important to determine whether the number is positive, negative, or zero, two's-complement numbers are slightly better.

Rounding

2.16. Using round-to-nearest, round the following decimal quantities to three significant digits:

    a.   1.234

    b.   8940.999

    c.   179.5

    d.   178.5

Solution

    a.   1.23

    b.   8940 (significant digits don't have to be to the right of the decimal point)

    c.   180 (round to even)

    d.   178 (round to even)

Floating-Point Representations (I)

2.17. Convert the following quantities to IEEE single-precision floating-point:

    a.   128

    b. -32.75

    c.   18.125

    d.   0.0625

Solution

    a. $128 = 2^7$, giving an exponent field of 134, a sign bit of 0, and a fraction field of 0 (because of the assumed 1). Therefore, $128 = $ 0b0100 0011 0000 0000 0000 0000 0000 0000 in single-precision floating-point format.

    b. $-32.75 = -100000.11_2$ or $-1.0000011_2 \times 2^5$. The single-precision floating-point representation of -32.75 is 0b1100 0010 0000 0011 0000 0000 0000 0000.

    c. $18.125 = 10010.001_2$ or $1.0010001_2 \times 2^4$, giving a single-precision floating-point representation of 0b0100 0001 1001 0001 0000 0000 0000 0000.

    d. $0.0625 = 0.0001_2$ or 1×2^{-4}, giving a single-precision floating-point representation of 0b0011 1101 1000 0000 0000 0000 0000 0000.

Floating-Point Representations (II)

2.18. What values are represented by the following IEEE single-precision floating-point numbers?

    a.   0b1011 1101 0100 0000 0000 0000 0000 0000

    b.   0b0101 0101 0110 0000 0000 0000 0000 0000

    c.   0b1100 0001 1111 0000 0000 0000 0000 0000

    d.   0b0011 1010 1000 0000 0000 0000 0000 0000

Solution

    a.   For this number, the sign bit $= 1$, exponent field $= 122$, so exponent $= -5$. Fraction field $= 100$ 0000 0000 0000 0000 0000, so this binary string represents $-1.1_2 \times 2^{-5} = -0.046875$

    b.   Here, we have a sign bit of 0, exponent field of 170, so the exponent is 43, and a fraction field of 110 0000 0000 0000 0000 0000, so the value of this number is $1.11_2 \times 2^{43} = 1.539 \times 10^{13}$ (to 4 significant digits)

    c. $-1.111_2 \times 2^4 = -30$

    d. $1.0_2 \times 2^{-10} = 0.0009766$ (to 4 significant digits)

NaNs and Denormalized Numbers

2.19. For each of the IEEE single-precision values below, explain what type of number (normalized, denormalized, infinity, 0, or NaN) they represent. If the quantity has a numeric value, give it.
  a. 0b0111 1111 1000 1111 0000 1111 0000 0000
  b. 0b0000 0000 0000 0000 0000 0000 0000 0000
  c. 0b0100 0010 0100 0000 0000 0000 0000 0000
  d. 0b1000 0000 0100 0000 0000 0000 0000 0000
  e. 0b1111 1111 1000 0000 0000 0000 0000 0000

Solution

  a. The exponent field of this number is all 1s, and its fraction field is not 0, so it's a NaN.
  b. This number has an exponent field of 0, a sign bit of 0, and a fraction field of 0, which is the IEEE floating-point representation for +0.
  c. This number has an exponent field of 132 and a fraction field of 100 0000 0000 0000 0000 0000. Since its exponent field is neither all 0s or all 1s, it represents a normalized number, with a value of $1.1_2 \times 2^5 = 48$.
  d. This number has an exponent field of all 0s, and its fraction field is nonzero, so it's a denormalized number. Its value is $-0.1_2 \times 2^{-126} = -2^{-127} = -5.877 \times 10^{-39}$ (to four significant digits).
  e. The exponent field of this number is all 1s, its fraction field is 0, and its sign bit is 1, so it represents $-$infinity.

Arithmetic on Floating-Point Numbers

2.20. Use IEEE single-precision floating-point numbers to compute the following quantities:
  a. 32×16
  b. $147.5 + 0.25$
  c. 0.125×8
  d. $13.25 + 4.5$

Solution

  a. $32 = 2^5$ and $16 = 2^4$, so the floating-point representations of these numbers are 0b0100 0010 0000 0000 0000 0000 0000 0000 and 0b0100 0001 1000 0000 0000 0000 0000 0000. To multiply them, we convert their fraction fields into a mantissa and multiply, while adding the exponent fields and subtracting the bias from the sum. This gives a resulting exponent field of 10001000 and a fraction field of 000 0000 0000 0000 0000 0000 once we remove the assumed 1 from the product of the mantissas. The resulting floating-point number is 0b0100 0100 0000 0000 0000 0000 0000 0000 $= 2^9 = 512$.
  b. $147.5 = 1.00100111_2 \times 2^7 =$ 0b0100 0011 0001 0011 1000 0000 0000 0000. $0.25 = 1.0_2 \times 2^{-2} =$ 0b0011 1110 1000 0000 0000 0000 0000 0000. Shifting the number with the smaller exponent (.25) to the right to make the exponents of both numbers equal gives $0.25 = 0.000000001_2 \times 2^7$. Adding the mantissas gives a sum of $1.001001111_2 \times 2^7 =$ 0b0100 0011 0001 0011 1100 0000 0000 0000.
  c. Converting these numbers to floating-point gives representations of 0b0011 1110 0000 0000 0000 0000 0000 0000 for 0.125, and 0b0100 0001 0000 0000 0000 0000 0000 0000 for 8. Multiplying the mantissas and adding the exponents gives a result of 0b0011 1111 1000 0000 0000 0000 0000 0000 $= 1$.

d. $13.25 = 1.10101_2 \times 2^3 = $ 0b0100 0001 0101 0100 0000 0000 0000 0000. $4.5 = 1.001_2 \times 2^2 = $ 0b0100 0000 1001 0000 0000 0000 0000 0000. Shifting 4.5 to the right one place to make the exponents the same gives $4.5 = 0.1001_2 \times 2^3$. Adding mantissas gives a result of $10.00111_2 \times 2^3$, so we have to shift this down one to get $1.000111_2 \times 2^4$. The single-precision floating-point representation of this is 0b0100 0001 1000 1110 0000 0000 0000 0000.

CHAPTER 3

Computer Organization

3.1   Objectives

The last two chapters laid the groundwork for our discussion of computer architecture by explaining how computer architects describe and analyze performance, and how computers represent and manipulate real-world values. In this chapter, we begin covering computer architecture *per se* by describing the basic building blocks that make up conventional computer systems: processors, memory, and I/O. We will also briefly describe how programs are represented internally by computer systems and how operating systems schedule programs and control the physical devices that make up a computer.

   After completing this chapter, you should

   1. Understand the basic concepts behind processors, memory, and I/O devices, and be able to describe their functions
   2. Be familiar with stored-program computer architecture
   3. Understand the basic functions of operating systems

3.2   Introduction

As shown in Fig. 3-1, most computer systems can be divided into three subsystems: the processor, the memory, and the input/output (I/O) subsystem. The processor is responsible for executing programs, the memory provides storage space for programs and the data they reference, and the I/O subsystem allows the processor and memory to control devices that interact with the outside world or store data, such as the CD-ROM, hard disk, and video card/monitor shown in the figure.

   In most systems, the processor has a single data bus that connects to a switch module, such as the PCI bridge found in many PC systems, although some processors integrate the switch module onto the same integrated circuit as the processor to reduce the number of chips required to build a system and thus the

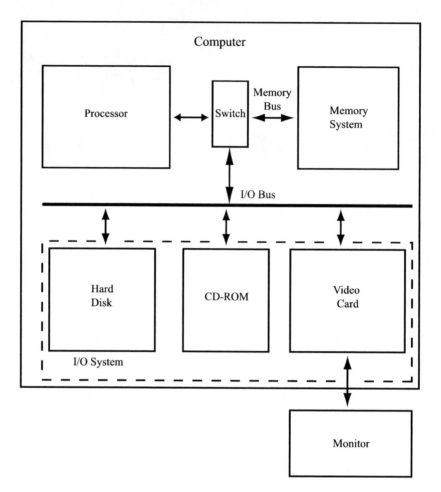

Fig. 3-1. Computer organization.

system cost. The switch communicates with the memory through a *memory bus*, a dedicated set of wires that transfer data between these two systems. A separate *I/O bus* connects the switch to the I/O devices. Separate memory and I/O buses are used because the I/O system is generally designed for maximum flexibility, to allow as many different I/O devices as possible to interface to the computer, while the memory bus is designed to provide the maximum-possible bandwidth between the processor and the memory system.

3.3   Programs

Programs are sequences of instructions that tell the computer what to do, although the computer's view of the instructions that make up a given program is often very different from the program writer's view. To the computer, a program is made up of a sequence of numbers that represent individual operations. These operations are known as *machine instructions* or just *instructions*, and the set of operations that a given processor can execute is known as its *instruction set*.

Almost all computers in use today are *stored-program computers* that represent programs as numbers that are stored in the same address space as data.[1] The stored-program abstraction (representing instructions as numbers stored in memory) was one of the major breakthroughs in early computer architecture. Prior to this breakthrough, many computers were programmed by setting switches or rewiring circuit boards to define the new program, which required a great deal of time and was prone to errors.

The stored-program abstraction provides two major advantages over previous approaches. First, it allows programs to be easily stored and loaded into the machine. Once a program has been developed and debugged, the numbers that represent its instructions can be written out onto a storage device, allowing the program to be loaded back into memory at some point in the future. On early systems, the most common storage device was punched cards or paper tape. Modern systems generally use magnetic media, such as hard disks. Being able to store programs like data eliminates errors in reloading the program (assuming that the device the program is stored on is error-free), while requiring a human to reenter the program each time it is used generally introduces errors that have to be corrected before the program runs correctly—imagine having to debug your word processor each time you started it up!

Second, and perhaps even more significant, the stored-program abstraction allows programs to treat themselves or other programs as data. Programs that treat themselves as data are called *self-modifying programs*. In a self-modifying program, some of the instructions in a program compute other instructions in the program. Self-modifying programs were common on early computers, because they were often faster than non-self-modifying programs, and because early computers implemented a small number of instructions, making some operations hard to do without self-modifying code. In fact, self-modifying code was the only way to implement a conditional branch on at least one early computer—the instruction set did not provide a conditional branch operation, so programmers implemented conditional branches by writing self-modifying code that computed the destination addresses of unconditional branch instructions as the program executed.

Self-modifying code has become less common on more-modern machines because changing the program during execution makes it harder to debug. As computers have become faster, ease of program implementation and debugging has become more important than the performance improvements achievable through self-modifying code in most cases. Also, memory systems with caches (discussed in Chapter 9) make self-modifying code less efficient, reducing the performance improvements that can be gained by using this technique.

---

[1] Stored-program computers are also sometimes called von Neumann computers, after John von Neumann, one of the developers of this concept.

3.3.1 PROGRAM DEVELOPMENT TOOLS

Programs that treat other programs as data, however, are very common and most program development tools fall into this category. These include *compilers* that convert programs from high-level languages such as C or FORTRAN into assembly language, *assemblers* that convert assembly-language instructions into the numeric representation used by the processor, and *linkers* that join multiple machine language programs into a single executable file. Also included in this category are *debuggers*, programs that display the state of another program as it executes to allow programmers to track the progress of a program and find errors.

The first stored-program computers were programmed directly in *machine language*, the numeric instruction representation used internally by the processor. To write a program, a programmer would determine the sequence of machine instructions needed to generate the correct result and would then enter the numbers that represented these instructions into the computer. This was a very time-consuming process, and it resulted in large numbers of programming errors.

The first step in simplifying program development came when assemblers were developed, allowing programmers to program in *assembly language*. In assembly language, each machine instruction has a text representation (such as ADD, SUB, or LOAD) that represents what it does, and programs are written using these assembly-language instructions. Once the program has been written, the programmer runs the assembler to convert the assembly-language program into a machine language program that can be executed on the computer. Figure 3-2 shows an example of an assembly-language instruction and the machine-language instruction that might be generated from it.

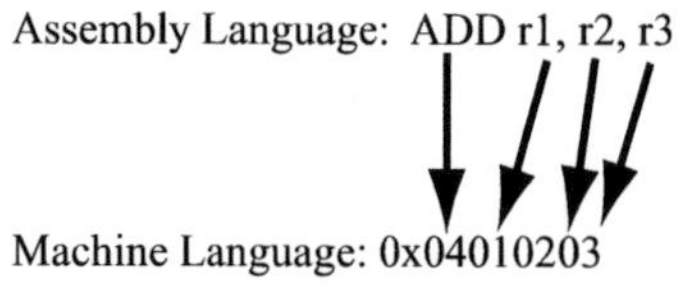

Assembly Language: ADD r1, r2, r3

Machine Language: 0x04010203

Fig. 3-2. Assembly language.

Using assembly language made programming much easier by allowing programmers to use an instruction format that is more easily understood by humans. Programming was still extremely tedious because of the small amount of work done by each instruction and because the instructions available to the programmer differed from machine to machine. If a programmer wanted to run a program on a different type of computer, the program had to be completely rewritten in the new computer's assembly language.

High-level languages, such as FORTRAN, COBOL, and C, were developed to address these issues. A high-level language instruction can specify much more work than an assembly-language instruction. Studies have shown that the average number of instructions written and debugged per day by a programmer is relatively independent of the language used. Since high-level languages allow programs to be written in many fewer instructions than assembly language, the time to implement a program in a high-level language is typically much less than the time to implement the program in assembly language.

Another advantage of writing programs in high-level languages is that they are more portable than programs written in assembly language or machine language. Programs written in high-level languages can be converted for use on different types of computer by recompiling the program using a compiler for the new computer. In contrast, assembly-language programs must be completely rewritten for the new system, which takes much more time.

The problem with high-level languages is that computers cannot execute high-level language instructions directly. Instead, a program called a *compiler* is used to convert the program into assembly language, which is then converted into machine language by an assembler. Figure 3-3 illustrates the process of developing and executing a program in a high-level language.

An alternative to compiling a program is to use an *interpreter* to execute the high-level language version of the program. Interpreters are programs that take high-level language programs as inputs and perform the steps defined by each instruction in the

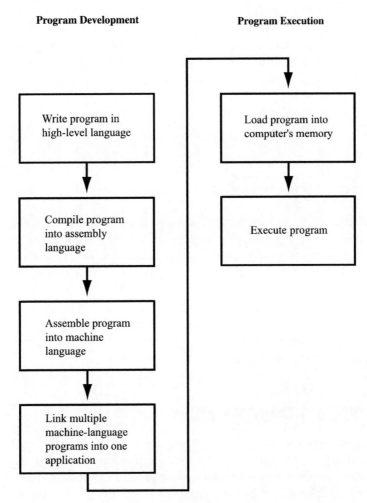

Program Development   **Program Execution**

Write program in high-level language

Load program into computer's memory

Compile program into assembly language

Execute program

Assemble program into machine language

Link multiple machine-language programs into one application

Fig. 3-3.   Program development.

high-level language program, generating the same result as compiling the program and then executing the compiled version. Interpreted programs tend to be much slower than compiled programs, because the interpreter has to examine each instruction in the source program as it occurs and then jump to a routine that performs the instruction. In many ways, this is similar to the compiler's task of determining the assembly-language instruction sequence that implements a given high-level language instruction, except that the interpreter must reinterpret each high-level language instruction each time it executes. If a program contains a loop that executes 10,000 times, the interpreter must interpret the loop 10,000 times, but the compiler only needs to compile it once.

Given their speed disadvantages, interpreters are much less common than compiled programs. They are mainly used in cases where it is important to be able to run a program on multiple different types of computer without recompiling it. In this case, using an interpreter allows each type of computer to execute the high-level language version of the program directly.

Compilers and assemblers have very different tasks. In general, there is a one-to-one mapping between assembly-language instructions and machine-language instructions, so all the assembler has to do is convert each instruction from one format to the other. A compiler, on the other hand, has to determine a sequence of assembly-language instructions that implement a high-level language program as efficiently as possible. Because of this, the execution time of a program written in a high-level language depends a great deal on how good the compiler is, while the execution time of a program originally written in assembly language depends completely on the set of instructions written by the programmer.

3.4   Operating Systems

On workstations, PCs, and mainframe computers, the *operating system* is responsible for managing the physical resources of the system, loading and executing programs, and interfacing with users. *Embedded systems*—computers designed for one specific task, such as controlling an appliance—often do not have operating systems because they only execute one program. The operating system is simply another program, one that knows about all the hardware in the computer, with one exception—it runs in *privileged* (or supervisor) mode, which allows it access to physical resources that user programs cannot control and gives it the ability to start or stop the execution of user programs.

3.4.1   MULTIPROGRAMMING

Most computer systems support *multiprogramming* (also called multitasking), a technique that allows the system to present the illusion that multiple programs are running on the computer simultaneously, even though the system may only have one processor. In a multiprogrammed system, user programs do not need to know which other programs are running on the system at the same time they are, or even how many other programs there are. The operating system and the hardware provide *protection* for programs, preventing any program from accessing another program's data unless the two programs have specifically arranged to access each other's data. Many multiprogrammed computers are also *multiuser* and allow more than one person to be logged in to the computer at once. Multiuser systems require that the operating system not only protect programs from accessing each other's data but prevent users from accessing data that is private to other users.

A multiprogrammed operating system presents the illusion that multiple programs are running simultaneously by switching between programs very rapidly, as illustrated in Fig. 3-4. Each program is allowed to execute for a fixed amount of time, known as a *timeslice*. When a program's timeslice ends, the operating system stops it, removes it from the processor, and loads another program into the processor. This process is known as a *context switch*. To do a context switch, the operating system copies the contents of the currently running program's register file (sometimes called the program's *context*) into memory, and then copies the contents of the next program's register file out of memory and into the register file. Programs cannot tell that a context switch has been performed—to them, it looks like they have been continuously running on the processor.

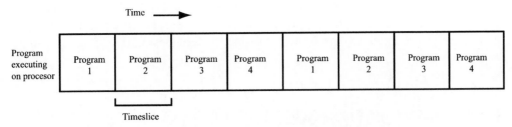

Fig. 3-4.   Multiprogrammed system.

Many computers context-switch 60 times per second, making timeslices 1/60th of a second, although some recent systems have started to context-switch more frequently. This has caused problems with programs that expect timeslices to be 1/60th of a second and use that information to time events or determine performance.

By context-switching 60 or more times per second, a computer can give each program an opportunity to execute sufficiently frequently that the system can prevent the illusion that a moderate number of programs are executing simulta-neously on the system. Obviously, as the number of programs on the system increases, this illusion breaks down—if the system is executing 120 programs, each program may only get a timeslice once every 2 seconds, which is enough of a delay for humans to notice. Multiprogramming can also increase the running time of applications, because the resources of the system are shared among all of the programs running on it.

3.4.2 PROTECTION

One of the main requirements of a multiprogrammed operating system is that it provide *protection* between programs running on the computer. This essentially means that the result of any program running on a multiprogrammed computer must be the same as if the program was the only program running on the computer. Programs must not be able to access other programs' data and must be confident that their data will not be modified by other programs. Similarly, programs must not be able to interfere with each other's use of the I/O subsystem.

Providing protection in a multiprogrammed or multiuser system requires that the operating system control the physical resources of the computer, including the processor, the memory, and the I/O devices. Otherwise, user programs could access any of the memory or other storage on the computer, gaining access to data that belongs to other programs or other users. This also allows the operating system to prevent more than one program from accessing an I/O device, such as a printer, at one time.

One technique that operating systems use to protect each program's data from other programs is *virtual memory*, which is described in detail in Chapter 10. Essentially, virtual memory allows each program to operate as if it were the only program running on the computer by *translating* memory addresses that the program references into the addresses used by the memory system. As long as the virtual memory system ensures that two programs' addresses don't translate into the same address, programs can be written as if they were the only program running on the machine, since no program's memory references will access data from another program.

3.4.3 PRIVILEGED MODE

To ensure that the operating system is the only program that can control the system's physical resources, it executes in *privileged mode*, while user programs execute in *user mode* (sometimes called unprivileged mode). Certain tasks, such as accessing an I/O device, performing context switches, or performing memory allocation, require that a program be in privileged mode. If a user-mode program tries to perform one of these tasks, the hardware prevents it from doing so and signals an error. When user-mode programs want to do something that requires privileged mode, they send a request to the operating system, known as a *system call*, that asks the operating system to do the operation for them. If the operation is something that the user program is allowed to do, the operating system performs the operation and returns the result to the user. Otherwise, it signals an error.

Because it controls the physical resources of the computer, the operating system is also responsible for the low-level user interface. When a user presses a key or otherwise sends input to the computer, the operating system is responsible for determining which program should receive the input and sending the input value to that program. Also, when a program wants to display some information for the user, such as printing a character on the monitor, it executes a system call to request that the operating system display the data.

3.5   Computer Organization

Figure 3-1 presented a high-level block diagram of a typical computer system. In this section, we present a brief introduction to each of the main subsystems: processor, memory, and I/O. The goal of this discussion is to give the reader enough high-level understanding of each subsystem to prepare them for later chapters that discuss each of these subsystems in more detail.

3.5.1   THE PROCESSOR

The processor is responsible for actually executing the instructions that make up programs and the operating system. As shown in Fig. 3-5, processors are made up of several building blocks: execution units, register files, and control logic. The execution units contain the hardware that executes instructions. This includes the hardware that fetches and decodes instructions, as well as the arithmetic logic units (ALUs) that perform actual computation. Many processors contain separate execution units for integer and floating-point computations because very different

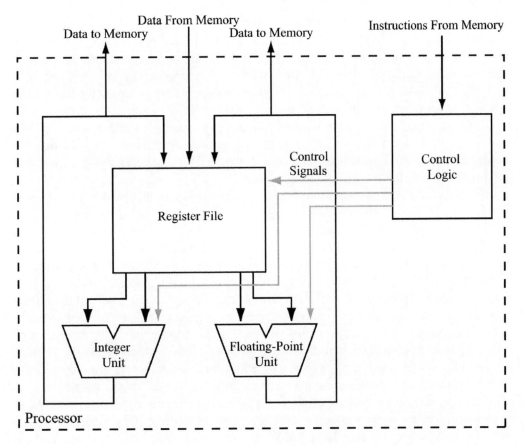

Fig. 3-5.   Processor block diagram.

hardware is required to handle these two data types. In addition, as we will see in Chapter 7, modern processors often use multiple execution units to execute instructions in parallel to improve performance.

The *register file* is a small storage area for data that the processor is using. Values stored in the register file can be accessed more quickly than data stored in the memory system, and register files generally support multiple simultaneous accesses. This allows an operation, such as an addition, to read all of its inputs from the register file at the same time, rather than having to read them one at a time. As we will see in Chapter 4, different processors access and use their register files in very different ways, but virtually all processors have a register file of some sort.

As might be guessed from its name, the control logic controls the rest of the processor, determining when instructions can be executed and what operations are required to execute each instruction. In early processors, the control logic was a very small fraction of the processor hardware compared to the ALUs and the register file, but the amount of control logic required has grown dramatically as processors have become more complex, making this one of the more difficult parts of a processor to design.

3.5.2 THE MEMORY SYSTEM

The memory system acts as a storage receptacle for the data and programs used by the computer. Most computers have two types of memory: *read-only memory* (ROM) and *random-access memory* (RAM). As its name suggests, the contents of the read-only memory cannot be modified by the computer but may be read. In general, the ROM is used to hold a program that is executed automatically by the computer every time it is turned on or reset. This program is called the bootstrap, or "boot" loader, and instructs the computer to load its operating system off of its hard disk or other I/O device. The name of this program comes from the idea that the computer is "pulling itself up by its own bootstraps" by executing a program that tells it how to load its own operating system.

The random-access memory, on the other hand, can be both read and written, and is used to hold the programs, operating system, and data required by the computer. RAM is generally volatile, meaning that it does not retain the data stored in it when the computer's power is turned off. Any data that needs to be stored while the computer is off must be written to a permanent storage device, such as a hard disk.

Memory (both RAM and ROM) is divided into a set of storage locations, each of which can hold 1 byte (8 bits) of data. The storage locations are numbered, and the number of a storage location (called its *address*) is used to tell the memory system which location the processor wants to reference. One of the important characteristics of a computer system is the width of the addresses it uses, which limits the amount of memory that the computer can address. Most current computers use either 32-bit or 64-bit addresses, allowing them to access either 2^{32} or 2^{64} bytes of memory.

Until Chapter 9, we will be using a simple random-access model of memory, in which all memory operations take the same amount of time. Our memory system will support two operations: load and store. Store operations take two operands, a value to be stored and the address that the value should be stored in. They place the specified value in the memory location specified by the address. Load operations take an operand that specifies the address containing the value to be loaded and return the contents of that memory location into their destination.

Using this model, the memory can be thought of as functioning similar to a large sheet of lined paper, where each line on the page represents a 1-byte storage location. To write (store) a value into the memory, you count down from the top of the page until you reach the line specified by the address, erase the value written on the line, and write in the new value. To read (load) a value, you count down from the top of the page until you reach the line specified by the address, and read the value written on that line.

Most computers allow more than 1 byte of memory to be loaded or stored at one time. Generally, a load or store operation operates on a quantity of data equal to the system's bit width, and the address sent to the memory system specifies the location of the lowest-addressed byte of data to be loaded or stored. For example, a 32-bit system loads or stores 32 bits (4 bytes) of data with each operation into the 4 bytes that start with the operation's address, so a load from location 424 would return a 32-bit quantity containing the bytes in location 424, 425, 426, and 427. To simplify the design of the memory system, some computers require loads and stores to be "aligned," meaning that the address of a memory reference must be a multiple of the size of the data being loaded or stored, so a 4-byte load must have an address that is a multiple of 4, an 8-byte store must have an address that is a multiple of 8, and so on. Other systems allow unaligned loads and stores, but take significantly longer to complete such operations than aligned loads.

An additional issue with multibyte loads and stores is the order in which the bytes are written to memory. There are two different ordering schemes that are used in modern computers: *little endian* and *big endian*. In a little-endian system, the least-significant (smallest value) byte of a word is written into the lowest-addressed byte, and the other bytes are written in increasing order of significance. In a big-endian system, the byte order is reversed, with the most significant byte being written into the byte of memory with the lowest address. The other bytes are written in decreasing order of significance. Figure 3-6 shows an example of how a little-endian system and a big-endian system would write a 32-bit (4-byte) data word to address 0x1000.

	0x1000	0x1001	0x1002	0x1003
Little Endian	ef	cd	ab	90
Big Endian	90	ab	cd	ef

Word = 0x90abcdef
Address = 0x1000

Fig. 3-6. Little endian versus big endian.

In general, programmers do not need to know the endianness of the system they are working on, except when the same memory location is accessed using loads and stores of different lengths. For example, if a 1-byte store of 0 into location 0x1000 was performed on the systems shown in Fig. 3-6, a subsequent 32-bit load from

0x1000 would return 0x90abcd00 on the little-endian system and 0x00abcdef on the big-endian system. Endianness is often an issue when transmitting data between different computer systems, however, as big-endian and little-endian computer systems will interpret the same sequence of bytes as different words of data. To get around this problem, the data must be processed to convert it to the endianness of the computer that will read it.

Memory system design has a tremendous impact on computer system performance and is often the limiting factor on how quickly an application executes. Both bandwidth (how much data can be loaded or stored in a given amount of time) and latency (how long a particular memory operation takes to complete) are critical to application performance. Other important issues in memory system design include protection (preventing different programs from accessing each other's data) and how the memory system interacts with the I/O system.

3.5.3 THE I/O SUBSYSTEM

The I/O subsystem contains the devices that the computer uses to communicate with the outside world and to store data, including hard disks, video displays, printers, and tape drives. I/O systems are covered in detail in Chapter 11. As shown in Fig. 3-1, I/O devices communicate with the processor through an I/O bus, which is separate from the memory bus that the processor uses to communicate with the memory system.

Using an I/O bus allows a computer to interface with a wide range of I/O devices without having to implement a specific interface for each I/O device. An I/O bus can also support a variable number of devices, allowing users to add devices to a computer after it has been purchased. Devices can be designed to interface with the bus, allowing them to be compatible with any computer that uses the same type of I/O bus. For example, almost all PCs and many workstations use the PCI bus standard for their I/O bus. All of these systems can interface to devices designed to meet the PCI standard. All that is required is a *device driver* for each operating system—a program that allows the operating system to control the I/O device. The downsides of using an I/O bus to interface to I/O devices is that all of the I/O devices on a computer must share the I/O bus and I/O buses are slower than dedicated connections between the processor and an I/O device because I/O buses are designed for maximum compatibility and flexibility.

I/O systems have been one of the least-studied aspects of computer architecture, even though their performance is critical to many applications. In recent years, the performance of I/O systems has become even more critical with the rising importance of database and transaction-processing systems, both of which depend heavily on the I/O subsystems of the computers they run on. This has made I/O systems an area of active research, particularly given the high prices that many companies are willing to pay for improvements in the performance of database and transaction-processing systems.

3.6   Summary

The purpose of this chapter has been to lay the groundwork for upcoming chapters by presenting an introduction to the major hardware building blocks of computer systems and the software components that interact with them. We discussed how computer systems are broken down into processors, memory systems, and I/O, and provided an introduction to each of these topics. This chapter also covered the different levels at which programs are implemented, ranging from the machine languages that processors execute to the high-level languages that humans typically use to program computers.

The next several chapters will concentrate on processor architecture, from programming models to techniques for improving performance like pipelining and instruction-level parallelism. After that, we will examine the memory system, discussing virtual memory, memory hierarchies, and cache memories. Finally, we will conclude with a discussion of I/O systems and an introduction to multi-processing.

 ## Solved Problems

Stored-Program Computers

3.1. The program for emacs (a UNIX text editor) is 2,878,448 bytes long on the computer being used to write this book. If a human could enter 1 byte of the program per second into the switches used to program a non-stored-program computer (which seems optimistic), how long would it take to start up the emacs program? If the human had an error rate of 0.001 percent in entering data, how many errors would be made in entering the program?

Solution

At 1 byte/s, the program would take 2,878,448 s, which is approximately 47,974 min, or 800 h, or 33.3 days. Obviously, a text editor would not be much use if it took over a month to start up.

An error rate of 0.001 percent is one error per 100,000 bytes, which would be extremely good for a human. Even so, the human would be expected to make approximately 29 errors in entering the program, each of which would have to be debugged and corrected before the program would run correctly.

Machine Language versus Assembly Language

3.2. **a.** What is the difference between machine language and assembly language?
b. Why is assembly language considered easier for humans to program in than machine language?

Solution

a. Machine-language instructions are the patterns of bits used to represent operations within the computer. Assembly language is a more human-readable version of machine language, in which each instruction is represented by a text string that describes what the instruction does.

b. In assembly-language programming, the assembler is responsible for converting assembly-language instructions into machine language, not the human. Humans generally find it easier to understand the text strings that represent assembly-language instructions than the numbers that encode machine language instructions. Also, relying on the assembler to translate assembly-language instructions into machine-language instructions eliminates the possibility of errors in generating the machine-language representation of each instruction.

Self-Modifying Programs

3.3. Why are self-modifying programs less common today than they were on early computers?

Solution

There are two main reasons. First, self-modifying code is harder to debug than non-self-modifying code, because the program that is executed is different from the one that was written. As computers have gotten faster, the performance advantages of self-modifying code have become less significant than the increased debugging difficulty.

Second, improvements in memory system design have reduced the performance improvement that can be gained through self-modifying code.

Compilers versus Assemblers

3.4. Explain briefly why the quality of a compiler has more impact on the execution time of a program developed using the compiler than the quality of an assembler has on programs developed using the assembler.

Solution

In general, there is a one-to-one mapping between assembly-language and machine-language instructions. An assembler's job is to translate each assembly-language instruction into its machine-language representation. Assuming the assembler does this translation correctly, the instructions in the resulting machine-language program are exactly the same as those in the source assembly-language program, just in a different encoding. Because the assembler does not change the set of instructions in a program, it has no impact on the execution time of the program.

In contrast, a compiler's job is to determine a sequence of assembly-language instructions that perform the computation specified by a high-level language program. Since the compiler is creating the sequence of assembly-language instructions for the program itself, the quality of the compiler has a great deal of impact on how long the resulting program takes to execute. Bad compilers create programs that do a great deal of unnecessary work and therefore run slowly, while good compilers eliminate this unnecessary work to deliver better performance.

Multiprogramming (I)

3.5. How does a multiprogrammed system present the illusion that multiple programs are running on the machine simultaneously? What factors can cause this illusion to break down?

Solution

Multiprogrammed systems rotate through the programs running on them very frequently—60 or more times per second. As long as the number of programs running on the system is relatively small, each program will get a chance to execute often enough that the system looks like it is executing all of the programs at the same time, in that they all appear to be making progress simultaneously.

If the number of programs running on the system gets too large—for example, approaching the number of context switches performed per second—users will be able to notice the gaps in time when a given program isn't making progress, and the illusion will break down. Even with a small number of programs running on the machine, it is often possible to tell that the machine is sharing its processor among the programs, because each program's rate of progress will be slower than if it had the machine to itself.

Multiprogramming (II)

3.6. If an 800-MHz computer context-switches 60 times per second, how many cycles are there in each time slice?

Solution

800 MHz $= 800,000,000$ cycles/s. $800,000,000/60 = 13,333,333$ cycles/timeslice.

Multiprogramming (III)

3.7. Suppose a given computer context-switches 60 times per second. If the human interacting with the computer notices any time a given operation takes more than 0.5 s to respond to an input, how many programs can be running on the computer and have the system guarantee that the human never notices a delay? (Assume that the system switches between programs in a round-robin fashion, that a program can always respond to an input during the first timeslice that it executes in after the input occurs, and that programs always execute for a full timeslice when they are selected to execute.) How many programs can be running before the human notices a delay at least half the time?

Solution

If the computer context-switches 60 times per second, there are 30 context switches in 0.5 s. Therefore, the computer can execute up to 30 programs and guarantee that each program gets a timeslice within 0.5 s of any user input. Since each program is guaranteed to respond to user inputs during its first timeslice after the input occurs, this will guarantee that the human never notices a delay.

For the human to only see a delay half of the time, there has to be a 50 percent chance that the program that an input is directed to gets a timeslice within 0.5 s after the input occurs. Since programs execute in round-robin fashion, this means that half of the programs have to execute within 0.5 s after the input. Since 30 programs execute in 0.5 s, there can be up to 60 programs running on the computer before the human notices a delay more than half the time.

Operating Systems (I)

3.8. Give two examples of problems that could occur if a computer allowed user programs to access I/O devices directly, rather than requiring them to go through the operating system.

Solution

The two examples described in this chapter are

1. Protection violations—If user programs can access data storage devices directly, then they can read or write data that belongs to other programs that they should not have access to.

2. Sequential access violation—A program might not be done with a device when its timeslice ends. If another program tries to use the device before the program gets another timeslice, the I/O operations of the two programs could become interleaved. This could result in unusual errors, such as the output of two programs being interleaved on the computer's monitor.

Another problem that wasn't discussed has to do with the fact that user programs are untrusted—they may have errors or may be actively malicious. If user programs can directly access I/O devices, they can send illegal operations or otherwise interfere with the ability of other programs to use the device. Having the operating system, which is a trusted program, control the devices eliminates this problem because the operating system can check to make sure any requested operation is legal before performing it.

Operating Systems (II)

3.9. Why is it necessary for a computer system to provide a privileged mode and a user mode for programs?

Solution

Privileged mode is the mechanism that computers use to prevent user programs from performing tasks that are limited to the operating system. Without a privileged execution mode, the hardware would be unable to tell whether the program attempting an operation were a user program or the operating system, preventing it from knowing whether the program should be allowed to perform the operation. Some systems provide more than two execution levels to allow different programs to be allowed access to different resources, but two levels are sufficient for most operating systems.

Register Files

3.10. Why does increasing the amount of data that can be stored in a processor's register file generally increase the performance of the processor?

Solution

Data in the register files can be accessed more quickly than data in the memory system. Therefore, being able to keep more data in the register file allows more data to be accessed at this faster speed, improving performance.

Memory Systems (I)

3.11. What is the difference between RAM and ROM?

Solution

Read-only memory (ROM) holds data that the processor can only read, not modify. It is used for things like the boot program that the system runs when the power is turned on. Random-access memory (RAM) can be both read and written. It is used to hold programs and data during operation of the computer.

Memory Systems (II)

3.12. Suppose that a computer's memory system did not have the random-access property—that is, that memory references took different amounts of time to complete depending on which address they referenced. How would this complicate the process of program development?

Solution

Non-random-access memory would require that programmers keep track of where a program's data was stored in memory in order to maximize performance. Programmers would want to store frequently accessed variables in locations that had short access times to reduce the total amount of time spent accessing memory. With random-access memory, the location of a variable in memory is irrelevant to its access time, so it doesn't matter where data is placed.

Big-Endian versus Little-Endian Addressing

3.13. The 32-bit value 0x30a79847 is stored to the location 0x1000. What is the value of the byte in address 0x1002 if the system is big endian? Little endian?

Solution

In a big-endian system, the most-significant byte in the word is stored in the address specified by the store operation, with successively lower-order bytes being stored in later locations. Therefore, the byte 0x98 will be stored in location 0x1002.

In a little-endian system, the lowest-order byte is stored in the location of the operation, and higher-order bytes are stored in successive locations. In this system, the value in location 0x1002 will be 0xa7 after the operation completes.

I/O Systems

3.14. What are the trade-offs involved in using a single I/O bus for all of the devices connected to a given system?

Solution

The trade-off is mainly one of bandwidth versus versatility. Using a single bus means that all of the devices attached to the processor have to share the bandwidth of the bus, limiting performance. However, using a single bus allows many devices to interface to a single system without requiring that the system designers provide separate interfaces for each possible device. Devices can be designed to match the interface of the bus, allowing the computer to interface to a wide range of devices, even ones that did not exist when the computer was being designed.

CHAPTER 4

Programming Models

4.1   Objectives

This chapter describes the programming models used on two types of processors: stack-based architectures and general-purpose register architectures. We begin with a discussion of the types of operations provided by most processors. A description of stack-based architectures and general-purpose register architectures follow. Each architecture's description includes a sample instruction set for that type of processor that will form the basis for examples and exercises throughout the rest of this book. The chapter concludes with a comparison of the two programming models and a discussion of how stacks are used to implement procedure calls, even on general-purpose register architectures.

After completing this chapter, you should

1. Be familiar with the different types of operations provided on most processors.
2. Understand stack-based architectures and be able to write short assembly-language programs in the instruction set described in this chapter.
3. Understand general-purpose register architectures and be able to write short assembly-language programs for these architectures.
4. Be able to compare general-purpose register architectures and stack-based architectures and describe situations in which each style would be more appropriate.
5. Understand procedure calls and how they are implemented.

4.2   Introduction

In the last chapter, we described programs as a set of machine instructions, without giving much detail about what instructions are or how they are implemented. In this chapter, we will cover two programming models for processors: stack-based architectures and general-purpose register (GPR) architectures. A processor's *programming model* defines how instructions access their operands and how instructions are described in the processor's assembly language, but not the set of operations that are provided by the processor. As we will see, processors with different programming models can provide very similar sets of operations but may require very different approaches to programming.

Figure 4-1 gives a high-level view of how instructions are executed that we will use in this chapter. Later chapters will give more detailed explanations of instruction execution. First, the processor fetches (reads) the instruction from memory. The address of the next instruction to be executed is stored in a special register known as the *program counter* (PC), which is sometimes called the *instruction pointer* (IP), so the processor can easily determine where it should look for the next instruction in memory.

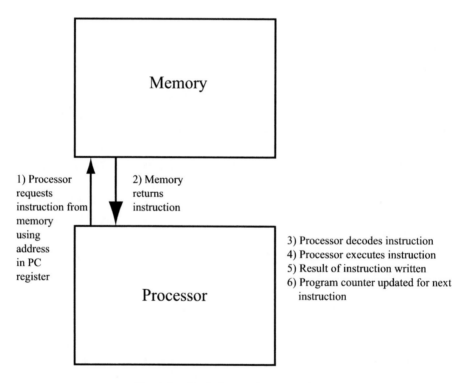

Fig. 4-1. Basic instruction execution.

Once the memory system has delivered the instruction to the processor, the processor examines the instruction to see what it has to do to complete the instruction, performs the operation specified by the instruction, and writes the result of the instruction into either a register or the memory system. The processor then updates the program counter to contain the address of the next instruction to be executed and repeats the process.

The remainder of this chapter begins with a discussion of the different types of instructions provided by most processors. We then give an introduction to stack-based architectures and present a sample instruction set for a stack-based architecture. A discussion of general-purpose register architectures follows, including a sample instruction set for these architectures. The chapter concludes with a discussion of how stacks are used to implement procedure calls on both stack-based and general-purpose register architectures.

4.3   Types of Instructions

One of the factors that differentiates processors is their *instruction sets*—the sets of basic operations provided by each processor. Early computers had very different instruction sets, and instruction set design was one of the main tasks of computer architects. As the field has progressed, the set of operations provided by processors has converged, and now almost all processors provide very similar sets of instructions, regardless of whether they use a stack-based or general-purpose register programming model. These basic operations can be divided into four categories: arithmetic operations, memory operations, comparisons, and control operations (branches).

4.3.1 ARITHMETIC OPERATIONS

Arithmetic operations perform basic computations, such as additions, multiplications, logical operations (AND, OR), and data copying. They generally take one or two inputs, and generate one output. In general, arithmetic operations read their inputs from and write their outputs to the register file, though some CISC (complex instruction set computer) architectures allow arithmetic operations to reference memory. CISC architectures are covered in more detail in the next chapter.

Figure 4-2 shows the set of arithmetic operations that we will be using in this book, which are representative of the arithmetic operations provided by most modern processors. Most processors provide a superset of these operations, often having multiple instructions that provide variations of a single operation. The operations presented here were selected as a compromise between completeness and complexity, with the goal of providing a rich enough instruction set to implement most programs without overwhelming the reader with complexity. Note that many of the instructions have integer and floating-point forms. This allows the hardware to determine whether it should treat the instruction's inputs as integers or floating-point quantities and determines which register file should be used on architectures that have separate integer and floating-point registers.

Most of the arithmetic operations presented in Fig. 4-2 are relatively self-explanatory, although two (ASH and LSH) deserve further explanation. These operations are examples of shift operations, operations that change the position of the bits in one of their inputs. Shift operations take the bits in their first input and move them left by a number of bit positions equal to the value of their second input (negative values of the second input indicate that the bits are shifted to the right). The differences between these operations lie in what values they insert into bit positions that are made vacant because a bit is shifted out of them but no bit is

Operation	Function
ADD	Adds its two integer operands
FADD	Adds its two floating-point operands
SUB	Subtracts its second integer operand from its first
FSUB	Subtracts its second floating-point operand from its first
MUL	Multiplies its two integer operands
FMUL	Multiplies its two floating-point operands
DIV	Divides its first integer input by its second
FDIV	Divides its first floating-point input by its second
MOV	Copies its input (of any type) to its output, both of which may be of any type
OR	Performs a logical OR on its two inputs, which can be of any type
AND	Performs a logical AND on its two inputs, which can be of any type
NOT	Performs logical negation on its input, which can be of any type
ASH	Shifts (arithmetic) its first input by the number of positions specified in its second input
LSH	Shifts (logical) its first input by the number of positions specified in its second input

Fig. 4-2.   Arithmetic operations.

available to shift into them (for example, what value goes into the low bit of a word that is left-shifted one place).

Logical shift (LSH) operations are the simpler of the two shift operations. Bits that are shifted out of the word are discarded, and zeroes are shifted into vacant bit positions.

EXAMPLE
On a system with 8-bit data words, what is the result of doing an LSH operation whose first input is 25 and whose second input is 2?

Solution

The 8-bit integer representation of 25 is 0b 0001 1001. Shifting this to the left two bit positions gives 0b0110 01xx, where the "x" bits indicate vacant bits. The LSH operation specifies that zeroes are shifted into vacant bit positions, so the final result is 0b0110 0100, which is the 8-bit binary representation of 100.

One thing to note from the example is that shifting an unsigned or positive integer binary value to the left has the effect of multiplying it by 2^n, where n is the number of bit positions that the value is shifted by. Similarly, shifting an unsigned or positive integer binary value to the right n positions divides it by 2^n, discarding any bits of remainder from the division. Shift operations are often faster than multiplications and divisions, so many compilers and programmers use them in preference to multiplication operations when multiplying or dividing numbers by powers of 2.

However, the LSH operation does not generate the correct result for dividing a negative integer by a power of 2 when either two's-complement or sign-magnitude integers are used. For example, the 8-bit two's-complement representation of -16 is 0b1111 0000. Using LSH to shift this quantity right 1 bit (a shift of -1 positions) gives 0b0111 1000, the two's-complement representation of 120, because shifting a 0 into the high bit position of a two's-complement integer makes the result a positive value.

On systems that use two's-complement integers, the ASH (arithmetic shift) operation preserves the sign of the shifted value by copying the high bit of the word into all bits that are made vacant by a right-shift. When shifting to the left, zeroes are copied into the vacant bits to generate the correct result for multiplying by two. Thus, ASH can be used to multiply and divide two's-complement numbers by powers of 2, with the caveat that using ASH to divide negative numbers by powers of 2 rounds to the next most negative integer rather than discarding the remainder. For example, using ASH to divide -31 by 2 in a two's-complement system will yield a result of -16.

EXAMPLE
What is the result of executing an ASH operation whose first input is -15 and whose second input is 3, when executed on a system that uses 8-bit two's-complement integers? What if the second input is -3?

Solution

The 8-bit two's-complement representation of -15 is 0b1111 0001. Shifting to the left by three places, we get 0b1000 1000, because ASH places zeroes in vacant bit positions when shifting to the left. This is the 8-bit two's-complement representation of -120, the result of multiplying 15 by 2^3.

Shifting -15 by -3 positions is a right-shift of three places, yielding a result of 0b1111 1110, because ASH copies the high bit of the number being shifted into the vacant bit positions when doing a right-shift. This is the 8-bit two's-complement representation for -2, the correct result of dividing 15 by 2^3 if we round to the next most negative integer.

ASH can be implemented on systems that use sign-magnitude numbers by keeping the value of the sign bit the same as it was on the input word and performing a logical shift on the magnitude portion of the word. When ASH is implemented in this fashion, division operations on both positive and negative integers round their result by discarding the remainder from the operation.

4.3.2 MEMORY OPERATIONS

Memory operations transfer data between the processor and the memory system. As will be discussed in Chapter 5, one of the big differences between RISC (reduced instruction set computer) and CISC architectures is whether memory can only be accessed through memory operations or whether other operations can access the memory system. For this book, we will assume that processors have two memory operations: load (LD) and store (ST).

Each of these operations operates on an amount of data equal to the word size of the machine, so a LD reads one word of data from the addresses starting at the address specified by its input, and a ST writes one word of data to the memory starting at the address specified by its address input. Many processors provide a larger set of load and store operations that operate on different amounts of data, but we will stick with just two for simplicity. See Fig. 4-3.

Operation	Function
LD	Loads the contents of the address specified by its input operand into its destination
ST	Stores the value contained in its second input into the address specified by its first input.

Fig. 4-3.   Memory operations.

4.3.3 COMPARISONS

As their name would suggest, comparison operations compare two or more values so that the program can make decisions. There is a great deal of variation among different processors in how they handle the output of comparison operations. Some processors write the results of the comparison into a register in the register file. Others provide a special register that holds the result of the most recent comparison operation. Architectures that use a special comparison result register have become less common in the recent past, as only having one place to put comparison results makes it impossible to perform multiple comparisons in parallel. Figure 4-4 shows a common set of comparison operations. Most processors also provide an equivalent set of floating-point comparison operations.

Operation	Function
EQ	Tests its two integer operands to see if they are equal
NEQ	Tests its two integer operands to see if they are not equal.
GT	Determines if its first integer operand is greater than its second
LT	Determines if its first integer operand is less than its second
GEQ	Determines if its first integer operand is greater than or equal to its second
LEQ	Determines if its first integer operand is less than or equal to its second

Fig. 4-4.   Comparison operations.

Comparison operations are generally used in conjunction with control operations to create a *conditional branch* that executes either one section of a program or another depending on the result of the comparison. This usage is so common that many processors provide conditional branch operations that combine a comparison and a branch into one instruction. For simplicity, the instruction sets presented later in this chapter for stack-based and general-purpose register architectures will omit the comparison instructions and provide only conditional branch instructions, since conditional branches are the most common use of comparisons.

4.3.4 CONTROL OPERATIONS

Control (branch) operations affect program flow by changing the processor's PC. When an operation other than a control operation executes, the hardware increments the program counter by the size of the instruction so that it now points to the next instruction in the program. For example, on an architecture in which instructions are 32 bits long, 4 would be added to the PC after each instruction was executed because 32 bits is 4 bytes.

When a control operation executes, the program counter is set to the input[1] of the control instruction, causing execution to jump to a different point in the program. Control operations, which are often called branches, can be divided into two categories: *unconditional* and *conditional*. Unconditional branches, also called jumps, always set the PC equal to their input when they execute. Conditional branches set the PC equal to their input if some condition, such as the result of a comparison, is true. Depending on the architecture, the comparison can be performed as part of the branch operation, or can have been performed by a separate instruction earlier in the program. Figure 4-5 shows a common set of control operations that we will assume our processors provide.

When programmers write assembly-language programs or compilers generate them from high-level language programs, they generally do not specify the destination addresses of branches as the address of the destination instruction in memory. Instead, instructions are labeled with text values, and branch instructions refer to these values. For example, in the (infinite) loop shown in Fig. 4-6, the label "loop_start" is associated with the instruction that immediately follows it. The branch instruction at the end of the loop uses the label "loop_start" as its target, indicating that the program should branch back to the instruction following the label after executing the branch. One of the duties of the assembler is to compute the address corresponding to each label and insert that address into any branch instruction that references the label. As we will discuss in more detail in the next chapter, these addresses are often expressed as offsets from the branch to its destination rather than the address of the destination in memory.

Using labels instead of numeric addresses has two advantages. First, it is much easier for the programmer to understand. Looking at the code example in Fig. 4-6, it

---

[1] Many processors provide different *addressing modes* for branch instructions that cause the branch instruction to perform a computation and set the PC to the result of the computation instead of just setting the PC to the value of its input. Addressing modes are described in more detail in the next chapter.

Operation	Function
BR (or JMP)	Sets the PC equal to the value of its input operand, causing the instruction at that address to be executed next.
BEQ	Sets the PC equal to the value of its first operand if its other two inputs are equal.
BNE	Sets the PC equal to the value of its first operand if its other two inputs are not equal.
BLT	Sets the PC equal to the value of its first operand if its second operand is less than its third operand.
BGT	Sets the PC equal to the value of its first operand if its second operand is greater than its third operand.
BLE	Sets the PC equal to the value of its first operand if its second operand is less than or equal to its third operand.
BGE	Sets the PC equal to the value of its first operand if its second operand is greater than or equal to its third operand.

Fig. 4-5.   Control operations.

is clear where the target of the branch instruction is, even if you don't know anything about the architecture of the processor. If the target were specified by a numeric address, you would have to know how much space each instruction takes up to be able to figure out the destination of each branch, and even that would take some work. The second advantage of using labels is that the address corresponding to a label can change if the instructions before the label change. If numeric addresses were used instead of labels, the destination of each branch would have to be changed every time the number of instructions before the branch changed. Instead, the programmer or compiler uses labels to specify the destination of each branch, and the assembler calculates the address of each label when the program is assembled.

```
loop_start:
        (instruction)
        (instruction)
        (instruction)
        BR loop_start;
```

Fig. 4-6.   Label example.

4.4   Stack-Based Architectures

In a stack-based architecture, the register file is invisible to the program. Instead, instructions read their operands from, and write their results to, a *stack*, a last-in-first-out (LIFO) data structure.

4.4.1 THE STACK

As illustrated in Fig. 4-7, a stack is a last-in-first-out (LIFO) data structure. The name *stack* comes from the fact that the data structure acts like a stack of plates or

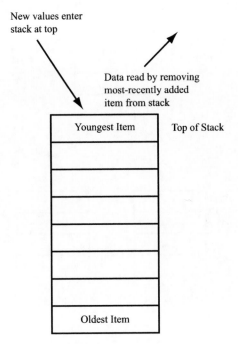

New values enter
stack at top

Data read by removing
most-recently added
item from stack

Youngest Item   Top of Stack

Oldest Item

Fig. 4-7. A stack.

other items—when a new plate is put on a stack of plates, it goes on the top, and it is the first plate removed when someone takes a plate off of the stack. Stacks consist of a set of locations, each of which can hold one word of data. When a value is added to the stack, it is placed in the *top* location of the stack, and all data currently in the stack is moved down one location. Data can only be removed from the top of the stack. When this is done, all other data in the stack moves up one location. In general, data cannot be read from a stack without disturbing the stack, although some processors may provide special operations to allow this.

Stacks support two basic operations: PUSH and POP. A PUSH operation takes one argument and places the value of the argument on the top of the stack, pushing all previous data down one location. A POP operation removes the top value from the stack and returns it, allowing the value to be used as the input to an instruction. Figure 4-8 shows how a set of PUSH and POP operations affect a stack.

Initially, the stack is empty. The first PUSH operation places the value 4 in the top-of-stack location. The second PUSH operation places 5 in the top of the stack, pushing the 4 down to the next location. A POP operation is then executed, which removes the 5 from the top of the stack and returns it. The 4 then moves up to the top of the stack. Finally, a PUSH 7 operation is executed, leaving 7 in the top of the stack and 4 in the next location down.

4.4.2 IMPLEMENTING STACKS

As an abstract data structure, stacks are assumed to be infinitely deep, meaning that an arbitrary amount of data can be placed on the stack by the program. In practice,

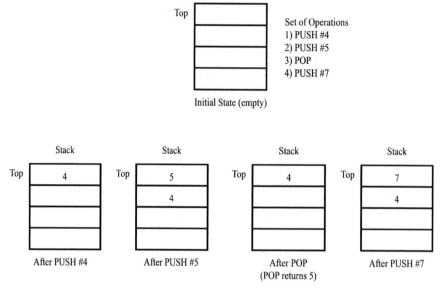

Fig. 4-8.   Stack example.

stacks are implemented using buffers in memory, which are finite in size. If the amount of data in the stack exceeds the amount of space allocated to the stack, a *stack overflow* error occurs.

Figure 4-9 shows how a stack is implemented in the memory system of a computer. A fixed location defines the bottom of the stack, and a pointer gives the location of the top of the stack (the location of the last value pushed onto the stack). When a value is pushed onto the stack, the top-of-stack pointer is incremented by the word size of the machine and the value being pushed is stored into memory at the address pointed to by the new value of the top-of-stack pointer. To pop a value off of the stack, the value in the location pointed to by the top-of-stack pointer is read, and the top-of-stack pointer is decremented by the word size of the machine. When the top-of-stack pointer and the bottom pointer are the same, the stack is empty, and an attempt to pop data off of the stack results in an error. Several variations on this approach are possible, including ones where the bottom pointer points to the highest address in the stack buffer and the stack grows toward lower addresses.

This approach results in a completely functional stack, but accessing the stack tends to be relatively slow, because of the latency of the memory system. If the stack were kept completely in memory, executing a typical arithmetic instruction, such as ADD, would require four memory operations: one to fetch the instruction, two to fetch the operands from the stack, and one to write the result back onto the stack. To speed up stack accesses, stack-based processors may incorporate a register file in the processor and keep the top N values (where N is the size of the register file) on the stack in the register file.

Figure 4-10 illustrates how this works. Essentially, the register file is treated as a separate memory buffer from the buffer in main memory, with its own top-of-stack pointer. Since the register file contains a fixed number of storage locations, a

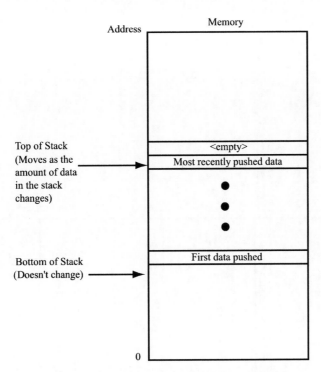

Fig. 4-9. Stack implementation in memory.

bottom-of-stack pointer is not required; the top-of-stack pointer simply keeps track of how many of the registers contain data. To push a value onto the stack, the register file top-of-stack pointer is incremented, and the value is copied into the register that it points to. When the register file becomes full, its contents are copied into the stack buffer in memory, and the top-of-stack pointers in both memory and the register file are adjusted to reflect that the register file is now empty and that the memory buffer contains more data. POP operations use a similar approach, with the register file being refilled from the buffer in memory when it becomes empty.

This approach can lead to a lot of memory accesses when the register file is nearly full or nearly empty and PUSHes and POPs alternate, because the register file is continually being copied to and from memory. Systems may choose to only half-empty or half-fill the register file when it over- or underflows to reduce this effect.

4.4.3 INSTRUCTIONS IN A STACK-BASED ARCHITECTURE

As stated above, instructions in a stack-based architecture get their operands from and write their results to the stack. When an instruction executes, it pops its operands off of the stack, performs the required computation, and pushes the result onto the top of the stack. Figure 4-11 shows an example of executing an ADD instruction on a stack-based architecture.

One of the significant advantages of stack-based architectures is that programs take up very little memory, because it is not necessary to specify where the source and destination of the operation are located. Thus, an instruction for a stack-based

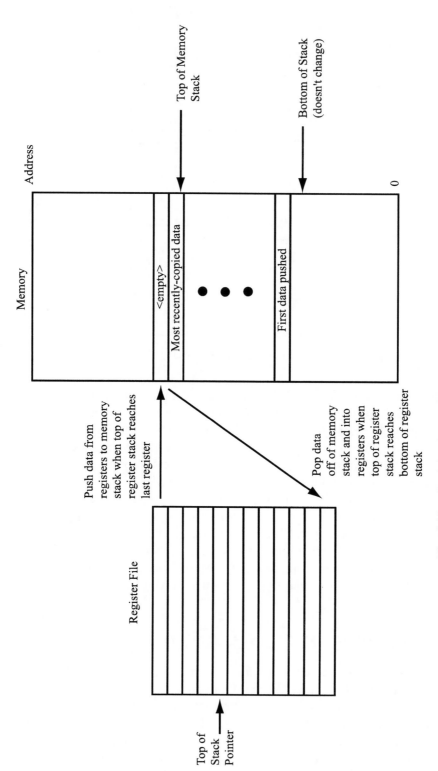

Fig. 4-10. Stack implementation using memory and registers.

ADD Instruction Execution

| Initial Stack | ADD pops the top two values off of the stack and adds them | ADD pushes its result onto the stack |

Top

3	8	7
4	12	8
8	<empty>	12
12	<empty>	<empty>

Fig. 4-11. Stack-based instruction execution.

processor can often be represented in just 1 byte that specifies the operation, although this can vary depending on how many operations the processor supports. The exception to this are PUSH instructions, whose operand is a constant specified in the instruction itself. Depending on the size of the constant allowed in the instruction, PUSH instructions can take 24 bits or more (8 bits to specify the operation and 16 bits of constant) to encode.

4.4.4 STACK-BASED INSTRUCTION SET

This section presents a sample instruction set for a stack-based processor, which we will use in programming exercises in this chapter. In describing this instruction set and the GPR instruction set presented later, we will use the following notation, which is frequently used in describing instructions:

"a $<-$ b": The value of b is placed in a.
(a): The memory location whose address is contained in a.
#X: The constant value X.
PC: The program counter. We will only refer to the PC in describing branch instructions. For non-branch instructions, it will be assumed that the PC is incremented to point to the next instruction without specifying this in the instruction description. This is done to simplify the instruction descriptions, and because the amount by which the PC is incremented varies depending on how the instructions are encoded into binary values, which we are not specifying here.

Variables such as a, b, and c are used to assign temporary names to data popped off of the stack and do not necessarily correspond to actual storage locations in the processor. This notation will not be required in describing the GPR instruction set, but it is used here to make the order of operands clearer for operations where the order of operands affects the result, such as subtractions.

We will use the value STACK to indicate a reference to the stack. When STACK is used as an input, the stack is popped and the top value returned. When STACK is used as a destination, the value written is pushed onto the stack. Thus, the ADD operation can be described by the following sequence:

```
a <- STACK
b <- STACK
STACK <- a + b
```

For simplicity, we will assume that the processor implements conditional branch operations, rather than separate comparisons and branches. For operations where the order of operations matters, the order was chosen to match the order used on RPN calculators, so that the sequence PUSH #4, PUSH #3, SUB computes 4 − 3.

Our example processor will execute the following instructions:

PUSH #X	STACK <- X
POP	a <- STACK (the value popped is discarded)
LD	a <- STACK STACK <- (a)
ST	a <- STACK (a) <- STACK
ADD	a <- STACK b <- STACK STACK <- a + b (integer computation)
FADD	a <- STACK b <- STACK STACK <- a + b (floating-point computation)
SUB	a <- STACK b <- STACK STACK <- b - a (integer computation)
FSUB	a <- STACK b <- STACK STACK <- b - a (floating-point computation)
MUL	a <- STACK b <- STACK STACK <- a × b (integer computation)
FMUL	a <- STACK b <- STACK STACK <- a × b (floating-point computation)
DIV	a <- STACK b <- STACK STACK <- b / a (integer computation)
FDIV	a <- STACK b <- STACK STACK <- b / a (floating-point computation)
AND	a <- STACK b <- STACK STACK <- a & b (bit-wise computation)

OR	a <- STACK
	b <- STACK
	STACK <- a | b (bit-wise computation)
NOT	a <- STACK
	STACK <- !a (bit-wise negation)
ASH	a <- STACK
	b <- STACK
	STACK <- a shifted by b positions (arithmetic shift)
LSH	a <- STACK
	b <- STACK
	STACK <- a shifted by b positions (logical shift)
BR	PC <- STACK
BEQ	a <- STACK
	b <- STACK
	c <- STACK
	PC <- c if b is equal to a
BNE	a <- STACK
	b <- STACK
	c <- STACK
	PC <- c if b is not equal to a
BLT	a <- STACK
	b <- STACK
	c <- STACK
	PC <- c if b is less than a
BGT	a <- STACK
	b <- STACK
	c <- STACK
	PC <- c if b is greater than a
BLE	a <- STACK
	b <- STACK
	c <- STACK
	PC <- c if b is less than or equal to a
BGE	a <- STACK
	b <- STACK
	c <- STACK
	PC <- c if b is greater than or equal to a

4.4.5 PROGRAMS IN A STACK-BASED ARCHITECTURE

Stack-based programs are simply sequences of instructions that get executed one after the other. Given a stack-based program and an initial configuration of the stack, the result of the program can be computed by applying the first instruction in the program, determining the state of the stack and memory after the first instruction completes and repeating with each successive instruction.

Writing programs for stack-based processors can be somewhat more difficult, because stack-based processors are better suited to postfix (RPN) notation than traditional infix notation. Infix notation is the traditional way of representing mathematical expressions, in which the operation is placed between the operands.

In postfix notation, the operation is placed after the operands. For example, the infix expression "2 + 3" becomes "2 3 +" in postfix notation. Once an expression has been recoded in postfix notation, converting it into a stack-based program is straightforward. Starting at the left, each constant is replaced with a PUSH operation to place the constant on the stack, and operators are replaced with the appropriate instruction to perform their operation.

EXAMPLE

Create a stack-based program that performs the following computation:

$$2 + (7 \times 3)$$

Solution

First, we need to convert the expression into postfix notation. This is best done by iteratively converting each subexpression into postfix, so $2 + (7 \times 3)$ becomes $2 + (7\ 3\times)$ and then $2\ (7\ 3\times)\ +$. We then convert the postfix expression into a series of instructions, as described above, giving

```
PUSH #2
PUSH #7
PUSH #3
MUL
ADD
```

To verify that this program is correct, we hand-simulate its execution. After the three PUSH statements, the stack contains the values 3, 7, 2 (starting from the top of the stack). The MUL instruction pops the 3 and the 7 off the stack, multiplies them, and pushes the result (21) onto the stack, making the stack contents 21, 2. The ADD pops these two values off of the stack and adds them, placing the result (23) onto the stack, which is the result of the computation. This matches the result of the original expression, so the program is correct.

4.5   General-Purpose Register Architectures

In a general-purpose register (GPR) architecture, instructions read their operands from and write their results to a random-access register file, similar to the one illustrated in Fig. 4-12. The general-purpose register file allows an instruction to access the registers in any order by specifying the number (also called the register ID) of the register to be accessed, much like the memory system allows the addresses in the memory to be accessed in any order. Another significant difference between a general-purpose register file and a stack is that reading the contents of a general-purpose register does not change them, unlike popping values off of a stack. Successive reads of a general-purpose register with no intervening writes will return

Register File

Register 0	<data>
Register 1	<data>
Register 2	<data>
Register 3	<data>
Register 4	<data>
Register 5	<data>
Register 6	<data>
Register 7	<data>

Fig. 4-12. General-purpose register file.

the same result, while successive stack pops will return the contents of the stack in LIFO order.

Many GPR architectures assign special meanings to some of the registers in the register file to make programming easier. For example, some processors hard-wire register 0 (r0) with the value 0 to make it easier to generate this common constant, and others make the program counter visible as one of the registers. The meanings are assigned by the hardware and cannot be changed by programs.

4.5.1 INSTRUCTIONS IN A GPR ARCHITECTURE

GPR processor instructions need to specify the registers that hold their input operands and the register where their result will be written. The most common format for this is the three-input instruction shown in Fig. 4-13. For most arithmetic instructions, the leftmost argument specifies the destination register of the instruction, while the other arguments specify the source registers[2]. Thus, the instruction ADD r1, r2, r3 instructs the processor to read the contents of registers r2 and r3, add them together, and write the result into r1. Formats for instructions that only have one input are also shown in the figure.

This instruction format is called "three-input" despite the fact that some operations have only two arguments to distinguish it from two-input instruction formats, in which one of the operand registers, such as the leftmost, is also the destination register. For example, the instruction ADD r1, r2 in a two-input instruction format tells the processor to add the contents of r1 and r2 and place the result in r1.

---

[2] Instruction encodings vary from processor to processor. In particular, some processors use the rightmost operand as their destination register, with other operands being the inputs to the instruction. We use the convention that the leftmost argument is the destination because that is the format used in many popular computer architecture texts.

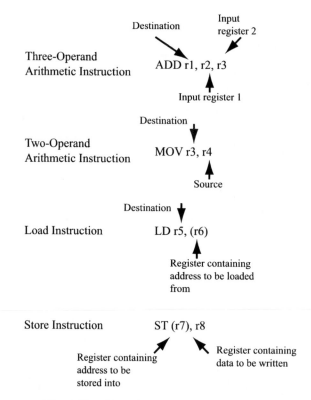

Fig. 4-13.   Three-input instruction formats.

Three-input instruction formats are more flexible than two-input formats, as they allow an instruction's input and output registers to be selected independently but require more bits to encode. Many current architectures have 32 or more registers, requiring at least 5 bits to encode the register ID of each register referenced by the instruction. On 16-bit and smaller architectures, this makes it difficult to encode a three-input instruction in a single word of data, making two-input instructions attractive. On more modern 32- and 64-bit architectures, this is not as much of a problem, and virtually all of these architectures use three-input instruction encodings. Because they have become dominant, this book will assume three-input encodings for GPR instructions unless otherwise specified.

One significant difference between stack-based and GPR architectures is the fact that, in a GPR architecture, the program can choose which values should be stored in the register file at any given time, allowing the program to keep its most-accessed data in the register file. In contrast, the LIFO access restrictions on a stack limit the program's ability to choose what data is in the register file at any time. On early computers, it was felt that this was an advantage for stack architectures, as they would automatically tend to keep the most-referenced data in the register file that formed the top of the stack. As compiler technology has advanced, *register allocation* techniques that select the values that should be kept in the register file have improved to the point where GPR architectures can generally make better use of their register files than stack-based architectures, leading to GPR architectures having higher performance than stack-based architectures.

4.5.2   A GPR INSTRUCTION SET

This section presents a sample instruction set for a GPR processor that will be used for the rest of the examples in this book. This architecture will be described using the same notation used in Section 4.4.4, with the extension that the notation "rX" refers to register X when that register contains an integer value. The notation "fY" will be used to refer to register Y when that register contains a floating-point value. This notation is used because many processors use separate register files for integer and floating-point data.

Our GPR instruction set will implement the same operations as the stack-based instruction set presented earlier, except that the GPR instruction set does not contain the PUSH and POP operations, since these operations are only used to manipulate the stack. The GPR instruction set does, however, contain a MOV operation for copying data from one register to another. We will use a three-input instruction format in this book and will assume that one but not both of the source operands in any instruction may be a constant instead of a register, using the #X notation to denote constants. Our GPR instruction set contains the following operations:

LD ra, (rb)[3]	ra <- (rb) (ra may be a floating-point register)
ST (ra), rb	(ra) <- rb (rb may be a floating-point register)
MOV ra, rb	ra <- rb (ra and/or rb may be floating-point registers
ADD ra, rb, rc	ra <- rb + rc (integer computation)
FADD fa, fb, fc	fa <- fb + fc (floating-point computation)
SUB ra, rb, rc	ra <- rb - rc (integer computation)
FSUB fa, fb, fc	fa <- fb - fc (floating-point computation)
MUL ra, rb, rc	ra <- rb × rc (integer computation)
FMUL fa, fb, fc	fa <- fb × fc (floating-point computation)
DIV ra, rb, rc	ra <- rb / rc (integer computation)
FDIV fa, fb, fc	fa <- fb / fc (floating-point computation)
AND ra, rb, rc	ra <- rb & rc (bit-wise computation)
OR ra, rb, rc	ra <- rb | rc (bit-wise computation)
NOT ra, rb	ra <- !rb (bit-wise negation)
ASH ra, rb, rc	ra <- rb shifted by rc positions (arithmetic shift)
LSH ra, rb, rc	ra <- rb shifted by rc positions (logical shift)
BR ra	PC <- ra
BR label	PC <- label
BEQ ra, rb, rc	PC <- ra if rb is equal to rc

---

[3] Note that memory operations in our GPR architecture use parentheses around the register name that specifies the address they reference. This notation is used to be consistent with the addressing modes presented in the next chapter.

BEQ label, rb, rc	PC <- label if rb is equal to rc
BNE ra, rb, rc	PC <- ra if rb is not equal to rc
BNE label, rb, rc	PC <- label if rb is not equal to rc
BLT ra, rb, rc	PC <- ra if rb is less than rc
BLT label, rb, rc	PC <- label if rb is less than rc
BGT ra, rb, rc	PC <- ra if rb is greater than rc
BGT label, rb, rc	PC <- label if rb is greater than rc
BLE ra, rb, rc	PC <- ra if rb is less than or equal to rc
BLE label, rb, rc	PC <- label if rb is less than or equal to rc
BGE ra, rb, rc	PC <- ra if rb is greater than or equal to rc
BGE label, rb, rc	PC <- label if rb is greater than or equal to rc

4.5.3 PROGRAMS IN A GPR ARCHITECTURE

Like programs for stack-based architectures, programs for GPR architectures are simply a sequence of individual instructions. To figure out what a short instruction sequence does, apply each of the instructions in sequence, updating the contents of the register file after each instruction. Programming a GPR processor is less structured than programming a stack-based architecture, since there are fewer restrictions on the order in which operations must execute. On a stack-based processor, operations must execute in an order that leaves the operands for the next operation on the top of the stack. On a GPR processor, any order that places the operands for the next instruction in the register file before that instruction executes is valid—operations that reference different registers can be arbitrarily reordered without making the program incorrect. As we will see in later chapters, many modern processors take advantage of this to reorder instructions at runtime to improve performance.

EXAMPLE

Write a GPR program to compute the function $2 + (7 \times 3)$. Assume that the architecture has 16 registers, r0–r15, and that all registers contain 0 at the start of the program. The result of the computation may be left in any register.

Solution

A program that does this is

```
MOV r1, #7
MOV r2, #3
MUL r3, r1, r2
MOV r4, #2
ADD r4, r3, r4
```

The first two MOV instructions place the values 7 and 3 in r1 and r2, respectively. The MUL multiplies them together and places the result in r3. The next MOV places 2 in r4, and the final ADD adds this constant with the result of the MUL to generate the final result.

There are two things to note about this solution. First, the choice of registers used was arbitrary—any choice that didn't overwrite a register value before it was used would work. Second, the final instruction overwrites one of its operands. Since we don't need to use the value in r4 again, this is fine and was done to illustrate that it is possible.

4.6 Comparing Stack-Based and General-Purpose Register Architectures

Stack-based and general-purpose register architectures differ mainly in their interfaces to their register files. In stack-based architectures, data is stored on a stack in memory. The processor's file may be used to implement the top portion of the stack to allow faster access to the stack.

In GPR architectures, the register file is a random-access device where each register can be independently read and written by the processor. On these architectures, the register file and the memory are completely independent, and programs are responsible for moving data between these two types of storage as necessary.

Stack-based architectures were used in some early computer systems for two reasons. First, because the operands and destination of an instruction in a stack-based architecture are implicit, instructions take fewer bits to encode than they do in general-purpose register architectures. This reduced the amount of memory taken up by programs, which was a significant issue on early machines. Second, stack-based architectures manage registers automatically, freeing programmers from the need to decide which data should be kept in the register file.

Another advantage of stack-based architectures is that the instruction set does not change if the size of the register file changes. This means that programs written for a stack-based processor can be run on future versions of the processor that have more registers, and they will see performance improvements because they are able to keep more of the stack in registers. Stack-based architectures are also very easy to compile to—so easy that some compilers generate stack-based versions of a program as part of the compilation process even when compiling for a GPR processor.

General-purpose register architectures have become dominant in more recent years because of improvements in technology and the switch to high-level languages. As memory capacities have increased and memory costs have decreased, the amount of space taken up by a program has become less important, making stack-based architectures' advantage in instruction size less important. More significantly, compilers for GPR architectures are generally able to achieve better performance with a given number of general-purpose registers than they are on stack-based architectures with the same number of registers because the compiler can choose which values to keep in the register file at any time and can use any value in the register file as the input to any instruction.

Because of their performance advantages and the decreasing importance of code size, virtually all recent workstation processors have been GPR architectures. Stack-based architectures are somewhat more attractive for embedded systems, in which low cost and low power consumption requirements often limit the amount of memory that can be included in a system, making code size more of a concern.

4.7   Using Stacks to Implement Procedure Calls

Procedure calls are an important part of virtually all computer languages. They allow commonly used functions to be written once and used whenever they are needed, and provide abstraction, making it easier for multiple people to collaborate on a program. However, several difficulties are involved in implementing procedure calls:

1.   Programs need a way to pass inputs to procedures that they call and to receive outputs back from them.

2.   Procedures need to be able to allocate space in memory for local variables without overwriting any data used by their calling program.

3.   Since procedures may be called from many different locations within a program and are often compiled separately from the program that calls them, it is generally impossible to determine which registers may be safely used by a procedure and which contain data that will be needed after the procedure completes.

4.   Procedures need a way to figure out where they were called from so that execution can return to the calling program when the procedure completes.

Most programming systems use a stack data structure to solve these problems. On GPR architectures, a stack is implemented in memory, such as the one illustrated in Fig. 4-9, while stack-based architectures can make use of the processor's main stack. When a procedure is called, a block of memory called a *stack frame* is allocated on the stack by incrementing the top-of-stack pointer by the number of locations in the stack frame. As illustrated in Fig. 4-14, a procedure's stack frame contains space for the contents of the calling program's register file, a pointer to the location that the procedure should branch to when it completes (its return address), the input arguments to the procedure, and the procedure's local variables.

When a procedure is called, the contents of the calling program's register file are copied into the stack frame, along with its return location and the inputs to the procedure. The procedure then uses the rest of the stack frame to hold its local variables. Since the number of input arguments and local variables varies from procedure to procedure, different procedures will have stack frames of different

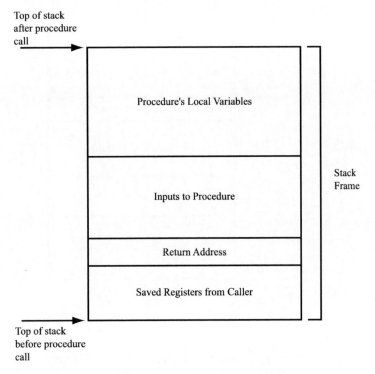

Top of stack
after procedure
call

Procedure's Local Variables

Inputs to Procedure

Return Address

Saved Registers from Caller

Stack
Frame

Top of stack
before procedure
call

Fig. 4-14. Stack frame.

sizes. The arrangement of data within the stack frame also varies from programming system to programming system.

When a procedure finishes, it jumps to the return address contained in the stack frame, and execution of the calling program resumes. The calling program reads its saved register file contents out of the stack frame and handles the procedure's result, which can be passed either in a register or on the stack. Finally, the top-of-stack pointer is restored to its position before the procedure was called, popping the stack frame off of the stack.

When a program makes nested procedure calls (procedures that call other procedures), each nested procedure allocates its stack frame on top of those already on the stack. For example, Fig. 4-15 shows the contents of the stack during the execution of procedure h(), which was called from within procedure g(). Procedure g() was called from within f(), which was called by the main program. As long as the stack does not overflow, procedure calls can be nested as deeply as necessary and each stack frame will be popped off of the stack when execution returns to its calling program.

4.7.1 CALLING CONVENTIONS

Different programming systems may arrange the data in a procedure's stack frame differently and may require that the steps involved in calling a procedure be

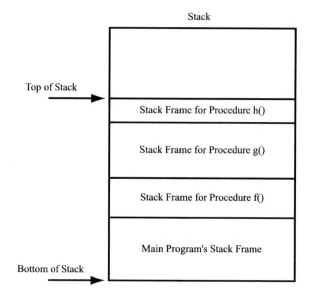

Fig. 4-15. Nested stack frames.

performed in different orders. The requirements that a programming system places on how a procedure is called and how data is passed between a calling program and its procedures are called *calling conventions*.

Many programming systems use their calling conventions to reduce the amount of data that needs to be copied to and from the stack during a procedure call. For example, a calling convention might specify a set of registers that are used to pass inputs and outputs between the calling program and the procedure. If a procedure's inputs and outputs fit in these registers, then it is not necessary to place them on the stack, reducing the number of memory references required. Programming systems generally also attempt to reduce the number of registers that must be saved and restored during a procedure call by identifying registers in the calling program whose values either will not be needed after the procedure call or whose values will not be overwritten by the procedure. These registers do not need to be saved or restored, reducing the cost of the procedure call.

4.8   Summary

This chapter has covered stack-based and general-purpose register architectures, two common programming models for processors. Stack-based processors use a last-in-first-out stack to hold the arguments to and results from their operations, while GPR architectures use a random-access register file. The two types of processors generally provide the same sorts of instructions, with a few exceptions, such as PUSH and POP instructions on a stack-based architecture.

Stack-based architectures were used in some early computer systems because they have very compact instruction encodings. Most instructions only need to specify the operation to be performed, since the stack is the source of their operands and the destination of their results. A few operations, such as PUSH, take constant operands, which increases the number of bits required to encode the operation. Stack-based architectures are also very easy to compile for, and they allow compatibility between processors with different numbers of registers because the register file is part of the stack and is invisible to the program.

General-purpose register file architectures allow the program to select which values are kept in the random-access register file. Combined with the fact that, unlike popping a value off of a stack, reading a value from a GPR register file does not remove the value from the register file, this generally allows GPR programs to achieve higher performance than stack-based programs, because they require fewer instructions to complete a calculation. As the cost of memory has decreased, making the compactness of stack-based programs less significant, this improved performance has made general-purpose register architectures the dominant programming model.

The rest of this book will assume a GPR processor model, since this matches most current processors. In the next chapter, we will discuss some of the details of processor design, including the RISC versus CISC debate and register file design.

 # Solved Problems

Shift Operations

4.1. What is the result of the following operations when executed on an 8-bit processor that uses a two's-complement representation for negative integers?
  a. LSH 14, 3
  b. ASH 17, 5
  c. LSH −23, −2
  d. ASH −23, −2

Solution

a. The 8-bit two's-complement integer representation of 14 is 0b0000 1110. Shifting left by three positions gives 0b0111 0000, which is the integer representation for 112. $112 = 14 \times 2^3$, checking the correctness of the result.

b. The 8-bit two's-complement integer representation of 17 is 0b0001 0001. Shifting left by five positions gives 0b0010 0000, the integer representation of 32. Here, the result of the shift does not equal 17×2^5 because 544 cannot be represented as an 8-bit two's-complement integer.

c. The 8-bit two's-complement integer representation of −23 is 0b1110 1001. Shifting by −2 positions is a right-shift of two positions. Doing this with a logical shift operation gives a result of 0b0011 1010, the integer representation of 58, illustrating that LSH does not implement division by a power of 2 on negative integers.

d. Here, the only difference from the last part is that we're using an arithmetic shift operation, which copies the high bit of the shifted value into all vacant bits when a right-shift is done. This gives a result of 0b1111 1010, which is the representation of −6. Thus,

ASH does implement division by powers of 2 when right-shifting negative integers, although it rounds to the next most negative integer instead of dropping fractions.

Labels

4.2. Why is it generally more convenient to use labels than actual addresses to specify the destination of branch instructions?

Solution

Labels have two advantages. First, they allow the programmer to specify the destination of a branch in a way that does not change as the program changes. If the destination of a branch were specified as either the distance from the start of the program to the destination or as the distance from the branch instruction to the destination, then the programmer might have to change the destination of each branch in the program every time the number of instructions in the program changed. Second, they make it easier for humans to read assembly-language programs. A programmer can find the destination of a branch whose destination is specified using a label without knowing anything about how much memory each instruction takes up, simply by looking for the label in the program.

Stack-Based Architectures (I)

4.3. Briefly explain how instructions in a stack-based architecture access their operands.

Solution

Instructions in a stack-based architecture read their operands from and write their results to the stack. Operands are popped off of the stack in LIFO order, and the result of the instruction is pushed onto the top of the stack.

Stack-Based Architectures (II)

4.4. What is the maximum number of values on the stack at any time during the execution of the following sequence of PUSH and POP operations, and what are the contents of the stack after the sequence completes?

```
PUSH #1
PUSH #2
PUSH #3
POP
PUSH #4
POP
POP
```

Solution

The maximum number of values on the stack is 3, which occurs after the PUSH #3 and again after PUSH #4. At the end of the sequence, only the value 1 remains on the stack.

Stack Implementation

4.5.   Why would it be a bad idea to implement a stack using just a processor's register file?

Solution

One of the benefits of a stack is that it presents the illusion of an infinitely large storage space to the programmer. Register files contain only a small number of storage locations, so a system that used only the register file to implement its stack would only be able to push a small amount of data onto the stack. Programmers using such a system would have to keep careful track of the amount of data on the stack at any time to avoid overflowing the stack, which would make the system much harder to program. Systems that allow the stack to expand into the memory when it overflows the register file are able to provide a much better approximation to the infinitely deep ideal stack.

Stack-Based Architecture Programming (I)

4.6.   What value remains on the stack after the following sequence of instructions?

```
PUSH #4
PUSH #7
PUSH #8
ADD
PUSH #10
SUB
MUL
```

Solution

After the three PUSH operations, the stack contains 8, 7, 4 (starting at the top). The ADD pops the 8 and the 7, then pushes 15 on the stack, making the stack contents 15, 4. The PUSH 10 makes the stack 10, 15, 4. The SUB pops 10 and 15 from the stack, subtracts 10 from 15, and pushes 5 back on the stack. (Remember that SUB subtracts the top value on the stack from the next value down, so that PUSH x, PUSH y, SUB generates x–y.) Finally, the MUL pops 5 and 4 from the stack and pushes 20, leaving 20 on the stack.

Stack-Based Architecture Programming (II)

4.7.   Write a stack-based program that computes the following function:
$5 + (3 \times 7) - 8$, assuming that the stack starts out empty.

Solution

First, we convert this expression to RPN, giving (5 (3 7×) +) 8 −). Note that the parentheses are completely unnecessary in RPN to generate the correct result. They are included solely to make parsing the RPN expression easier for the reader.

Then, the expression is translated into instructions:

```
PUSH #5
PUSH #3
PUSH #7
MUL
ADD
PUSH #8
SUB
```

Stack-Based Architecture Programming (III)

4.8. Assuming the stack starts out empty, write a stack-based program that computes $((10 \times 8) + (4 - 7))^2$.

Solution

Because our processor does not provide an instruction to compute the square of a value, we need to compute $(10 \times 8) + (4 - 7)$ twice, so that the stack contains two copies of this result, and then multiply them. (It would also be possible to store the result into memory and load it into the stack twice.) As we will see in Problem 4.13, a GPR architecture can compute this much more efficiently by using the same register as both of the inputs to a MUL operation.

Transforming the computation into RPN and then into instructions gives the following program:

```
PUSH 10
PUSH 8
MUL
PUSH 4
PUSH 7
SUB
ADD [At this point, the stack contains only the first result of
(10 × 8) + (4 - 7)]
PUSH 10
PUSH 8
MUL
PUSH 4
PUSH 7
SUB
ADD [At this point, the stack contains two copies of
(10 × 8) + (4 - 7)]
MUL
```

GPR Architectures (I)

4.9. Briefly explain how instructions in a GPR architecture access their operands.

Solution

In a GPR architecture, instructions read their operands from and write their results to a random-access register file. Each instruction specifies both the registers containing its operands and the register where its result should be written.

GPR Architectures (II)

4.10. Briefly explain the difference between two-operand and three-operand instruction formats.

Solution

In a two-operand instruction format, one of the input registers to an instruction is also the instruction's output register. In a three-input instruction format, each instruction's input and output registers are specified independently. Three-operand instructions are more flexible than two-operand instructions, but they require more bits to encode.

GPR Programming (I)

4.11. Assuming that all registers start out containing 0, what is the value of r7 after the following instruction sequence is executed?

```
MOV r7, #4
MOV r8, #3
ADD r9, r7, r7
SUB r7, r9, r8
MUL r9, r7, r7
```

Solution

The two MOV instructions put the values 4 and 3 in r7 and r8, respectively. The ADD instruction adds 4 (the value of r7) to 4 (the value of r7), getting 8, and places that in r9. The SUB instruction subtracts 3 from 8, getting 5, and puts that in r7. Finally, the MUL instruction multiplies 5 and 5 to get 25, and puts that value in r9. Therefore, the value in r7 at the end of the instruction sequence is 5.

GPR Programming (II)

4.12. Write a GPR assembly-language program that performs the following computation, assuming that all registers start out containing 0. The final result may be left in any register.

$$5 + (3 \times 7) - 8.$$

Solution

Here is one such program, but there are many acceptable variations:

```
MOV r1, #5
MOV r2, #3
MOV r3, #7
MOV r4, #8
MUL r5, r2, r3
ADD r6, r1, r5
SUB r7, r6, r4
```

GPR Programming (III)

4.13. Assuming all registers start out containing 0, write a GPR program that computes $((10 \times 8) + (4 - 7))^2$. The final result may be left in any register.

Solution

Again, here is one of many programs that compute this function:

```
MOV  r1,  #10
MOV  r2,  #8
MOV  r3,  #4
MOV  r4,  #7
MUL  r5,  r1,  r2
SUB  r6,  r3,  r4
ADD  r7,  r5,  r6
MUL  r8,  r7,  r7
```

Comparing Stack-Based and GPR Architectures (I)

4.14. Give two advantages of stack-based architectures over GPR architectures.

Solution

This chapter has discussed three advantages of stack-based architectures:

1. Instructions in a stack-based architecture take up less memory than GPR architecture instructions, because stack-based architecture instructions do not have to specify the registers containing their sources or the register where their result should be written.

2. The register file in a stack-based architecture is invisible to the programmer, being the top part of the stack. As a result, future implementations of a stack-based architecture can contain different numbers of registers and still run programs written for the old processor. In contrast, the number of registers in a GPR architecture is encoded into the instruction set by the number of bits allocated for each register name, preventing programs written for a GPR processor from running on a GPR processor with a different number of registers.

3. The stack provides the illusion of an infinitely deep storage area, so programs do not have to worry about overflowing the amount of storage in the register file.

Listing any two of these advantages is a correct answer to the problem.

Comparing Stack-Based and GPR Architectures (II)

4.15. Give two advantages of GPR architectures over stack-based architectures.

Solution

The two main advantages of GPR architectures over stack-based architectures are as follows:

1. Reading a register in a GPR architecture does not affect its contents, while reading a value off of the top of the stack removes the value from the stack. When a given value is used more than once in a program, a GPR architecture can allocate that value to a register and read it repeatedly when it is needed. In contrast, stack-based architectures must either

use instructions to duplicate the value on the stack each time it is used as the input to an instruction or store the value in memory and reload it each time it is used.

2. GPR programs can choose which values to keep in the register file, while stack-based architectures are limited by the LIFO nature of the stack. Register allocation techniques in modern compilers are good enough at keeping the most-referenced values in the program in the register file that they require fewer memory references to complete a given program on a GPR architecture than on a stack-based architecture, improving performance.

Comparing Stack-Based and GPR Architectures (III)

4.16. Why have GPR architectures become dominant over stack-based architectures?

Solution

The key advantages of stack-based architectures are their smaller program size and lack of need for register allocation, while GPR architectures are capable of achieving better performance when the programmer/compiler does a good job of allocating values to registers. In early computers, memory was very expensive, so reducing program size was important. Also, many of the currently used register allocation techniques had not been developed.

As technology has advanced, memory has become cheap, making the reduced program size of stack-based architectures less important. Also, most programming is now done in high-level languages, and compilers contain sophisticated register allocation algorithms that make good use of the register file in a GPR architecture. Because of this, the performance advantages of GPR architectures have become more significant than the code size advantage of stack-based architectures, making GPR architectures better choices for most processor designs.

Stack Frames

4.17. A program is running on an architecture with 32 registers, each 32 bits wide. Addresses on this system are also 32 bits long. The program calls a procedure that takes four 32-bit arguments and allocates eight 32-bit internal variables. How large is the procedure's stack frame? (Assume that all of the calling program's registers must be saved.)

Solution

The stack frame has to be large enough to hold the caller's register file contents, the return address, the procedure's inputs, and its local variables. This is $(32 + 1 + 4 + 8) = 45$ 32-bit values for this procedure, or 180 bytes.

Processor Design

5.1 Objectives

This chapter provides an introduction to processor design, breaking down some of the abstractions we have used in previous chapters and preparing for the next two chapters, which discuss techniques for improving processor performance. After completing this chapter, you should

1. Understand the difference between instruction set architecture and processor microarchitecture
2. Be familiar with the difference between RISC and CISC instruction sets, and be able to convert program fragments written for one style for execution on the other
3. Understand addressing modes and how they impact performance
4. Understand the basics of register file design, and be able to discuss how trade-offs in register file organization affect the implementation cost of the register file

5.2 Introduction

This chapter begins a three-chapter sequence on processor design by covering instruction set architecture and the basics of processor microarchitecture. The next chapter builds on this by discussing pipelining, a technique that improves performance by overlapping the execution of multiple instructions. Chapter 7 completes our coverage of processor architecture by discussing instruction-level parallelism.

Processor design has typically been divided into two subcategories: instruction set architecture and processor microarchitecture. Instruction set architecture refers to the design of the set of operations that the processor executes and includes the choice of programming model, number of registers, and decisions about how data is accessed. Processor microarchitecture describes how instructions are implemented and includes factors such as how long it takes to execute instructions, how many instructions may be executed at one time, and how processor modules such as the register file are designed. These definitions are somewhat vague, and there is a great deal of overlap between the two areas, so it is often difficult to decide whether a given aspect of computer architecture counts as instruction set architecture or microarchitecture. A good working definition is that any aspect of the processor that an assembly-language programmer needs to know about to write a correct program is part of the instruction set architecture, and that any aspect that only affects performance, not correctness, is part of the microarchitecture.

5.3   Instruction Set Architecture

When most computer programming was done in assembly language, instruction set architecture was considered the most important part of computer architecture, because it determined how difficult it was to obtain optimal performance from the system. Over the years, instruction set architecture has become less significant, for several reasons. First, most programming is now done in high-level languages, so the programmer never interacts with the instruction set. Second, and more significant, consumers have come to expect *compatibility* between different generations of a computer system, meaning that they expect programs that ran on their old system to run on their new system without changes. As a result, the instruction set of a new processor is often required to be the same as the instruction set of the company's previous processor, sometimes with a few additional instructions, meaning that most of the design effort for a processor goes into improving the microarchitecture to increase performance.

In the previous chapter, we covered one of the most significant decisions involved in designing a processor's instruction set architecture (ISA)—the selection of a programming model. As was discussed in that chapter, the GPR programming model has become dominant and will be assumed for the remainder of this book. In this chapter, we cover four of the most significant remaining issues in instruction set architecture: the RISC versus CISC debate, selection of addressing modes, the use of fixed- or variable-length instruction encodings, and multimedia vector instructions.

5.3.1 RISC VERSUS CISC

Before the 1980s, there was a great deal of focus on reducing the "semantic gap" between the languages used to program computers and machine languages. It was believed that making machine languages more like high-level programming languages would result in better performance by reducing the number of instructions required to implement a program and would make it easier to compile high-level language programs into machine language. The end result of this was the design of instruction sets that contained very complex instructions.

As compiler technology improved, researchers began to consider whether systems with complex instructions, known as complex instruction set computers (CISC), delivered better performance than systems based around simpler instruction sets. This second class of system was known as reduced instruction set computers (RISC).

The primary argument in favor of CISC computers is that CISC computers generally require fewer instructions than RISC computers to perform a given computation, so a CISC computer will have higher performance than a RISC computer that executes instructions at the same rate. In addition, programs written for CISC architectures tend to take less space in memory than the same programs written for a RISC architecture. The main argument in favor of RISC computers is that their simpler instruction sets often allow them to be implemented at higher clock rates than CISC computers, allowing them to execute more instructions in the same amount of time. If a RISC processor's increased clock rate allows it to execute its programs in less time than a CISC processor takes to execute its programs (which require fewer instructions), the RISC processor will have higher performance.

There was a great deal of controversy in the computer architecture community during the 1980s and early 1990s about which of the two approaches was better, and depending on how you look at it, either approach can be said to have won. The vast majority of ISAs introduced since the 1980s have been RISC architectures, arguing that RISC is superior. On the other hand, the Intel x86 (IA-32) architecture, which uses a CISC instruction set, is the dominant PC/workstation architecture in terms of number of processors sold, arguing that CISC architectures have won.

Over the last 20 years, there has been a fair amount of convergence between RISC and CISC architectures, making it somewhat difficult to determine whether an architecture is RISC or CISC. RISC architectures have incorporated some of the most useful complex instructions from CISC architectures, relying on their micro-architecture to implement these instructions with little impact on the clock cycle, and CISC architectures have dropped complex instructions that were not used sufficiently often to justify their implementation.

One clear delineation between RISC and CISC architectures is that RISC architectures are *load-store architectures*, meaning that only load and store instructions may access the memory system. The GPR architecture described in Chapter 4 is a load-store architecture.

In many CISC architectures, arithmetic and other instructions may read their inputs from or write their outputs to the memory system, instead of the register file. For example, a CISC architecture might allow an ADD operation of the form ADD (r1), (r2), (r3), where the parentheses around a register name indicates that the register contains the address in memory where the operand can be found or the result should be placed. Using this notation, the instruction ADD (r1), (r2), (r3) instructs the processor to add the value contained in the memory location whose address is stored in r2 to the value contained in the memory location whose address is stored in r3, and store the result into memory at the address contained in r1.

The difference between load-store architectures and architectures that can merge memory references with other operations is an excellent example of the trade-offs between RISC and CISC architectures. Because RISC architectures are implemented using the load-store model, a RISC processor would require several instructions to implement the single CISC ADD operation described above. However, the hardware required to implement the CISC processor would be more complex, since it would have to be able to fetch instruction operands from memory, so the CISC processor would probably have a longer cycle time (or would require more cycles to execute each instruction) than the RISC processor.

EXAMPLE

In our GPR load-store architecture, how many instructions are required to implement the same function as the CISC ADD operation described above? Assume that the appropriate memory addresses are present in r1, r2, and r3 at the start of the instruction sequence.

Solution

Four instructions are required:

```
LD  r4, (r2)
LD  r5, (r3)
ADD r6, r4, r5
ST  (r1), r6
```

This example shows that a RISC architecture may require many more operations to implement a function than a CISC architecture, although it is something of an extreme example. It also shows that RISC architectures generally require more registers to implement a function than CISC architectures, since all of the inputs of an instruction must be loaded into the register file before the instruction can execute. However, RISC processors have the advantage that breaking a complex CISC operation into multiple RISC operations can allow the compiler to schedule the RISC operations for better performance. For example, if memory references take multiple cycles to execute (as they generally do), a compiler for a RISC architecture can place other instructions between the LD instructions in the example and the ADD. This gives the LD instructions time to complete before their results are needed by the ADD, preventing the ADD from having to wait for its inputs. In contrast, the CISC instruction has no choice but to wait for its inputs to come back from the memory system, potentially delaying other instructions.

5.3.2 ADDRESSING MODES

As we have discussed, one of the major differences between RISC and CISC architectures is the set of instructions that can access memory. A related issue that affects both RISC and CISC architectures is the choice of which *addressing modes* the architecture supports. An architecture's addressing modes are the set of syntaxes and methods that instructions use to specify a memory address, either as the target address of a memory reference or as the address that a branch will jump to.

Depending on the architecture, some of the addressing modes may only be available to some of the instructions that reference memory. Architectures that allow any instruction that references memory to use any addressing mode are described as *orthogonal*, because the choice of addressing mode is independent from the choice of instruction.

So far, we have used only two addressing modes: register addressing for load instructions, store instructions, and CISC instructions that reference memory; and label addressing for branch instructions. In register addressing, an instruction reads the value out of a register and uses that as the address of the memory reference or branch target. We use the syntax (rx) to indicate that the register addressing mode is being used. An instruction set that provided only register addressing would be possible, since any address could be computed using arithmetic instructions and stored in a register. Processors provide other addressing modes because they reduce the number of instructions required to compute addresses, thereby improving performance.

The second addressing mode that we have seen so far is label addressing, in which a branch instruction specifies its destination as a label that is placed on an instruction elsewhere in the program. As was discussed in the last chapter, these text labels do not appear in the machine-language version of the program. In fact, most branch instructions do not explicitly contain their destination addresses at all. Instead, the assembler/linker translates the label into an *offset* (which can be either positive or negative) from the location of the branch instruction to the location of its target. In effect, the branch instruction tells the processor how far away the target instruction is from it, rather than exactly where the target instruction is located. The processor adds the offset to the branch instruction's PC to get the destination address of the branch.

Using offsets rather than explicit addresses for label addressing has two advantages. First, it reduces the number of bits required to encode the instruction. Most branches have targets that are relatively close to the branch, so a small number of bits can be used to encode the offset. When a branch has a target that is far away, the target address can be calculated by other instructions and a register or similar addressing mode used. Second, using offsets instead of explicit addresses in branch instructions allows the loader to place the program at different locations in the memory without having to change the program. If explicit addresses were used, the destination address of each branch would have to be recomputed every time the program was loaded. This feature is particularly useful for operating system libraries that are dynamically linked into the program at runtime, as these libraries have no ability to predict which address they will be loaded into.

EXAMPLE
An assembly-language "BR label1" instruction is assembled and linked as part of a larger program. The linker calculates the offset from the branch instruction to label1 as 0x437 bytes. If the branch instruction is loaded into address 0x4000, what is the target address of the branch? How about if the instruction is loaded into address 0x4400?

Solution

The target address of the branch is the sum of the address of the branch (the PC when the branch executes) and the offset. When the branch is loaded into address 0x4000, the target address is 0x4437 (0x4000 + 0x437). When the branch is loaded into address 0x4400, the target address is 0x4837.

Another addressing mode that is provided by many processors is *register plus immediate addressing*. In register plus immediate mode, which is typically expressed as imm(rx), the value of the specified register is added to the immediate (constant) value specified in the instruction to generate a memory address.

EXAMPLE

If the value of r4 is 0x13000, what address is referenced by the instruction LD −0x80(r4)?

Solution

The label plus immediate addressing mode adds the value of the immediate to the value of the register to get the destination address. Adding −0x80 to 0x13000 gives 0x12F80, the address referenced by the load.

Register plus immediate mode is extremely useful in accessing data structures, which tend to have fields that are located at fixed offsets from the start of the data structure. Using this addressing mode, a program that needs to reference different fields of a data structure can simply load the starting address of the data structure into a register and then use register plus immediate mode to access the different fields of the data structure, reducing the number of instructions required to perform address computations and the number of registers required to store addresses.

Many other addressing modes have been implemented in ISAs over the years. In general, they are variations on the register plus immediate mode. For example, some ISAs allow you to add a label offset and an immediate, or a label offset, a register value, and an immediate.

One problem with all addressing modes that compute their address rather than taking it straight from a register is that these addressing modes increase the execution time of instructions that use them, since the processor must perform a computation before the address can be sent to the memory system. To provide flexibility in addressing without increasing memory latency, some architectures provide *postincrementing* addressing modes instead of register plus immediate-style addressing modes. These addressing modes, which we will use the syntax imm[rx][1] for, read their address out of the specified register, send that address to the memory system, and then add the specified immediate to the value of the register. This result is then written back into the register file. Because the address is sent directly from

---

[1] Unlike the other syntaxes we use for addressing modes, this syntax is not standard for the industry. Different architectures use different syntaxes to describe postincrement addressing. For example, at least one architecture has separate instructions for postincrementing and nonpostincrementing addressing modes.

the register file to the memory system, these instructions execute more quickly than register plus immediate addressing mode instructions, but they still reduce the number of instructions required to implement a program as compared to ISAs that only provide register addressing.

Effectively, each use of a postincrementing addressing mode computes the address for the next instruction to reference the register. Thus, a sequence of register plus immediate addressing mode references can be easily transformed into a sequence of postincrementing addressing mode references. Postincrementing addressing mode is also useful when accessing an array of equally sized data structures, as the last reference to each address can increment the register containing the address to point at the next data structure.

EXAMPLE

Convert the following sequence of instructions written for an ISA that provides register plus increment addressing mode to run on an ISA that has only register and postincrementing addressing modes. (*Hint*: Exactly one additional instruction is required.)

```
LD  r4,  8(r1)
LD  r5,  12(r1)
ST  16(r1),  r8
```

Solution

The thing to remember here is that postincrementing addressing mode instructions change the value of their address register. Register plus increment addressing mode just computes the address to be sent to the memory system, leaving the value in the address register the same. Thus, each postincrementing instruction needs to increment by the offset from the address it references to the address referenced by the next instruction, which will generally be different than the immediate added to the address register in register plus immediate mode. This gives the following code sequence:

```
    ADD r1, r1, #8 /* increment the original address register
by the offset to the address used by the first LD. */
    LD r4, 4[r1] /* The second LD has an offset of 12 bytes
from the original value of r1. Since we've already offset
r1 by 8 bytes, just increment by 4 more */
    LD r5, 4[r1] /* Just need to add 4 more bytes to get from
the address referenced by this load to the one referenced
by the store */
    ST (r1), r8 /* No need to postincrement */
```

5.3.3   MULTIMEDIA VECTOR INSTRUCTIONS

Many processor families have recently added multimedia vector instructions to their ISAs. These instructions, which include the MMX extensions to the x86 ISA, are intended to improve performance on multimedia applications, such as video decompression and audio playback. These applications have several traits that make it possible to significantly improve their performance with a small number of new instructions. First, they perform the same sequence of operations on a large number of independent data objects, such as 8×8 blocks of compressed pixels. This trait is often described as *data parallelism*, because multiple data objects can be processed at the same time. The second important trait of these applications is that they operate on data that is much smaller than the 32-bit or 64-bit data words found in most modern processors. Video pixels, which are often described by 8-bit red, green, and blue color values, are an example of this. Each of the color values is generally computed independently, meaning that 24 bits of a 32-bit ALU are idle during the computation.

Multimedia vector instructions treat the processor's data word as a collection of smaller data objects, as shown in Fig. 5-1, which shows how a multimedia vector instruction might process a 32-bit data word. Instead of operating on a 32-bit quantity, the data word is treated as a collection of four 8-bit quantities or two 16-bit quantities. Most of the multimedia vector instruction sets can operate on longer data types, such as 64-bit or 128-bit quantities, allowing more operations to be done in parallel.

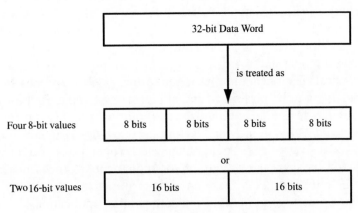

Fig. 5-1. Multimedia vector data types.

Many multimedia vector instructions allow the option to operate in *saturating arithmetic mode.* In saturating arithmetic, computations that overflow the number of bits in their representation return the maximum value that the representation can represent, and computations that underflow return 0. For example, adding 0xaa and 0xbc in 8-bit saturating arithmetic has a result of 0xff instead of 0x66. Saturating arithmetic is useful when it is desirable to have a computation be limited by its maximum value. For example, increasing the amount of red in a pixel that is already extremely red should result in a pixel that has the maximum allowable amount of redness, instead of a pixel that has very little redness because the computation has wrapped around to a small value.

When a multimedia vector instruction executes, it performs its computation in parallel on each of the smaller objects within its input word, as shown in Fig. 5-2, which illustrates a 32-bit vector addition, treating the 32-bit word as four 8-bit

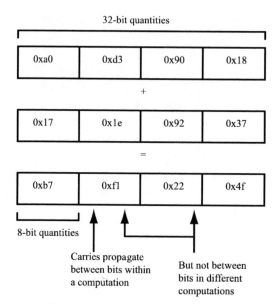

Fig. 5-2. Multimedia vector addition.

unsigned quantities. Saturating arithmetic is not used in this example. Each of the four parallel additions executes in parallel, and the results of any one addition do not affect the other additions. In particular, note that carries propagate normally within each 8-bit computation but do not propagate between different computations.

Multimedia vector instructions can significantly improve a processor's performance on data-parallel applications that operate on small data types by allowing multiple computations to be performed in parallel. For example, 32-bit multimedia vector operations can be used to compute the red color values of four different pixels simultaneously, potentially improving performance by up to a factor of 4. The hardware required to implement multimedia vector operations is typically fairly small, as most of the hardware required to implement a processor's nonvector operations can be reused, making these operations attractive to computer architects who expect their processors to be used for data-parallel applications.

5.3.4 FIXED-LENGTH VERSUS VARIABLE-LENGTH INSTRUCTION ENCODINGS

Once the set of instructions that a processor will support has been selected, a computer architect must select an encoding for the ISA, which is the set of bits that will be used to represent the instructions in the memory of the computer. Generally, architects want to find an encoding that is both compact and requires little logic to decode, meaning that it is simple for the processor to figure out which instruction is represented by a given bit pattern in the program. Unfortunately, these two goals are somewhat in conflict.

Fixed-length instruction set encodings use the same number of bits to encode each instruction in the ISA. Fixed-length encodings have the advantage that they are simple to decode, reducing the amount of decode logic required and the latency of the decode logic. Also, a processor that uses a fixed-length ISA encoding can easily predict the location of the next instruction to be executed (assuming that the current instruction is not a branch). This makes it easier for the processor to use pipelining, the subject of the next chapter, to improve performance by overlapping the execution of multiple instructions.

Variable-length instruction set encodings use different numbers of bits to encode the instructions in the ISA, depending on the number of inputs to the instruction, the addressing modes used, and other factors. Using a variable-length encoding, each instruction takes only as much space in memory as it requires, although many systems require that all instruction encodings be an integer number of bytes long. Using a variable-length instruction set can reduce the amount of space taken up by a program, but it greatly increases the complexity of the logic required to decode instructions, since parts of the instruction, such as the input operands, may be stored in different bit positions in different instructions. Also, the hardware cannot predict the location of the next instruction until the current instruction has been decoded enough to know how long the current instruction is.

Given the pros and cons of fixed- and variable-length instruction encodings, fixed-length encodings are more common in recent architectures. Variable-length encodings are mainly used in architectures where there is a large variance between the amount of space required for the longest instruction in the ISA and the average instruction in the ISA. Examples of this include stack-based architectures, because many operations do not need to specify their inputs, and CISC architectures, which often contain a few instructions that can take a large number of inputs.

This ends our discussion of instruction set architecture. We have covered the RISC versus CISC debate, one of the most famous controversies in computer architecture, the impact of addressing modes on a processor's ISA, and the pros and cons of fixed-length and variable-length instruction encodings. Also, we have prescribed a brief introduction to multimedia vector instructions, a recent extension to processor ISAs that improves performance on data-parallel applications.

The rest of this chapter will begin our discussion of processor microarchitecture, which will continue in the next two chapters. We will start with a more in-depth discussion of how processors execute instructions than has been presented so far, and we will continue with a discussion of register file design. For simplicity, we will assume a RISC-style processor for the rest of our discussion of processor architecture, although the concepts we will cover are generally applicable to CISC architectures as well.

5.4 Processor Microarchitecture

As described earlier, processor microarchitecture includes all of the details about how a processor is implemented. The ISA specifies how the processor is programmed, and the microarchitecture specifies how it is built. Obviously, the ISA has a great deal of impact on the microarchitecture. An ISA that contains only simple operations can be implemented using a simple, straightforward microarchitecture, while an ISA containing complex operations generally requires a complex microarchitecture to implement.

In Chapter 3, we presented the processor block diagram that is reproduced here as Fig. 5-3. This diagram breaks the processor down into three main subsystems: the execution units, the register file, and the control logic. Together, the execution units and the register file are often described as the processor's *datapath*, as data and instructions flow through them in a regular fashion. The control logic is more irregular and very processor-specific.

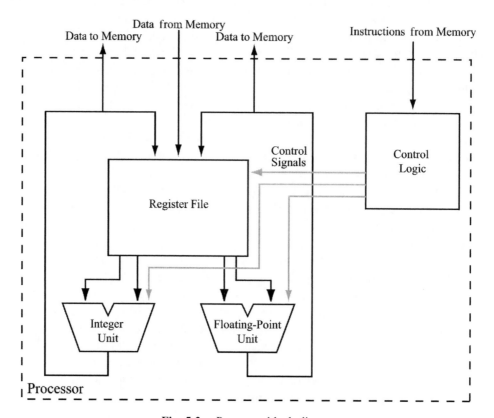

Fig. 5-3.   Processor block diagram.

5.4.1 EXECUTION UNITS

Figure 5-4 shows the steps involved in executing an instruction and how the different modules of the processor interact during instruction execution. First, the processor fetches the instruction from the memory. The instruction is then *decoded* to determine what instruction it is and what its input and output registers are. The decoded instruction is represented as a set of bit patterns that tell the hardware how to execute the instruction. These bit patterns are sent on to the next section of the execution unit, which reads the instruction's inputs from the register file. The decoded instruction and the values of the input registers are forwarded to the hardware that computes the result of the instruction, and the result is written back into the register file.

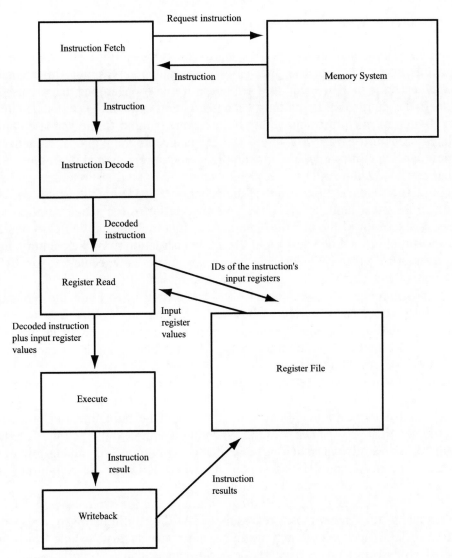

Fig. 5-4. Instruction execution.

Instructions that access the memory system have a similar execution flow, except the output of the execution unit is sent to the memory system, either as the address of a load operation or as the address and data of a store operation. When the result of a load returns from the memory system, it is written into the register file, similar to the way the result of a computation is written into the register file.

Many execution units are implemented using a physical structure similar to the one shown in the figure. Modules that implement the different steps in instruction execution are physically laid out next to each other in a line, with short wires connecting them. As the instruction executes, data flows through the line from one module to the next, with each module performing its task in sequence.

5.4.2 MICROPROGRAMMING

In a *microprogrammed* processor, the hardware does not directly execute the instructions in the ISA. Instead, the hardware executes very simple micro-operations, and each instruction specifies a sequence of micro-operations that are used to implement the instruction. Essentially, each instruction in the ISA is translated into a short program of microinstructions by the hardware, similar to the way a compiler translates each instruction in a high-level language program into a sequence of assembly-language instructions. For example, a microprogrammed processor might translate the instruction ADD r1, r2, r3 into six micro-operations: one that reads the value of r2 and sends it to one input of the adder, one that reads the value of r3 and sends it to the other input of the adder, one that performs the actual addition, one that writes the result of the addition into r1, one that increments the PC to point to the next instruction, and one that fetches the next instruction from the memory. Each micro-operation generally takes one processor cycle to execute, so an ADD instruction would require six cycles to complete in such a system.

Microprogrammed processors contain a small memory that holds the sequences of microinstructions used to implement each instruction in the ISA. To execute an instruction, a microprogrammed processor accesses this memory to locate the set of microinstructions required to implement the ISA instruction, and then executes the microinstructions in sequence.

Microprogramming became popular because the technologies used to implement early computers (vacuum tubes, discrete transistors, and small-scale integrated circuits) limited the amount of hardware that could be built into the processor, and computer architects wanted to design ISAs with complex instructions to reduce the number of instructions required to implement a program. By using microprogramming, architects could build simple hardware and then microprogram that hardware to execute complex instructions.

Modern processors tend not to use microprogramming for two reasons. First, it is now practical to implement most processors's ISAs directly in hardware because of advances in VLSI technology, making microcode unnecessary. Second, microprogrammed processors tend to have lower performance than nonmicroprogrammed processors because of the overhead involved in fetching each microinstruction from the microinstruction memory.

5.4.3 REGISTER FILE DESIGN

So far, we have treated the register file as a single device that contains both integer and floating-point data. Most processors do not implement their register files in this fashion. Instead, they implement separate register files for floating-point and integer data. Integer register files are referenced using the "rx" syntax we have used so far for register names, while floating-point registers are referenced as "fx." Using this syntax makes it clear which register file is being referenced for instructions, such as loads and stores, that may need to reference both register files. Arithmetic instructions are generally restricted to accessing the appropriate register file for the type of computation they perform, although some arithmetic instructions are allowed to transfer data between register files.

Processors implement separate register files for two reasons. First, it allows the register files to be placed physically close to the execution units that need them. The integer register file can be placed close to units that perform integer operations, and the floating-point register file can be placed close to the floating-point execution units. This reduces the length of the wires that connect the register files to the execution units, and therefore the amount of time required to send data from the register file to the execution units.

The second reason why processors implement separate integer and floating-point register files is that separate register files take up less space on processors that execute more than one instruction per cycle. The details of this are beyond the scope of this book, but the size of a register file grows as approximately the square of the number of simultaneous reads and writes that the register file allows. To execute one instruction per cycle, a register file typically needs to allow two reads and one write per cycle, since some arithmetic operations read two registers and write one. Each additional operation that the processor wants to execute in a cycle typically increases the number of simultaneous reads/writes (called ports) by three. Dividing the register file into integer and floating-point register files reduces the number of ports required on each register file. Since the area of a register file grows faster than linearly with the number of ports, the two separate register files take up less area than one register file that provides the same number of ports.

5.5   Summary

The goal of this chapter has been to provide an introduction to processor design, in preparation for the next two chapters, which provide more in-depth discussions of two techniques that are widely used to improve processor performance: pipelining and instruction-level parallelism. The chapter began with a discussion of the distinction between instruction set architecture and processor microarchitecture. Instruction set architecture is the design of the instructions that a processor provides, including the programming model, the set of operations provided, the addressing modes that the processor supports, and the choice of which instructions may access memory. Processor microarchitecture covers the details of how the processor is implemented. In general, instruction set architecture refers to any aspect of the architecture that is visible to an assembly-language programmer, while processor microarchitecture covers details that affect how quickly a program executes. There is substantial overlap between these two categories. For example, an instruction set architecture that provides a number of complex instructions may require a processor microarchitecture that gives lower performance than a microarchitecture that implements only simpler instructions.

Within instruction set architecture, we discussed the distinction between RISC and CISC instructions, the central element of which is the requirement that RISC architectures be load-store architectures, while most CISC architectures allow other operations to reference memory as well. The impact of addressing modes and instruction set encodings on program size, performance, and the complexity of the hardware required to implement the processor was discussed. Finally, an introduction to multimedia vector instructions, a relatively new addition to many instruction sets, was provided.

Our introduction to processor microarchitecture included a block diagram of the data flow through a processor, with a discussion of the function of each element in the flow. We then briefly discussed microprogramming, a technique commonly used to implement processors in the past, but one that is rarely used today because of its impact on performance. Our processor microarchitecture discussion then concluded with coverage of the trade-offs involved in register file design.

In the next chapter, we will discuss pipelining, a technique that improves processor performance by overlapping the execution of multiple instructions. This allows a higher clock rate and improves the rate at which instructions are executed. Pipelining is often combined with instruction-level parallelism, the subject of Chapter 7, to produce processors that issue multiple instructions in each cycle and overlap instruction execution to increase the number of clock cycles in a second.

 # Solved Problems

Instruction Set Architecture

5.1. What is a load-store architecture, and what are the pros and cons of such an architecture as compared to other GPR architectures?

Solution

A load-store architecture is one in which only load and store instructions can access the memory system. In other GPR architectures, some or all of the other instructions may read their operands from or write their results to the memory system. The primary advantage of non-load-store architectures is the reduced number of instructions required to implement a program and lower pressure on the register file. The advantage of load-store architectures is that limiting the set of instructions that can access the memory system makes the microarchitecture simpler, which often allows implementation at a higher clock rate. Depending on whether the clock rate increase or the decrease in number of instructions is more significant, either approach can result in greater performance.

RISC versus CISC (I)

5.2. Rewrite the following CISC-style program fragment so that it executes correctly on a RISC (load-store) processor that executes the GPR ISA outlined in the previous chapter. Assume that the GPR ISA provides only the register addressing mode, and that there are enough registers in the processor to hold any temporary values that you need to generate.

```
ADD r3, (r1), (r2)
SUB r4, r3, (r5)
MUL (r6), r7, r4
```

Solution

This program fragment makes four memory references as part of arithmetic operations. To execute the fragment, we need to replace each of those with an explicit load or store. Here's a code fragment that does that:

```
LD r10, (r1)
LD r11, (r2)
ADD r3, r10, r11
LD r12, (r5)
SUB r4, r3, r12
MUL r13, r7, r4
ST (r6), r13
```

RISC versus CISC (II)

5.3. Rewrite the following program fragment that is written using the GPR instruction set for execution on a CISC processor that provides the same instruction set as the GPR processor but allows the register addressing mode to be used on the input operands or destination of any instruction. (Yes, the code fragment will execute correctly as written on such a processor. Your goal should be to reduce the number of instructions as much as possible.) Assume that the program ends after the last instruction in the fragment, so that the only goal of the program should be to have the correct value written into memory at the end.

```
LD r1, (r2)
LD r3, (r4)
LD r5, (r6)
LD r7, (r8)
DIV r9, r1, r3
ADD r10, r9, r5
SUB r11, r7, r10
ST (r12), r11
```

Solution

The general approach here is to replace all of the load and store instructions with memory references in arithmetic instructions. A program that does this is as follows:

```
DIV r9, (r2), (r4)
ADD r10, r9, (r6)
SUB (r12), (r8), r10
```

Addressing Modes (I)

5.4. Why does adding addressing modes like register plus immediate to an ISA tend to improve performance?

Solution

Adding additional addressing modes to an ISA tends to improve performance by reducing the number of instructions required to compute addresses. For example, if a data structure contains four data words, register plus immediate addressing can be used to access all of them, with only one address computation required to change the pointer to point to the next data structure. If an architecture only provided the register addressing mode, an ADD instruction would be required to calculate the address of each element in the data structure.

Addressing Modes (II)

5.5. Why are postincrementing addressing modes often found on processors that need to have a very short cycle time?

Solution

Postincrementing addressing modes allow different elements of a data structure to be accessed without explicit instructions to compute addresses, but they don't require that the processor perform an addition before sending the address to the memory system, because they add the immediate offset to the contents of the register after the address is sent to the memory system. This allows memory-referencing instructions to compute addresses that will be used by later memory-referencing instructions without increasing the latency to complete a memory reference.

Addressing Modes (III)

5.6. Rewrite the following program fragment to take advantage of register plus immediate addressing mode. Assume that no register values are used outside of the program fragment and that the code fragment will execute on a load-store processor.

```
ADD r2, r3, #8
LD r4, (r2)
ADD r1, r4, r8
ADD r5, r3, #16
LD r6, (r5)
MUL r7, r1, r6
ADD r9, r3, #24
ST (r9), r7
```

Solution

All of the ADD operations that take r3 as an input can be folded into the LD or ST operations that follow them using register plus immediate addressing mode, to give the following program:

```
LD r4, 8(r3)
ADD r1, r4, r8
LD r6, 16(r3)
MUL r7, r1, r6
ST 24(r3), r7
```

Addressing Modes (IV)

5.7. Rewrite the program from Problem 5.6 to take advantage of postincrementing addressing mode. The value in r3 is allowed to be different at the end of the program from the value at the beginning. You may not use register plus immediate addressing mode anywhere in the program, but you may use register addressing mode.

Solution

The first ADD operation is still required to compute the address used by the first LD. The LD operations can then compute the address for the next memory operation. Remember that the increment value for each operation should be the difference between the address referenced by the next operation and the one referenced by the current operation, not the offset from the original value in the register containing the address.

```
ADD r3, r3, #8
LD r4, 8[r3]
ADD r1, r4, r8
LD r6,8[r3]
MUL r7, r1, r6
ST (r3), r7
```

Multimedia Vector Instructions (I)

5.8. If a program operates on 8-bit data types and a processor's multimedia vector instructions operate on 64-bit data words, what is the maximum-possible speedup that can be achieved by using multimedia vector instructions? Assume that all instructions take the same amount of time to execute.

Solution

Eight 8-bit values can fit in a 64-bit word. Therefore, the processor can perform eight 8-bit operations in parallel using multimedia vector instructions. If all instructions in the program were replaced with multimedia vector instructions, the program would require 1/8th the number of instructions as the original program, for a maximum speedup of 8.

Multimedia Vector Instructions (II)

5.9. If two registers contain the values 0xab0890c2 and 0x4598ee50, what is the result of adding them using
  a.   Multimedia vector operations that operate on 8-bit data?
  b.   Multimedia vector operations that operate on 16-bit data?
  Assume that saturating arithmetic is not being used.

Solution

To find the result of using multimedia vector operations, we simply divide the input data words into chunks of the appropriate size and add them. This gives the following separate additions and final result (all numbers are in hexadecimal):

  a.   (ab + 45), (08 + 98), (90 + ee), (c2 + 50) → 0xf0a07e12

  b.   (ab08 + 4598), (90c2 + ee50) → 0xf0a07f12

Fixed-Length versus Variable-Length Encodings (I)

5.10. What are the pros and cons of fixed-length and variable-length instruction encodings?

Solution

Variable-length instruction encodings reduce the amount of memory that programs take up, since each instruction takes only as much space as it requires. Instructions in a fixed-length encoding scheme all take up as much storage space as the longest instruction in the ISA, meaning that there is some number of wasted bits in the encoding of instructions that take fewer operands, don't allow constant inputs, and so forth.

However, variable-length instruction sets require more-complex instruction decode logic than fixed-length instruction sets, and they make it harder to calculate the address of the next instruction in memory. Therefore, processors with fixed-length instruction sets can often be implemented at higher clock rates than processors with variable-length instruction sets.

Fixed-Length versus Variable-Length Encodings (II)

5.11. A given processor has 32 registers, uses 16-bit immediates, and has 142 instructions in its ISA. In a given program, 20 percent of the instructions take one input register and have one output register, 30 percent have two input registers and one output register, 25 percent have one input register, one output register, and take an immediate input as well, and the remaining 25 percent have one immediate input and one output register.

    a. For each of the four types of instructions, how many bits are required? Assume that the ISA requires that all instructions be a multiple of 8 bits in length.

    b. How much less memory does the program take up if a variable-length instruction set encoding is used as opposed to a fixed-length encoding?

Solution

    a. With 142 instructions, 8 bits are required to determine which instruction an instruction is ($128 < 142 < 256$). 32 registers means that 5 bits are required to encode register ID, and we know that 16 bits are required for each immediate. Given that, it's just a matter of adding up the fields required for each type of instruction.

        One register input, one register output: $8 + 5 + 5$ bits $= 18$ bits, which rounds up to 24.

        Two input registers, one output register: $8 + 5 + 5 + 5 = 23$ bits, which rounds up to 24.

        One input register, one output register, and an immediate: $8 + 5 + 5 + 16$ bits $= 34$ bits, which rounds up to 40 bits.

        One input immediate, one output register: $8 + 16 + 5$ bits $= 29$ bits, which rounds up to 32 bits.

    b. Since the largest instruction type requires 40-bit instructions, the fixed-length encoding will have 40 bits per instruction. Each instruction type in the variable encoding will use the number of bits given in Part a. To find the average number of bits per instruction in the variable-length encoding, we multiply the number of bits for each instruction type by that type's frequency and add the results. This gives (20 percent $\times$ 24 bits) + 30 percent $\times$ 24 bits) + (25 percent $\times$ 40 bits) + (25 percent $\times$ 32 bits) $= 4.8 + 7.2 +$

$10 + 8 = 30$ bits on average. Therefore, the variable-length encoding requires 25 percent less space than the fixed-length encoding for this program.

Datapath Design

5.12. If it takes 5 ns to read an instruction from memory, 2 ns to decode the instruction, 3 ns to read the register file, 4 ns to perform the computation required by the instruction, and 2 ns to write the result into the register file, what is the maximum clock rate of the processor?

Solution

The time for an instruction to pass through the processor must be greater than the clock cycle time of the processor. The total time to execute an instruction is just the sum of the times to perform each step, or 16 ns. The maximum clock rate is 1/cycle time, or 62.5 MHz.

Microprogramming

5.13. **a.** Why was microprogramming used on many early processors?
   b. Why have modern processors gone away from this technique?

Solution

a. Microprogramming allowed relatively complex instructions to be implemented using small amounts of hardware.

b. Microprogramming has become less commonly used because the increased amount of hardware available to computer architects and the less complex instruction sets used in current processors allow instructions to be directly implemented in hardware. This generally provides better performance than microprogramming, so architects choose to implement instructions directly rather than microprogramming them.

Register File Design

5.14. **a.** Why do many processors implement integer and floating-point register files as separate register files?
   b. Give two ways in which using one register file for both integer and floating-point data might be better than separate register files.

Solution

a. There are two arguments for separate register files. First, on processors that execute multiple instructions in each cycle, having separate register files reduces the total area required for the register file because register files grow quadratically with the number of simultaneous accesses they support (ports). Second, having separate register files allows each of the register files to be located closer to the execution units than access it, reducing wire delay. Since integer and floating-point values are mostly independent—few values are operated on by both integer and floating-point instructions—separate register files are the choice for most processors.

b. One reason is that having a single register file for integer and floating-point data would let the number of registers used for integer and floating-point data vary depending on the needs of the program. With separate register files, the number of registers available for each type of data is fixed—if a program references a large number of integer values but few floating-point values, it cannot easily use the floating-point registers to store integer values that do not fit in the integer register file. If the processor had one combined register file, the program could use it to hold whatever combination of integer and floating-point data gave the best performance.

A second reason is that, while integer and floating-point values are mostly independent, there are some cases where both integer and floating-point instructions operate on a value. In this case, explicit operations are required to move the value between the two register files if the processor implements separate integer and floating-point register files. If the processor implemented a single combined register file, both types of instructions could access the value from the combined register file.

CHAPTER 6

Pipelining

6.1 Objectives

This chapter covers pipelining, a technique for improving processor performance. Pipelining allows a processor to overlap the execution of several instructions so that more instructions can be executed in the same period of time.

After completing this chapter, you should be able to

1. Describe pipelining and how it works
2. Compute the cycle time of a processor with different degrees of pipelining
3. Determine how long (in both processor cycles and time) it takes to execute small code segments on pipelined processors
4. Describe result forwarding and discuss how it affects execution time
5. Compute the execution time of small code segments on pipelined processors with result forwarding

6.2 Introduction

Early computers executed instructions in a very straightforward fashion: The processor fetched an instruction from memory, decoded it to determine what the instruction was, read the instruction's inputs from the register file, performed the computation required by the instruction, and wrote the result back into the register file. Instructions that accessed memory were slightly different, but each instruction was completely finished before execution of the next one began. The problem with this approach is that the hardware needed to perform each of these steps (instruction fetch, instruction decode, register read, instruction execution, and register write-back) is different, so most of the hardware is idle at any given moment, waiting for the other parts of the processor to complete their part of executing an instruction.

In many ways, this is similar to baking several loaves of bread by making the dough for one loaf, letting that loaf rise, baking the loaf, and then repeating the entire process. While each of the steps in baking each loaf of bread has to be done in order and takes a set amount of time, one person could bake several loaves of bread much faster by making the dough for the second loaf while the dough for the first loaf is rising, making the dough for the third loaf while the second loaf was rising and the first loaf baking, and continuing this process with each loaf so that there were three loaves of bread in progress at any time. Each loaf of bread would take the same amount of time to make, but the number of loaves made in a given amount of time would increase.

Pipelining is a technique for overlapping the execution of several instructions to reduce the execution time of a set of instructions. Similar to the baking analogy, each instruction takes the same amount of time to execute in a pipelined processor as it would in a nonpipelined processor (longer, actually, because pipelining adds hardware to the processor), but the rate at which instructions can be executed is increased by overlapping instruction execution.

When we discuss pipelining, and computer performance in general, two terms are often used: latency and throughput. *Latency* is the amount of time that a single operation takes to execute. *Throughput* is the rate at which operations get executed (generally expressed as operations/second or operations/cycle). In a nonpipelined processor, throughput = 1/latency, since each operation executes by itself. In a pipelined processor, throughput > 1/latency, since instruction execution is overlapped. The latency of a pipelined processor is still important, however, as it determines how often dependent instructions may be executed.

6.3 Pipelining

To implement pipelining, designers divide a processor's datapath into sections, and place *pipeline latches* between each section, as shown in Fig. 6-1. At the start of each cycle, the pipeline latches read their inputs and copy them to their outputs, which then remain constant throughout the rest of the cycle. This breaks the datapath into several sections, each of which has a latency of one clock cycle, since an instruction cannot pass through a pipeline latch until the start of the next cycle.

The amount of the datapath that a signal travels through in one cycle is called a *stage* of the pipeline, and designers often describe a pipeline that takes *n* cycles as an *n*-stage pipeline. In Fig. 6-1, the pipeline has five stages. Stage 1 is the fetch instruction block and its associated pipeline latch, stage 2 is the decode instruction block and its pipeline latch, and stages 3, 4, and 5 are the subsequent blocks of the pipeline. Computer architects differ on whether a pipeline latch is the last part of a stage or the first part of the next stage, so an alternate division of the pipeline into stages would be to count the fetch instruction block as stage 1, the first pipeline latch and the decode instruction block as stage 2, and so on.

Figure 6-2 shows how instructions flow through the pipeline in Fig. 6-1. On cycle 1, the first instruction enters the instruction fetch (IF) stage of the pipeline and stops at the pipeline latch between the instruction fetch and instruction decode (ID) stages of the pipeline. On cycle 2, the second instruction enters the instruction fetch stage, while instruction 1 proceeds to the instruction decode stage. On the third cycle,

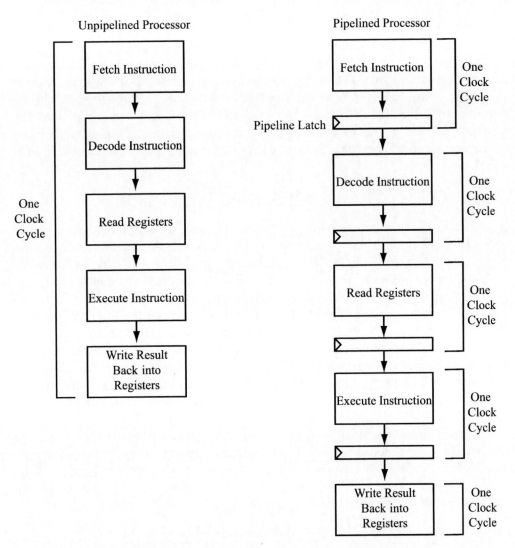

Fig. 6-1. Pipelined versus nonpipelined processor.

Cycle

		1	2	3	4	5	6	7
	IF	Instruction 1	Instruction 2	Instruction 3	Instruction 4	Instruction 5	Instruction 6	Instruction 7
	ID		Instruction 1	Instruction 2	Instruction 3	Instruction 4	Instruction 5	Instruction 6
Pipeline Stage	RR			Instruction 1	Instruction 2	Instruction 3	Instruction 4	Instruction 5
	EX				Instruction 1	Instruction 2	Instruction 3	Instruction 4
	WB					Instruction 1	Instruction 2	Instruction 3

Fig. 6-2. Instruction flow in a pipelined processor.

instruction 1 enters the register read (RR) stage, instruction 2 is in the instruction decode stage, and instruction 3 enters the instruction fetch stage.

Instructions proceed through the pipeline at one stage per cycle until they reach the register write-back (WB) stage, at which point execution of the instruction is complete. Thus, on cycle 6 in the example, instructions 2 through 6 are in the pipeline, while instruction 1 has completed and is no longer in the pipeline. The pipelined processor is still executing instructions at a rate (throughput) of one instruction per cycle, but the latency of each instruction is now 5 cycles instead of 1.

6.3.1   CYCLE TIME OF PIPELINED PROCESSORS

If you consider just the number of cycles required to execute a given set of instructions, it looks like pipelining doesn't increase the performance of the processor. In fact, as we'll see later, pipelining a processor generally increases the number of clock cycles it takes to execute a program, because some instructions get held up in the pipeline waiting for the instructions that generate their inputs to execute. The performance benefit of pipelining comes from the fact that, because less of the logic in the datapath gets executed in a single cycle in a pipelined processor, pipelined processors can have reduced cycle times (more cycles/second) than unpipelined implementations of the same processor. Since the pipelined processor has a throughput of one instruction/cycle, the total number of instructions executed per unit time is higher in the pipelined processor, giving better performance.

The cycle time of a pipelined processor is dependent on four factors: the cycle time of the unpipelined diversion of the processor, the number of pipeline stages, how evenly the datapath logic is divided among the stages, and the latency of the pipeline latches. If the logic can be divided evenly among the pipeline stages, the clock period of the pipelined processor is[1]

$$\text{Cycle Time}_{\text{Pipelined}} = \frac{\text{Cycle Time}_{\text{Unpipelined}}}{\text{Number of Pipeline Stages}} + \text{Pipeline Latch Latency}$$

since each stage contains the same fraction of the original logic, plus one pipeline latch. As the number of pipeline stages increases, the pipeline latch latency becomes a greater and greater fraction of the cycle time, limiting the benefit of dividing a processor into a very large number of pipeline stages.

EXAMPLE

An unpipelined processor has a cycle time of 25 ns. What is the cycle time of a pipelined version of the processor with 5 evenly divided pipeline stages, if each pipeline latch has a latency of 1 ns? What if the processor is divided into 50 pipeline stages?

---

[1] A slightly higher clock rate can be achieved by taking advantage of the fact that an n-stage pipeline requires only $n - 1$ pipeline latches by assigning enough additional logic to the last stage of the pipeline to make its total latency equal to that of the other pipeline stages including their pipeline latches. See Exercise 6.5 for an example of this.

Solution

Applying the above equation, cycle time for the 5-stage pipeline = (25 ns/5)+ 1 ns = 6 ns. For the 50-stage pipeline, cycle time = (25 ns/50)+ 1 ns = 1.5 ns. In the 5-stage pipeline, the pipeline latch latency is only 1/6th of the overall cycle time, while the pipeline latch latency is 2/3 of the total cycle time in the 50-stage pipeline. Another way of looking at this is that the 50-stage pipeline has a cycle time 1/4 that of the 5-stage pipeline, at a cost of 10 times as many pipeline latches.

Often, the datapath logic cannot easily be divided into equal-latency pipeline stages. For example, accessing the register file in a processor might take 3 ns, while decoding an instruction might take 4 ns. When deciding how to divide a datapath into pipeline stages, designers must balance the desire to have each stage have the same latency with the difficulty of dividing the datapath into pipeline stages at different points and the amount of data that has to be stored in the pipeline latch, which determines the amount of space that the latch takes up on the chip. Some parts of the datapath, such as the instruction decode logic, are irregular, making it hard to split them into stages. Other parts generate a large number of intermediate data values which would have to be stored in the pipeline latch. For these sections, it is often more efficient to place the pipeline latch at a point where there are fewer intermediate results, and thus fewer bits that have to be stored in the latch, than to place the pipeline latch at a point that divides the datapath into more even sections. When a processor cannot be divided into equal-latency pipeline stages, the clock cycle time of the processor is equal to the latency of the longest pipeline stage plus the pipeline latch delay, since the cycle time has to be long enough for the longest pipeline stage to complete and store its result in the pipeline latch between it and the next stage.

EXAMPLE

Suppose an unpipelined processor with a 25-ns cycle time is divided into 5 pipeline stages with latencies of 5, 7, 3, 6, and 4 ns. If the pipeline latch latency is 1 ns, what is the cycle time of the resulting processor?

Solution

The longest pipeline stage is 7 ns. Adding a 1-ns pipeline latch to this stage gives a total latency of 8 ns, which is the cycle time.

6.3.2 PIPELINE LATENCY

While pipelining can reduce a processor's cycle time and thereby increase instruction throughput, it increases the latency of the processor by at least the sum of all the pipeline latch latencies. The latency of a pipeline is the amount of time that a single instruction takes to pass through the pipeline, which is the product of the number of pipeline stages and the clock cycle time.

EXAMPLE

If an unpipelined processor with a cycle time of 25 ns is evenly divided into 5 pipeline stages using pipeline latches with 1-ns latency, what is the total latency of the pipeline? How about if the processor is divided into 50 pipeline stages?

Solution

This is the same pipeline as the first example in Section 6.3.1, in which we determined that the cycle time of the 5-stage pipeline was 6 ns and the cycle time of the 50-stage pipeline was 1.5 ns. Given that, we can compute the latency of each pipeline by multiplying the cycle time by the number of stages in the pipeline. This gives a latency of 30 ns for the 5-stage pipeline and 75 ns for the 50-stage pipeline.

This example shows the impact pipelining can have on latency, particularly as the number of stages grows. The 5-stage pipeline has a latency of 30 ns, 20 percent longer than the original 25-ns unpipelined processor, while the 50-stage pipeline has a latency of 75 ns, three times that of the original processor! Pipelines with uneven pipeline stages use the same formula, although they see an even greater increase in latency, because the cycle time must be long enough to accommodate the longest stage of the pipeline, even if the other stages are much shorter.

EXAMPLE

Suppose an unpipelined processor with a 25-ns cycle time is divided into 5 pipeline stages with latencies of 5, 7, 3, 6, and 4 ns. If the pipeline latch latency is 1 ns, what is the latency of the resulting pipeline?

Solution

This is the same pipeline as the second example from Section 6.3.1 and has a cycle time of 8 ns. Since there are 5 stages in the pipeline, the total latency of the pipeline is 40 ns.

6.4 Instruction Hazards and Their Impact on Throughput

As described above, pipelining increases processor performance by increasing instruction throughput. Because several instructions are overlapped in the pipeline, cycle time can be reduced, increasing the rate at which instructions execute. In the ideal case, the throughput of a pipeline is simply 1/cycle time, so a 5-stage pipeline with a 6-ns cycle time and an unpipelined cycle time of 25 ns would have an ideal throughput of $\frac{1}{6\,\text{ns}} = 1.67 \times 10^8$ instructions/s, a more than $4\times$ improvement over the unpipelined processor's throughput of 4×10^7 instructions/s.

However, there are a number of factors that limit a pipeline's ability to execute instructions at its peak rate, including dependencies between instructions, branches, and the time required to access memory. In this chapter, we will discuss how instruction dependencies and branches affect the execution time of programs on pipelined processors. Later chapters will cover techniques for improving memory system performance.

Instruction *hazards* (*dependencies*) occur when instructions read or write registers that are used by other instructions. They are divided into four categories, depending on whether the two instructions involved read or write each other's registers. Read-after-read (RAR) hazards, as shown in Fig. 6-3, occur when two instructions both read from the same register. RAR hazards don't cause a problem for the processor because reading a register doesn't change the register's value. Therefore, two instructions that have an RAR hazard can execute on successive cycles (or on the same cycle, in processors that can execute more than one instruction/cycle).

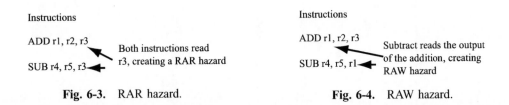

Fig. 6-3. RAR hazard.   **Fig. 6-4.** RAW hazard.

Read-after-write (RAW) hazards occur when an instruction reads a register that was written by a previous instruction, as shown in Fig. 6-4. RAW hazards are also known as *data dependencies* or *true dependencies*, because they occur when an instruction needs to use the result of another instruction.

When a RAW hazard occurs, the reading instruction cannot proceed past the register read stage of the pipeline until the writing instruction has passed through the write-back stage, because the data that the reading instruction needs is not available until then. This is called a *pipeline stall* or *bubble*. Note that the reading instruction can proceed through the instruction fetch and instruction decode stages of the pipeline before the writing instruction completes, because the reading instruction does not need the value produced by the writing instruction until it reaches the register read stage.

Figure 6-5 shows how the instructions in Fig. 6-4 would flow through the five-stage example pipeline we've been using. During cycles 1 through 4, both instructions flow through the pipeline at one stage per cycle. In cycle 4, the subtract instruction attempts to read r5 and r1, its input registers, and determines that r1 cannot be read because the ADD has not written its result into r1 yet. (The hardware the subtract uses to determine this will be discussed later in this chapter.)

In cycle 5, the subtract would normally enter the execute stage, but it is prevented from doing so because it was not able to read r1 on cycle 4. Instead, the hardware inserts a special no-operation (NOP) instruction, known as a bubble, into the

| Pipeline Stage | | Cycle | | | | | | |
	1	2	3	4	5	6	7	8
IF	ADD r1, r2, r3	SUB r4, r5, r1						
ID		ADD r1, r2, r3	SUB r4, r5, r1					
RR			ADD r1, r2, r3	SUB r4, r5, r1	SUB r4, r5, r1	SUB r4, r5, r1		
EX				ADD r1, r2, r3	(bubble)	(bubble)	SUB r4, r5, r1	
WB					ADD r1, r2, r3	(bubble)	(bubble)	SUB r4, r5, r1

Fig. 6-5. Pipelined execution with stall.

execute stage of the pipeline, and the subtract tries to read its input registers again on cycle 5. The result of the ADD is still unavailable on cycle 5 because the ADD has not completed the writeback stage yet, so the subtract cannot enter the execute stage on cycle 6. On cycle 6, the SUB is able to read r1, and it proceeds into the execute stage on cycle 7. Thus, the RAW dependency between these two instructions has caused a two-cycle delay in the pipeline.

Write-after-read (WAR) hazards, shown in Fig. 6-6, and write-after-write (WAW) hazards (Fig. 6-7) occur when the output register of an instruction has been either read or written by a previous instruction. These hazards are sometimes called *name dependencies*, as they occur because the processor has a finite number of registers. If the processor had an infinite number of registers, it could use a different register for the output of each instruction, and WAW and WAR hazards would never occur.

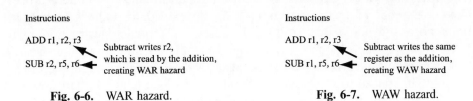

Instructions

ADD r1, r2, r3

SUB r2, r5, r6⬅   Subtract writes r2, which is read by the addition, creating WAR hazard

Fig. 6-6.   WAR hazard.

Instructions

ADD r1, r2, r3

SUB r1, r5, r6⬅   Subtract writes the same register as the addition, creating WAW hazard

Fig. 6-7.   WAW hazard.

If a processor executes instructions in the order that they appear in the program and uses the same pipeline for all instructions, WAR and WAW hazards do not cause delays because of the way instructions flow through the pipeline. Since the output register of an instruction is written in the writeback stage of the pipeline, instructions with WAW hazards will enter the writeback stage in the order in which they appear in the program and write their results into the register in the right order. There is even less of a problem with instructions that have WAR hazards, because the register read stage of the pipeline occurs before the writeback stage. By the time an instruction enters the writeback stage of the pipeline, all previous instructions in the program have already passed through the register read stage and read their input values. Therefore, the writing instruction can go ahead and write its destination register without causing any problems.

If a processor's instructions do not all have the same latency, WAW and WAR hazards can cause problems, because it is possible for a low-latency instruction to complete before a longer-latency instruction that appeared earlier in the program. These processors must keep track of name dependencies between instructions and stall the pipeline as necessary to resolve these hazards. WAR and WAW hazards are also an issue in out-of-order processors, which allow instructions to execute in different orders than the original program to improve performance. These processors will be discussed in more detail in the next chapter, along with register renaming, a hardware technique to reduce the performance impact of name dependencies.

6.4.1 BRANCHES

Branch instructions can also cause delays in pipelined processors, because the processor cannot determine which instruction to fetch next until the branch has executed. Effectively, branch instructions, particularly conditional branches, create data dependencies between the branch instruction and the instruction fetch stage of the pipeline, since the branch instruction computes the address of the next instruction that the instruction fetch stage should fetch. Figure 6-8 shows how a branch instruction would execute on our five-stage pipeline. The PC is updated at the end of the cycle that the branch instruction is in the execute stage, allowing the next instruction to be fetched on the following cycle.

The delay between when a branch instruction enters the pipeline and the time at which the next instruction enters the pipeline is often called the processor's *branch delay*. Branch delays are sometimes called *control hazards*, because the delay is due to the control flow of the program. The pipeline illustrated in Fig. 6-8 has a four-cycle branch delay.

Branch delays have a significant impact on the performance of modern processors, and a number of techniques have been developed to address them. One technique is to add hardware to allow the result of a branch instruction to be computed earlier in the pipeline. For example, if our pipeline computed the new value of the PC in the register read stage instead of the execute stage, the branch delay would be reduced to three cycles. Another technique is to add hardware that predicts the destination address of each branch before the branch completes, allowing the processor to begin fetching instructions from that address earlier in the pipeline. These *branch prediction* techniques are beyond the scope of this book, but they significantly improve the performance of modern processors.

6.4.2 STRUCTURAL HAZARDS

A final cause of stalls in pipelined processors are *structural hazards*. Structural hazards occur when the processor's hardware is not capable of executing all the instructions in the pipeline simultaneously. For example, if the register file did not have enough ports to allow an instruction in the WB stage to write its result into the register file in the same cycle that another instruction in the RR stage read from the register file, it would be necessary to stall any instruction in the RR stage if there was also an instruction in the WB stage on that cycle. (Choosing to stall the instruction in the WB stage to allow the instruction in the RR stage to proceed would be a poor choice, as the stall in the WB stage would prevent instructions in the EX stage from advancing.)

Structural hazards within a single pipeline are relatively rare on modern processors, because their hardware and instruction sets have been designed to support pipelining. However, processors that execute more than one instruction in a cycle, which are covered in the next chapter, often have restrictions on the types of instructions that the hardware can execute simultaneously. For example, a processor might be able to execute two instructions in each cycle, but only if one of the instructions was an integer operation and the other a floating-point computation.

6.4.3 SCOREBOARDING

Pipelined processors need to keep track of which registers will be written by instructions that are already in the pipeline, so that subsequent instructions can

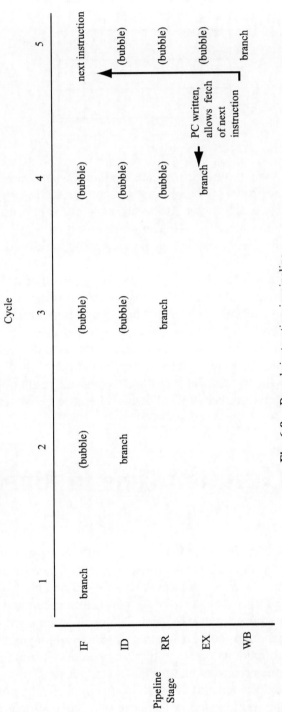

Fig. 6-8. Branch instruction in pipeline.

Presence Bit   Register

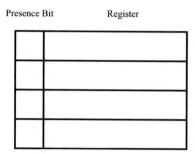

Fig. 6-9. Register scoreboard.

determine whether their input registers are available when they reach the register read stage. To do this, most processors use a technique called *register scoreboarding*. In scoreboarding, a bit, known as the *presence* bit, is added to each register in the register file, as shown in Fig. 6-9. The presence bit records whether the register is available for reading (full) or waiting for an instruction to write its output value (empty).

When an instruction enters the register read stage, the hardware checks to see if all of its input registers are full. If so, the hardware reads the values of all the input registers, marks the output register of the instruction empty, and allows the instruction to proceed to the execute stage on the next cycle. If not, the hardware holds the instruction in the register read stage until its input values become full, inserting bubbles into the execute stage on each cycle until this happens. When an instruction reaches the writeback stage and writes its result into its destination register, that register is marked full, allowing operations that read the register to proceed.

6.5 Predicting Execution Time in Pipelined Processors

An unpipelined processor must complete the execution of each instruction before it begins the execution of the next. This means that dependencies between instructions generally do not affect the execution time of a program on an unpipelined processor, because the result of each instruction has been fully computed before any later instruction in the program begins execution. Thus, on an unpipelined processor, the execution time of a program can be computed by simply adding together the execution times of all of the instructions that the processor executes in running the program.

On a pipelined processor, computing the execution time of a program is more complicated because dependencies between instructions affect a program's execution time. In the ideal case, no pipeline stalls occur, and one instruction passes from the register read stage to the execute stage in each cycle. In this case, the execution time (in cycles) of a program is equal to the depth of the pipeline plus the number of instructions in the program minus 1, because the first instruction passes through the pipeline in a number of cycles equal to the pipeline depth, and the other instructions proceed through at one instruction per cycle. Multiplying the execution time in cycles by the clock cycle time gives the execution time of the program in seconds. When programs contain dependencies that cause pipeline stalls, however, we need to be able to determine how many stalls occur to predict the execution time of a program.

One way to compute the execution time of a program on a pipelined processor is to draw a pipeline diagram, similar to Fig. 6-5, for the program, but this becomes impractical for large programs. Instead, a better approach is to separate the execution time of the program into two parts: the pipeline latency and the time required to *issue* all of the instructions in the program. An instruction is said to have issued when it passes from the register read stage into the execute stage, because the register read stage is generally the last point in the pipeline where an instruction can stall. Once an instruction enters the execute stage, it is guaranteed to proceed through the pipeline at one stage per cycle until it reaches the last stage and completes. The time to issue all of the instructions begins in the cycle when the first instruction issues, ends in the cycle when the last instruction issues, and includes all of the cycles during which pipeline stalls cause bubbles to be issued into the execute stage.

Using this model, the execution time (in cycles) of a program is equal to the pipeline latency plus the time to issue all of the instructions minus 1 (again, because the first instruction travels through the pipeline in a number of cycles equal to the pipeline depth). In the ideal case, the number of cycles required to issue all of the instructions in a program is equal to the number of instructions in the program, because one instruction issues each cycle. In almost all cases, however, dependencies cause stalls during the execution of a program, which increase the number of cycles required to issue the instructions in the program.

To help compute the time required to issue the instructions in a program, architects define the *instruction latency* of each instruction type in a pipeline as the delay between the time at which an instruction of that type issues and the time at which a dependent instruction may issue. For example, the pipeline in Fig. 6-5 has an instruction latency of three cycles for non-branch instructions, because a dependent instruction may enter the execute stage three cycles after the instruction which generates its data. Branch instructions have instruction latencies of four cycles, as shown in Fig. 6-8. (Think of the instruction that executes after a branch as being dependent on the result of the branch.)

In a pipelined processor, each instruction will issue on either the cycle after the instruction before it in the program issues or the cycle after the latencies of all of the instructions it is dependent on complete, whichever is later. Thus, the number of cycles required to issue all of the instructions in a program can be computed by proceeding sequentially through the program to determine when each instruction can issue.

EXAMPLE

On the sample pipeline we've been using, which has instruction latencies of 3 cycles for non-branch instructions and 4 cycles for branch instructions, what is the execution time of the following instruction sequence?

```
ADD  r1,  r2,  r3
SUB  r4,  r5,  r6
MUL  r8,  r2,  r1
ASH  r5,  r2,  r1
OR   r10, r11, r4
```

Solution

Our sample pipeline has five stages, so the pipeline latency is 5 cycles. To compute the issue time of the instruction sequence, assume that the ADD issues on cycle n. The SUB is independent of the ADD, so it can issue on cycle $n + 1$, the cycle after the previous instruction in the program issues. The MUL depends on the ADD, so it can't issue until cycle $n + 3$, because the ADD has a latency of 3 cycles. The ASH is also dependent on the ADD, but it can't issue until cycle $n + 4$, because the MUL issues on cycle $n + 3$. The OR is independent of the previous instructions, so it issues on cycle $n + 5$. Therefore, it takes 6 cycles to issue all of the instructions in the program. Using the formula, the execution time of the program is 5 cycles (pipeline latency) + 6 cycles (time to issue the instructions in the program) $- 1 = 10$ cycles. Figure 6-10 shows a pipeline diagram of the execution of this set of instructions, confirming the 10-cycle execution time.

This example also illustrates an important factor in achieving good performance on pipelined processors—scheduling instructions to avoid pipeline stalls. Because the SUB instruction did not use the result of the ADD, it was able to execute on the cycle immediately following the ADD. If the SUB and MUL instructions had been reversed, the MUL instruction would still have had to wait until three cycles after the ADD executed for its input data to be ready, and the SUB would have been unable to issue until four cycles after the ADD. Compilers for pipelined processors must understand the details of the pipeline to be able to place instructions in an order which maximizes performance.

EXAMPLE

What is the execution time of this sequence on a 7-stage pipeline with a 2-cycle instruction latency for non-branch instructions, but a 5-cycle branch instruction latency? Assume the branch is not taken, so the DIV is the next instruction executed after it.

```
BNE  r4,  #0,  r5
DIV  r2,  r1,  r7
ADD  r8,  r9,  r10
SUB  r5,  r2,  r9
MUL  r10, r5,  r8
```

Solution

The pipeline has 7 stages, so the pipeline latency is 7 cycles. To compute the number of cycles required to issue the program, assume the BNE executes on cycle n. The pipeline has a 5-cycle branch latency, so the DIV executes on

Pipeline Stage	1	2	3	4	5	6	7	8	9	10
IF	ADD r1, r2, r3	SUB r4, r5, r6	MUL r8, r2, r1	ASH r5, r2, r1	OR r10, r11, r4	OR r10, r11, r4				
ID		ADD r1, r2, r3	SUB r4, r5, r6	MUL r8, r2, r1	ASH r5, r2, r1	ASH r5, r2, r1	OR r10, r11, r4			
RR			ADD r1, r2, r3	SUB r4, r5, r6	MUL r8, r2, r1	MUL r8, r2, r1	ASH r5, r2, r1	OR r10, r11, r4		
EX				ADD r1, r2, r3	SUB r4, r5, r6	(bubble)	MUL r8, r2, r1	ASH r5, r2, r1	OR r10, r11, r4	
WB					ADD r1, r2, r3	SUB r4, r5, r6	(bubble)	MUL r8, r2, r1	ASH r5, r2, r1	OR r10, r11, r4

Cycle

Fig. 6-10. Pipelined execution example.

cycle $n + 5$. The ADD has no data dependency on the DIV, so it executes on cycle $n + 6$. The SUB has a data dependency on the DIV, so it can't execute before cycle $n + 7$, which is the first cycle on which it is possible for the SUB to execute, because the ADD issued on cycle $n + 6$.

The MUL has data dependencies on both the SUB and the ADD. The ADD issued on cycle $n + 6$, so an instruction that depended only on the ADD could issue on cycle $n + 8$. However, the SUB issued on cycle $n + 7$, so instructions that depend on it can't issue until cycle $n + 9$. Therefore, the MUL issues on cycle $n + 9$, and it takes a total of 10 cycles to issue all of the instructions in the program.

Therefore, the total execution time of this program is 7 cycles (pipeline latency) + 10 cycles (time to issue) − 1 = 16 cycles.

6.6 Result Forwarding (Bypassing)

As illustrated in Fig. 6-11, much of the delay caused by data dependencies is due to the amount of time required to write the result of an instruction into the register file and then read it out as the input to another instruction. The result of the ADD instruction is computed in the execute stage of the pipeline in cycle 4, but the SUB instruction is unable to issue until cycle 7 because the result of the ADD is not written into the register file until cycle 5, allowing the subtract to read it on cycle 6. If the result of the ADD could be sent to the subtract instruction directly, without going through the register file, the subtract could issue on cycle 5 without any pipeline stalls.

Virtually all pipelined processors incorporate a technique known as result forwarding, or *bypassing*, that forwards the results of the execute stage(s) directly to instructions in the previous stages of the pipeline, allowing these instructions to proceed without waiting for the result to be written into the register file. In general, the instruction latency of non-branch instructions in a pipeline with bypassing is equal to the number of execute stages in the pipeline, because the output of an instruction is not computed until it completes the last execute stage, but an instruction's inputs are required when it enters the first execute stage. Bypassing does not usually improve the latency of branch operations, because the results of branch instructions are not written into the register file.

Figure 6-12 shows how bypassing would be implemented on our five-stage pipeline. In addition to the conventional writeback path, connections are added that send the output of the execute stage directly to the input of the execute stage and to the register read stage. If the instruction in the register read stage depends on the output of the instruction in the execute stage, it obtains its input from the bypass path at the start of the next cycle, as it enters the execute stage. Similarly, an instruction in the instruction decode stage that depends on the instruction in the execute stage obtains its input from the bypass path on the next cycle, while it is in register read stage, instead of having to wait until its input can be read out of the register file. There is no need to forward the result of an instruction to the instruction

Pipeline Stage	Cycle 1	Cycle 2	Cycle 3	Cycle 4	Cycle 5	Cycle 6	Cycle 7	Cycle 8
IF	ADD r1, r2, r3	SUB r4, r5, r1						
ID		ADD r1, r2, r3	SUB r4, r5, r1					
RR			ADD r1, r2, r3	SUB r4, r5, r1	SUB r4, r5, r1	SUB r4, r5, r1		
EX				ADD r1, r2, r3	(bubble)	(bubble)	SUB r4, r5, r1	
WB					ADD r1, r2, r3	(bubble)	(bubble)	SUB r4, r5, r1

But isn't read until this cycle

Value of r1 generated in this cycle

Fig. 6-11. Data delay.

Pipelined Processor

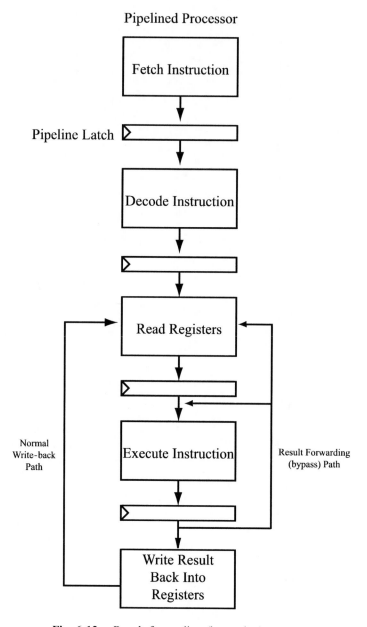

Fig. 6-12.   Result forwarding (bypassing).

decode stage, because the result of an instruction in the execute stage will have been written into the register file by the time the instruction in the instruction fetch stage reaches the register read stage.

Different processors implement bypassing in different ways, although the basic idea remains the same. For example, some processors eliminate the need for the bypass path that connects the output of the execute stage to the register read stage by using register files that are written in the first half of a clock cycle and read in the second. If such a register file is used, an instruction in the write-back stage writes its result during the first half of the clock cycle, allowing an instruction in the register read stage to read it during the second half of the clock cycle. This optimization alone would reduce the non-branch instruction latency of our sample pipeline to two cycles, and adding the bypass path from the output of the execute stage to the input of the execute stage would then reduce the non-branch instruction latency to one cycle.

EXAMPLE

What is the execution time (in cycles) of the code fragment from Fig. 6-5 if result forwarding is added to our 5-stage pipeline?

Solution

Result forwarding reduces the latency of non-branch instructions to one cycle, becuase our 5-stage pipeline has only one execute stage. This reduces the issue time of the code fragment to two cycles. The total execution time becomes 5 cycles (pipeline latency) $+ 2$ cycles (issue time) $- 1 = 6$ cycles.

6.7 Summary

Pipelining improves processor performance by overlapping the execution of multiple instructions. While one instruction is being executed, the next instruction is reading its input registers, another instruction is being decoded, and so on. Since each stage of instruction execution requires different hardware, pipelining can greatly improve performance at a relatively low hardware cost.

The peak performance of a pipelined system is determined by how many pipeline stages the system contains, how even the division of execution into pipeline stages is, and how much delay is added for the pipeline registers in each pipeline stage. If the division of the processor into pipeline stages is uneven, the clock rate is limited by the latency of the longest stage. Even if the processor can be divided into even pipeline stages, the impact of pipelining diminishes as the number of pipeline stages increases, because the delay added by the pipeline latches becomes a significant portion of the cycle time.

The actual performance of a pipelined system is generally limited by data dependencies within a program. We have discussed three types of data dependencies: read-after-write, write-after-read, and write-after-write. WAR and WAW dependencies are also known as name dependencies, as they only occur because the processor has a limited number of registers to store results in, which must be reused over the course of a program's execution. Branches also limit a pipeline's performance, because the processor must stall until the branch has completed execution.

Result forwarding, or bypassing, is used to reduce the delay caused by RAW dependencies. In addition to writing the result of an instruction back into the register file, bypassing sends the result of an instruction directly to instructions in the pipeline that need it, reducing the latency of non-branch instructions.

In the next chapter, we will discuss instruction-level parallelism, which further improves processor performance by allowing independent instructions to execute simultaneously. Pipelining and instruction-level parallelism combine well, and most modern processors employ both techniques to improve performance.

 Solved Problems

Pipelining (I)

6.1. Why does pipelining improve performance?

Solution

In an unpipelined processor, each instruction is executed completely before execution of the next instruction begins. In a pipelined processor, instruction execution is divided into stages, and execution of the next instruction starts as soon as the current instruction has completed the first stage. This increases the rate at which instructions can be executed, improving performance.

Another way to describe this is that pipelining divides the processor's datapath into stages that are separated by pipeline latches. In an unpipelined processor, an instruction must be able to get all the way through the datapath within a single clock cycle. In a pipelined processor, an instruction must only be able to get through one stage of the pipeline in each cycle, allowing the clock cycle to be much shorter than in an unpipelined processor. Since a pipelined processor can still start executing one instruction during each clock cycle, shortening the clock cycle increases the rate at which instructions can be executed, improving performance.

Pipelining (II)

6.2. What are the limits on how much a processor's performance can be improved using pipelining?

Solution

There are two main limitations. First, as the number of pipeline stages increases, the fraction of the latency of each stage that is due to the pipeline latch increases. In the extreme, pipelining can't reduce the clock cycle time down below the latency of the pipeline latch required for each stage.

The second limitation comes from data dependencies and branch delays. Instructions that depend on the results of other instructions have to wait for those instructions to complete, creating pipeline stalls (bubbles), and instructions that follow branches have to wait for the branch to complete so that the processor knows which instruction to execute next. This means that the pipeline will execute less than one instruction per cycle on average. As the pipeline gets deeper, the delay between dependent instructions will get longer, meaning that more and more of the processor's time will be spent waiting for pipeline stalls. Bypassing can reduce this problem somewhat, but it cannot eliminate it completely, since very deep pipelines will have to have more than one execute stage, meaning that the delay between the execution of dependent instructions will be more than one cycle.

Even Pipelining

6.3. Given an unpipelined processor with a 10 ns cycle time and pipeline latches with 0.5 ns latency, what are the cycle times of pipelined versions of the processor with 2, 4, 8, and 16 stages if the datapath logic is evenly divided among the pipeline stages? Also, what is the latency of each of the pipelined versions of the processor?

Solution

$$\text{Cycle Time}_{\text{Pipelined}} = \frac{\text{Cycle Time}_{\text{Unpipelined}}}{\text{Number of Pipeline Stages}} + \text{Pipeline Latch Latency (from Sect. 6.3.1)}$$

Applying this formula, we get cycle times of 5.5, 3, 1.75, and 1.125 ns, showing the diminishing returns of pipelining as the pipeline latch latency becomes a significant part of the overall cycle time.

To compute the latency of each processor, we simply multiply the cycle time by the number of pipeline stages, giving latencies of 11, 12, 14, and 18 ns.

Pipeline to Achieve Clock Rate

6.4. For the processor from the last exercise, how many stages of pipelining are required to achieve a cycle time of 2 ns? 1 ns?

Solution

Here, we want to solve for the number of pipeline stages, so we rewrite the cycle time formula to get the following:

$$\text{Number of Stages} = \frac{\text{Cycle Time}_{\text{Unpipelined}}}{\text{Cycle Time}_{\text{Pipelined}} - \text{Pipeline Latch Latency}}$$

Applying this gives 6.67 as the number of pipeline stages required to achieve a 2 ns cycle time. Since you can't have a fractional number of pipeline stages, this rounds up to 7. The formula gives 20 as the number of pipeline stages required to achieve a 1 ns clock rate.

Minimum Cycle Time

6.5. For the processor and pipeline latch latencies in Problem 6.3, what is the minimum cycle time achievable with a 4-stage pipeline if additional logic is assigned to the final stage to balance the additional latency of the pipeline latches in the other stages?

Solution

In this pipeline, the total latency of each stage will be the same, even though some stages contain pipeline latches and others do not. A simple way to compute the cycle time in this case is to find the total latency of the original datapath plus the pipeline latches, and then divide by the number of stages. The latency of the original datapath is 10 ns. A 4-stage pipeline requires 3 pipeline latches. Each pipeline latch has a latency of 0.5 ns, so the pipeline latches add 1.5 ns to the datapath latency, giving a total latency of 11.5 ns. Dividing this by the number of stages (4) gives 2.875 ns as the clock time of the pipeline processor with this design.

Uneven Pipelining

6.6. Suppose that an unpipelined processor has a cycle time of 25 ns, and that its datapath is made up of modules with latencies of 2, 3, 4, 7, 3, 2, and 4 ns (in that order). In pipelining this processor, it is not possible to rearrange the order of the modules (for example, putting the register read stage before the instruction decode stage) or to divide a module into multiple pipeline stages (for complexity reasons). Given pipeline latches with 1 ns latency:

a. What is the minimum cycle time that can be achieved by pipelining this processor?

b. If the processor is divided into the fewest number of pipeline stages that allow it to achieve the minimum latency from part 1, what is the latency of the pipeline?

c. If you are limited to a 2-stage pipeline what is the minimum cycle time?

d. What is the latency for the pipelines from part 3?

Solution

a. If there is no limit on the number of pipeline stages, then the minimum cycle time is determined by the latency of the longest module in the datapath plus the pipeline latch time. This gives a cycle time of 7 ns + 1 ns = 8 ns.

b. To answer this, we need to know how many pipeline stages the processor requires to operate at a cycle time of 8 ns. We can group any set of adjacent modules with total latencies of 7 ns or less into a single stage. Doing this gives 5 pipeline stages. 5 stages × 8 ns cycle time = 40 ns latency.

c. For minimum cycle time, we want to divide the modules into stages with as even latencies as possible. For two stages, this gives stage latencies of 16 ns and 9 ns (or the reverse order). Since we only need one pipeline latch between the two stages, we can divide the logic into a 9 ns first stage and a 16 ns second stage. Adding the pipeline latch to the first stage gives us a 16 ns clock rate.

d. 16 ns × 2 stages = 32 ns latency.

Instruction Hazards (I)

6.7. **a.** Identify all of the RAW hazards in this instruction sequence:

```
DIV  r2,  r5,  r8
SUB  r9,  r2,  r7
ASH  r5,  r14, r6
MUL  r11, r9,  r5
BEQ  r10, #0,  r12
OR   r8,  r15, r2
```

b. Identify all of the WAR hazards in the previous instruction sequence.

c. Identify all of the WAW hazards in the instruction sequence.

d. Identify all of the control hazards in this instruction sequence.

Solution

a. RAW hazards exist between the DIV instruction and the SUB instruction, between the ASH and the MUL, between the SUB and MUL, and between the DIV and the OR.

b. WAR hazards exist between the DIV and the ASH instructions, and between the DIV and the OR instructions.

c. There are no WAW hazards in this instruction sequence.

d. There is only one control hazard in this sequence, between the BEQ instruction and the OR instruction.

Instruction Hazards (II)

6.8. When reordering instructions to improve performance, which types of instruction hazards represent ordering constraints that must be maintained if the reordered program is to generate the same result as the original program, and why?

Solution

Control, RAW, WAW, and WAR hazards represent ordering constraints. RAW hazards indicate that the reading instruction uses the result of the writing instruction, and moving the reading instruction before the writing instruction will cause the reading instruction to see the wrong value of the writing instruction's output register. WAW hazards occur when multiple instructions write the same register. Changing the order of two instructions with a WAW hazard will cause a different instruction to write the output register last, leaving a different value in the register for any subsequent readers. WAR hazards occur when a register is reused. Moving the writing instruction before the reading instruction will cause the reading instruction to see the new value of the output register, rather than the old value, which it was intended to see.

Branch (control) hazards result from branch instructions that compute the address of the next instruction fetch, and create ordering constraints. Moving an instruction that was above a branch below the branch causes the instruction to only be executed if the branch is not taken, while moving an instruction that was below a branch above the branch has the reverse effect, causing an instruction that was only intended to be executed when the branch is not taken to be executed each time the instruction sequence executes.

RAR hazards do not represent ordering constraints. Reading a register does not change its value, so multiple reads may be done in any order. Structural hazards arise because of the limitations of the processor, not because of dependencies between instructions, so they do not generally impose constraints on the ordering of instructions in a program.

Pipelined Execution

6.9. Assuming no result forwarding and the five-stage sample pipeline of Section 6.3, draw a pipeline execution diagram similar to Fig. 6-2 for the following code fragment:

```
ADD  r1, r2, r3
SUB  r4, r5, r6
MUL  r8, r9, r10
DIV  r12, r13, r14
```

Solution

There are no instruction hazards in this code fragment, so instructions proceed through the pipeline at one stage per cycle.

Pipelined Execution With Hazards (I)

6.10. Assuming no result forwarding and the five-stage sample pipeline of Section 6.3, draw a pipeline execution diagram similar to Fig. 6-2 for the following code fragment:

```
ADD  r1,  r2,  r3
SUB  r4,  r5,  r6
MUL  r8,  r9,  r4
DIV  r12, r13, r14
```

Solution

Here, there is a RAW hazard between the SUB instruction, which writes r4, and the MUL instruction, which reads r4. Therefore, the MUL instruction will not be able to read its input registers until after the SUB instruction has completed the WB stage, creating a pipeline stall.

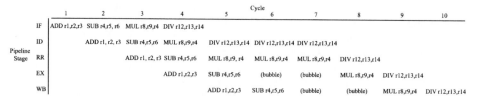

Pipelined Execution With Hazards (II)

6.11. Assuming no result forwarding and the five-stage sample pipeline of Section 6.3, draw a pipeline execution diagram similar to Fig. 6-2 for the following code fragment. Assume that the branch represented by the BEQ instruction is not taken.

```
ADD  r1,  r2,  r3
SUB  r4,  r5,  r6
BEQ  r2,  #0,  r9
DIV  r12, r13, r14
```

Solution

Here, the stall occurs because the BEQ instruction must complete the execution stage before the instruction fetch stage knows what address the next instruction should be fetched from, causing a stall. In general, processors have a direct path from the execution unit to the instruction fetch stage, allowing them to fetch the next instruction on the cycle after a branch reaches the execution stage.

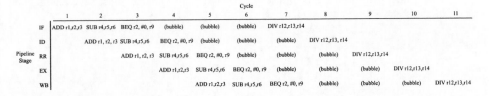

Execution Time on Pipelines

6.12. What is the execution time (in cycles) of the following instruction sequence on our example five-stage pipeline (without bypassing)? Assume the branch is not taken. If the processor has a 2-ns clock cycle, what is the execution time in ns?

```
ADD  r1, r4, r7
BEQ  r2, #0, r1
SUB  r8, r10, r11
MUL  r12, r13, r14
```

Solution

The pipeline has a depth of 5 stages, giving a pipeline latency of 5 cycles. The BEQ instruction depends on the result of the ADD, so it issues on cycle $n + 3$, assuming the ADD issues on cycle n. The SUB has to wait for the four-cycle branch delay of the BEQ, so it issues on cycle $n + 7$, and the MUL issues on cycle $n + 8$, giving 9 cycles as the time to issue this program. Total execution time is $5 + 9 - 1 = 13$ cycles.

At 2 ns/cycle, this is 26 ns.

Instruction Ordering

6.13. a. What is the execution time (in cycles) of the following instruction sequence on our five-stage pipeline (without bypassing)?

```
ADD  r3, r4, r5
SUB  r7, r3, r9
MUL  r8, r9, r10
ASH  r4, r8, r12
```

b. Can the execution time of the instruction sequence be improved by reordering the instructions without changing the result of the computation? If so, show the instruction sequence with the shortest execution time and give its execution time.

Solution

a. The five-stage pipeline has a latency of 5 cycles. Assuming the ADD issues on cycle n, the SUB can issue on cycle $n + 3$ because it depends on the ADD, which has a 3-cycle instruction latency. The MUL is independent of the ADD and SUB, so it issues on cycle

$n + 4$, and the ASH issues on cycle $n + 7$, because it depends on the MUL. Therefore, it takes 8 cycles to issue all of the instructions in the program, and the execution time is $5 + 8 - 1 = 12$ cycles.

b.   Yes, there is a better ordering. The ordering with the shortest execution time is as follows:

```
ADD  r3,  r4,  r5
MUL  r8,  r9,  r10
SUB  r7,  r3,  r9
ASH  r4,  r8,  r12
```

In this sequence, the only pipeline stall that occurs is between the MUL and the SUB instructions, because the SUB can't execute until 3 cycles after the ADD executes. The dependency between the MUL and the ASH does not cause any stalls because the MUL completes before the cycle after the SUB enters the execute stage, which is the first opportunity for the ASH to enter the execute stage. Therefore, it takes 5 cycles to issue all of the instructions in the sequence. The execution time of this sequence is $5 + 5 - 1 = 9$ cycles.

Instruction Ordering (II)

6.14.   Compute the execution time of the following instruction sequence on our five-stage pipeline without bypassing. Then, find the reordering of the instructions that gives the shortest execution time and compute that execution time.

```
MUL  r10,  r11,  r12
SUB  r8,  r10,  r15
ADD  r13,  r14,  r0
ASH  r15,  r2,  r3
OR   r7,  r5,  r6
```

Solution

The execution time of the original sequence is 11 cycles. A reordering that gives minimal execution time is as follows:

```
MUL  r10,  r11,  r12
ADD  r13,  r14,  r0
OR   r7,  r5,  r6
SUB  r8,  r10,  r15
ASH  r15,  r2,  r3
```

The execution time of this ordering is 9 cycles, because no pipeline stalls occur. Note that it would not be possible to move the ASH instruction before the SUB instruction because of the WAR hazard between these instructions.

Bypassing (I)

6.15.   Why does bypassing usually eliminate or reduce stalls due to data dependencies, but has no effect on stalls due to control hazards?

Solution

Bypassing eliminates the time required to write a result back into the register file and read the result out of the register file in pipelines without bypassing. For data dependencies, this is a significant fraction of the instruction latency, so bypassing improves performance. Because the transmission of the result address from a branch instruction to the instruction fetch stage does not go through the register file, bypassing does not improve the performance of branch instructions. Another way of looking at this is that the base pipeline already has a bypass path from the execution unit to the instruction fetch stage, so no improvement is gained from adding additional bypass paths.

Bypassing (II)

6.16. What is the execution time of the code sequence in Problem 6.12 if bypassing is added to our base pipeline?

Solution

The execution time would be 11 cycles. Since our base pipeline has only one execute stage, bypassing reduces the instruction latency of non-branch instructions to one cycle. This eliminates the two cycles of delay between the ADD and the branch, but not the branch delay.

Comprehensive Example

6.17. This exercise will consider the seven-stage pipeline shown in Fig. 6-13.
  a. If the clock period of this pipeline is 4 ns, what is the latency of the pipeline in cycles and ns?
  b. Draw a pipeline execution diagram for this pipeline, showing how each of the following instruction sequences flow through the pipeline. Assume that the pipeline does not implement bypassing.

  Sequence 1:
  ```
  ADD r1, r2, r3
  SUB r4, r1, r5
  ```
  Sequence 2: (assume branch not taken)
  ```
  BNE r9, #3, r8
  OR r12, r14, r15
  ```

  c. Based on these diagrams, what are the non-branch and branch instruction latencies for this pipeline?
  d. Given the branch and non-branch instruction latencies for this pipeline, what is the execution time of the code sequence in Problem 6.12 on this pipeline?
  e. If result forwarding were implemented on this pipeline, what would the non-branch and branch instruction latencies be?
  f. What would the execution time of the code sequence from Problem 6.12 be on this pipeline with result forwarding?

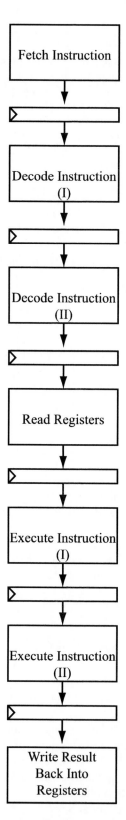

Fig. 6-13. Seven-stage pipeline.

Solution

a.   The pipeline has seven stages. Therefore, the latency of the pipeline is seven cycles. At 4ns/cycle, this is 28 ns.

b.   *Sequence 1:*

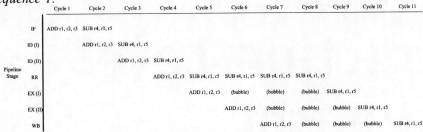

Sequence 2:

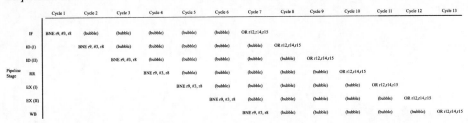

c.   Non-branch instruction latency: 4 cycles. Branch instruction latency: 6 cycles.

d.   The execution time would be 18 cycles.

e.   The non-branch latency would become 2 cycles because of the two execute stages. The branch latency would remain 6 cycles because result forwarding does not improve branch latency.

f.   16 cycles.

CHAPTER 7

Instruction-Level Parallelism

7.1 Objectives

This chapter covers a variety of techniques for exploiting *instruction-level parallelism* (ILP) by executing independent instructions at the same time. After completing this chapter, you should

1. Understand the concepts behind instruction-level parallelism and why it is used
2. Understand and be able to discuss the differences between superscalar and VLIW (very long instruction word) processors
3. Be able to predict the execution time of short instruction sequences on processors that exploit instruction-level parallelism
4. Be able to predict the impact that out-of-order execution will have on the execution time of programs
5. Be familiar with loop unrolling and software pipelining, two compiler techniques that improve the performance of programs on ILP processors

7.2 Introduction

In the last chapter, we discussed pipelining, an important technique that increases computer performance by overlapping the execution of multiple instructions. This allows instructions to be executed at a higher rate than would be possible if each instruction had to wait for the previous instruction to complete before it could begin execution. In this chapter, we explore techniques to exploit instruction-level parallelism by executing multiple instructions simultaneously, further improving performance. Modern processors typically employ both pipelining and techniques that exploit instruction-level parallelism, and we will assume that all of the ILP processors discussed in this chapter are pipelined unless otherwise specified.

Pipelining improves performance by increasing the rate at which instructions can be executed. However, as we saw in the last chapter, there are limits to how much pipelining can improve performance. As more and more pipeline stages are added to a processor, the delay of the pipeline register required in each stage becomes a significant component of the cycle time, reducing the benefit of increasing the pipeline depth. More significantly, increasing the pipeline depth increases branch delay and instruction latency, increasing the number of stall cycles that occur between dependent instructions.

Since the combination of technological constraints and diminishing returns from additional pipelining limits the maximum clock rate of a processor in a given fabrication process, architects have turned to parallelism to improve performance by performing multiple tasks at the same time. Parallel computer systems tend to take one of two forms: multiprocessors and instruction-level parallel processors, which vary in the size of the tasks that are executed in parallel. In multiprocessor systems, which are covered in Chapter 12, relatively large tasks, such as procedures or loop iterations, are executed in parallel. In contrast, instruction-level parallel processors execute individual instructions in parallel.

Processors that exploit instruction-level parallelism have been much more successful than multiprocessors in the general-purpose workstation/PC market because they can provide performance improvements on conventional programs, while this has not been possible on multiprocessors. In particular, superscalar processors can achieve speedups when running programs that were compiled for execution on sequential (non-ILP) processors without requiring recompilation. The other architecture that will be covered in this chapter, VLIW processors, requires that programs be recompiled for the new architecture but achieves very good performance on programs written in sequential languages such as C or FORTRAN when these programs are recompiled for a VLIW processor.

A high level block diagram of an instruction-level parallel processor is shown in Fig. 7-1. The processor contains multiple execution units to execute instructions, each of which reads its operands from and writes its results to a single, centralized register file. When an operation writes its result back to the register file, that result becomes visible to all of the execution units on the next cycle, allowing operations to execute on different units from the operations that generate their inputs. Instruction-level parallel processors often have complex bypassing hardware that forwards the results of each instruction to all of the execution units to reduce the delay between dependent instructions.

The instructions that make up a program are handled by the instruction issue logic, which issues instructions to the units in parallel. This allows control flow changes, such as branches, to occur simultaneously across all of the units, making it much easier to write and compile programs for instruction-level parallel processors.

In Fig. 7-1, all of the execution units have been drawn as identical modules. In most actual processors, some or all of the execution units are only able to execute a subset of the processor's instructions. The most common division is between integer

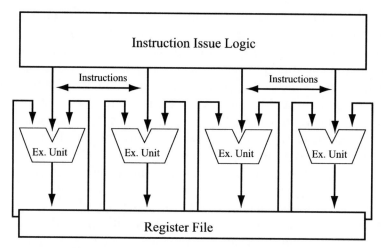

Fig. 7-1. Instruction-level parallel processor.

operations and floating-point operations, because these operations require very different hardware. Implementing these two sets of hardware as separate execution units increases the number of instructions that can be executed simultaneously without significantly increasing the amount of hardware required. On other processors, some of the integer execution units may be constructed to execute only some of the processor's integer operations, generally the most commonly executed operations. This reduces the size of these execution units, although it means that some combinations of independent integer instructions cannot be executed in parallel.

7.3 What is Instruction-Level Parallelism?

Instruction-level parallel processors exploit the fact that many of the instructions in a sequential program do not depend on the instructions that immediately precede them in the program. For example, consider the program fragment in the left side of Fig. 7-2. Instructions 1, 3, and 5 are dependent on each other because instruction 1 generates a data value that is used by instruction 3, which generates a result that is used by instruction 5. Instructions 2 and 4 do not use the results of any other instructions in the fragment and do not generate any results that are used by instructions in the fragment. These dependencies require that instructions 1, 3, and 5 be executed in order to generate the correct result, but instructions 2 and 4 can be

```
1: LD r1, (r2)
2: ADD r5, r6, r7        Cycle 1:  LD r1, (r2)      ADD r5, r6, r7
3: SUB r4, r1, r4        Cycle 2:  SUB r4, r1, r4    MUL r8, r9, r10
4: MUL r8, r9, r10       Cycle 3:  ST (r11), r4
5: ST (r11), r4
```

Fig. 7-2. Instruction-level parallelism example.

executed before, after, or in parallel with any of the other instructions without changing the results of the program fragment.

On a processor that executes one instruction at a time, the execution time of this program would be at least five cycles, even on an unpipelined processor with an instruction latency of one cycle. In contrast, an unpipelined processor that is capable of executing two instructions simultaneously could execute the program fragment in three cycles if each instruction had a latency of one cycle, as shown in the right half of the figure. Because instructions 1, 3, and 5 are dependent, it is not possible to reduce the execution time of the fragment any further by increasing the number of instructions that the processor can execute simultaneously.

This example illustrates both the strengths and the weaknesses of instruction-level parallelism. ILP processors can achieve significant speedups on a wide variety of programs by executing instructions in parallel, but their maximum performance improvement is limited by instruction dependencies. In general, as more execution units are added to a processor, the incremental performance improvement that results from adding each execution unit decreases. Going from one execution unit to two gives substantial reductions in execution time. However, as the number of execution units is increased to four, eight, or more, the additional execution units spend most of their time idle, particularly if the program has not been compiled to take advantage of the additional execution units.

7.4 Limitations of Instruction-Level Parallelism

The performance of ILP processors is limited by the amount of instruction-level parallelism that the compiler and the hardware can locate in the program. Instruction-level parallelism is limited by several factors: data dependencies, name dependencies (WAR and WAW hazards), and branches. In addition, a given processor's ability to exploit instruction-level parallelism may be limited by the number and type of execution units present in the processor and by restrictions on which instructions in the program can be examined to locate operations that can be performed in parallel.

RAW dependencies limit performance by requiring that instructions be executed in sequence to generate the correct results, and they represent a fundamental limitation on the amount of instruction-level parallelism available in programs. Instructions with WAW dependencies must also issue sequentially to ensure that the correct instruction writes its destination register last. Instructions with WAR dependencies can issue in the same cycle, but not out of order, because instructions read their inputs from the register file before they issue. Thus, an instruction that reads a register can issue in the same cycle as an instruction that writes the register and appears later in the program, because the reading instruction will read its input registers before the writing instruction generates the new value of its destination register. Later in this chapter, we will discuss *register renaming*, a hardware technique that allows instructions with WAR and WAW dependencies to be executed out of order without changing the results of the program.

Branches limit instruction-level parallelism because the processor does not know which instructions will be executed after a branch until the branch has completed. This requires the processor to wait for the branch to complete before any instructions after the branch can be executed. As mentioned in the last chapter, many processors incorporate branch prediction hardware to reduce the impact of branches on execution time by predicting the destination address of a branch before the branch is executed.

EXAMPLE

Consider the following program fragment :

```
ADD r1, r2, r3
LD r4, (r5)
SUB r7, r1, r9
MUL r5, r4, r4
SUB r1, r12, r10
ST (r13), r14
OR r15, r14, r12
```

How long would this program take to issue on a processor that allows two instructions to be executed simultaneously? How about on a processor that allows four instructions to be executed simultaneously? Assume that the processor can execute instructions in any order that does not violate data dependencies, that all instructions have latencies of one cycle, and that all of the processor's execution units can execute any of the instructions in the fragment.

Solution

On a processor that allows two instructions to be executed simultaneously, this program will take four cycles to issue. One sample sequence is shown in the following, but there are several sequences that take the same number of cycles.

```
Cycle 1: ADD r1, r2, r3      LD r4, (r5)
Cycle 2: SUB r7, r1, r9      MUL r5, r4, r4
Cycle 3: SUB r1, r12, r10    ST (r13), r14
Cycle 4: OR r15, r14, r12
```

If the processor can execute four instructions simultaneously, the program can issue in two cycles, as follows:

```
Cycle 1: ADD r1, r2, r3  LD r4, (r5)  ST (r13), r14  OR r15, r14, r12
Cycle 2: SUB r7, r1, r9  MUL r5, r4, r4  SUB r1, r12, r10
```

Note that, regardless of the number of instructions that the processor can execute simultaneously, it is not possible to issue this program fragment in only one cycle, because of the RAW dependencies between the ADD r1, r2, r3 and SUB r7, r1, r9 instructions and between the LD r4, (r5) and MUL r5, r4, r4 instructions. Also, note that the SUB r7, r1, r9 and SUB r1, r12, r10 instructions, which have a WAR dependence, are issued in the same cycle.

7.5   Superscalar Processors

Superscalar processors rely on hardware to extract instruction-level parallelism from sequential programs. During each cycle, the instruction issue logic of a superscalar processor examines the instructions in the sequential program to determine which instructions may be issued on that cycle. If enough instruction-level parallelism exists within a program, a superscalar processor can execute one instruction per execution unit per cycle, even if the program was originally compiled for execution on a processor that could only execute one instruction per cycle.

This capability is one of the greatest advantages of superscalar processors and is the reason why virtually all workstation and PC CPUs are superscalar processors. Superscalar processors can run programs that were originally compiled for purely sequential processors, and they can achieve better performance on these programs than processors that are incapable of exploiting instruction-level parallelism. Thus, users who buy systems containing superscalar CPUs can install their old programs on those systems and see better performance on those programs than was possible on their old systems.

The ability of superscalar processors to exploit instruction-level parallelism on sequential programs does not mean that compilers are irrelevant for systems built around superscalar processors. In fact, good compilers are even more critical to the performance of superscalar systems than they are on purely sequential processors. Superscalar processors can only examine a small *window* of the instructions in a program at one time to determine which instructions can be executed in parallel. If a compiler is able to schedule a program's instructions so that large numbers of independent instructions occur within this window, a superscalar processor will be able to achieve good performance on the program. If most of the instructions within the window at any time are dependent on each other, a superscalar processor will not be able to run the program much faster than a sequential processor would. In Section 7.9, we will discuss techniques that a compiler can use to improve the performance of programs on superscalar processors.

7.6   In-Order versus Out-of-Order Execution

One of the significant complexity/performance trade-offs in the design of a superscalar processor is whether the processor is required to execute instructions in the order that they appear in the program (in-order execution), or whether the processor can execute instructions in any order that does not change the result of the program (out-of-order execution). Out-of-order execution can provide much better performance than in-order execution but requires much more complex hardware to implement.

7.6.1 PREDICTING EXECUTION TIMES ON IN-ORDER PROCESSORS

In the previous chapter, we divided the execution time of programs on pipelined processors into the time to issue all of the instructions in the program and the pipeline latency of the processor, giving

$$\text{Execution Time (in Cycles)} = \text{Pipeline Latency} + \text{Issue Time} - 1$$

On pipelined ILP processors, we can use the same expression for the execution time of a program, but calculating the issue time becomes somewhat more complex because the processor can issue more than one instruction in a cycle. Since the pipeline latency of a processor does not vary from program to program, most of the exercises in this chapter will focus on determining the issue time of programs on ILP processors.

On in-order superscalar processors, the issue time of a program can be determined by stepping sequentially through the code to determine when each instruction can issue, similar to the technique used for pipelined processors that execute only one instruction per cycle. The key difference between an in-order superscalar processor and a non-superscalar pipelined processor is that a superscalar processor can issue an instruction in the same cycle as the previous instruction in the program if the data dependencies allow, as long as the number of instructions issued in the cycle does not exceed the number of instructions that the processor can execute simultaneously. On processors where some or all of the execution units can only execute some instructions, the set of instructions issued on a given cycle must match the limitations of the execution units.

EXAMPLE
How long would the following sequence of instructions take to execute on an in-order processor with two execution units, each of which can execute any instruction? Load operations have a latency of two cycles, and all other operations have a latency of one cycle. Assume that the pipeline depth is 5 stages.

```
LD  r1, (r2)
ADD r3, r1, r4
SUB r5, r6, r7
MUL r8, r9, r10
```

Solution

The pipeline latency of this processor is five cycles. Assuming that the LD issues on cycle n, the ADD cannot issue until cycle $n + 2$ because it is dependent on the LD. The SUB is independent of the ADD and the LD, so it also issues on cycle $n + 2$. (It cannot issue in cycle n or $n + 1$ because the processor must issue instructions in order.) The MUL is also independent of all previous instructions, but must wait until cycle $n + 3$ to issue, because the processor can only issue two instructions per cycle. Therefore, it takes four cycles to issue all of the instructions in the program, and the execution time is $5 + 4 - 1 = 8$ cycles.

7.6.2 PREDICTING EXECUTION TIMES ON OUT-OF-ORDER PROCESSORS

Determining the issue time of a sequence of instructions on an out-of-order processor is significantly more difficult than determining the issue time of the same sequence on an in-order processor, because there are many possible orders in which the instructions could execute. In general, the best approach is to start by examining the sequence of instructions to locate the dependencies between instructions. Once the dependencies between instructions are understood, they can then be assigned to issue cycles to minimize the delay between the execution of the first and last instructions in the sequence.

The effort required to find the best-possible ordering of a set of instructions grows exponentially with the number of instructions in the set, since all possible orderings must potentially be considered. Thus, we will assume that the instruction logic in a superscalar processor places some restrictions on the order in which instructions issue in order to simplify the instruction issue logic. The assumption we will make is that the processor issues an instruction in the first cycle in which the dependencies within the program allow it to issue[1]. If more instructions can issue in a cycle than the processor has execution units, the processor will take a greedy approach and issue the instructions that occur earliest in the program, even if issuing the instructions in a different order would reduce the time required to issue the sequence. When the compiler is able to control when instructions issue, such as in the VLIW processors that are discussed in Section 7.8, we will assume that the compiler considers all possible instruction orderings to find the one with the shortest execution time, since the compiler is able to devote more effort to instruction scheduling than the issue logic.

With this greedy instruction issue assumption, finding the issue time of a sequence of instructions on an out-of-order processor becomes much easier. Starting at the first instruction in the sequence, proceed through the instructions, assigning each instruction to the earliest cycle on which all of its input operands are available, the number of instructions already assigned to issue in the cycle is less than the number of instructions that the processor can issue simultaneously, and the set of instructions to be issued does not violate the limitations of the processor's execution units, even if this means that an instruction issues before an instruction that appears

---

[1] This is a simplifying assumption that may or may not be true on any particular out-of-order processor. The order in which instructions issue on an out-of-order processor is strongly dependent on the details of the processor's instruction issue logic, and different processors may have different policies.

later in the original program. Repeating this process for all of the instructions in the sequence will determine how long the sequence takes to issue.

EXAMPLE

How long would the following sequence of instructions take to issue on an out-of-order processor with two execution units, each of which can execute any instruction? Load operations have a latency of 2 cycles, and all other operations have a latency of 1 cycle. (This is the same sequence as the example that was used to illustrate in-order instruction issue.)

```
LD  r1, (r2)
ADD r3, r1, r4
SUB r5, r6, r7
MUL r8, r9, r10
```

Solution

The only dependency in this sequence is between the LD and the ADD instructions (a RAW dependency). Because of this dependency the ADD instruction must issue at least two cycles after the LD. The SUB and the MUL could both issue in the same cycle as the LD. Using our greedy assumption, the SUB and the LD issue in cycle n, the MUL issues in cycle $n + 1$, and the ADD issues in cycle $n + 2$, giving a three-cycle issue time for this program.

7.6.3 IMPLEMENTATION ISSUES FOR OUT-OF-ORDER PROCESSORS

On in-order processors, the *instruction window* (the number of instructions the processor examines to select instructions to issue in each cycle) can be relatively small, since the processor is not allowed to issue an instruction until all of the instructions that appear before it in the program have been issued. On a processor with n execution units, only the next n instructions in the program can possibly be issued in a given cycle, so an instruction window length of n instructions is generally sufficient.

Out-of-order processors require much larger instruction windows than in-order processors, to give them as much opportunity as possible to find instructions that can issue in a given cycle. However, the size of the instruction logic grows quadratically with the number of instructions in the instruction window, since each instruction in the window must be compared to all other instructions to determine the dependencies between them. This makes large instruction windows expensive to implement in terms of the amount of hardware required.

The procedure presented earlier for determining the execution time of an instruction sequence on an out-of-order processor assumed that the processor's instruction window was large enough to allow the processor to examine all of the instructions in the sequence simultaneously. If this is not the case, predicting execution time becomes much more difficult, as it becomes necessary to keep track of which instructions are contained within the instruction window on any given cycle and only select instructions to issue from within that set.

Handling interrupts and program exceptions is another difficult implementation issue on out-of-order processors. If instructions can execute out of order, it becomes very difficult to determine exactly which instructions have executed when an instruction takes an exception or when an interrupt occurs. This makes it hard for the programmer to determine the cause of an exception and makes it hard for the system to return to execution of the original program when an interrupt handler completes.

To combat this, virtually all out-of-order processors use a technique called *in-order retirement*. When an instruction generates its result, the result is only written into the register file if all earlier instructions in the program have completed. Otherwise, the result is saved until all earlier instructions have completed, and only then written into the register file. Since results are written into the register file in order, the hardware can simply discard all results that are waiting to be written into the register file when an exception or interrupt occurs. This presents the illusion that instructions are being executed in order, allowing programmers to debug errors relatively easily and making it possible to resume execution of the program at the next instruction when an interrupt handler completes. Processors that use this technique generally use bypassing logic or other techniques to forward the result of an instruction to dependent instructions before the result is written into the register file. This allows dependent instructions to issue as soon as an instruction generates its result, rather than having to wait until the instruction's result is written back into the register file.

7.7   Register Renaming

WAR and WAW dependencies are sometimes referred to as "name dependencies," because they are a result of the fact that programs are forced to reuse registers because of the limited size of the register file. These dependencies can limit instruction-level parallelism on superscalar processors, because it is necessary to ensure that all instructions that read a register complete the register read stage of the pipeline before any instruction overwrites that register.

Register renaming is a technique that reduces the impact of WAR and WAW dependencies on parallelism by dynamically assigning each value produced by a program to a new register, thus breaking WAR and WAW dependencies. Figure 7-3 illustrates register renaming. Each instruction set has an *architectural register file*, which is the set of registers that the instruction set uses. All instructions specify their inputs and outputs out of the architectural register file. On the processor, a larger register file, known as the *hardware register file*, is implemented instead of the architectural register file. Renaming logic tracks mappings between registers in the architectural register file and the hardware register file.

Whenever an instruction reads a register in the architectural register file, the register ID is sent through the renaming logic to determine which register in the hardware register file should be accessed. When an instruction writes a register in

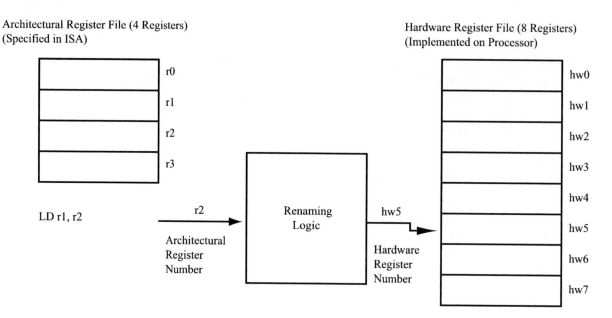

Architectural Register File (4 Registers)
(Specified in ISA)

Hardware Register File (8 Registers)
(Implemented on Processor)

Fig. 7-3. Register renaming.

the architectural register file, the renaming logic creates a new mapping between the architectural register that was written and a register in the hardware register file. Subsequent instructions that read the architectural register access the new hardware register and see the result of the instruction.

Figure 7-4 illustrates how register renaming can improve performance. In the original (before renaming) program, a WAR dependence exists between the LD r7, (r3) and SUB r3, r12, r11 instructions. The combination of RAW and WAR dependencies in the program forces the program to take at least three cycles to issue, because the LD must issue after the ADD, the SUB cannot issue before the LD, and the ST cannot issue until after the SUB.

Before Renaming
ADD r3, r4, r5
LD r7, (r3)
SUB r3, r12, r11
ST (r15), r3

After Renaming
ADD hw3, hw4, hw5
LD hw7, (hw3)
SUB hw20, hw12, hw11
ST (hw15), hw20

Fig. 7-4. Register renaming example

With register renaming, the first write to r3 maps to hardware register hw3, while the second maps to hw20 (these are just arbitrary examples). This remapping converts the original four-instruction dependency chain into 2 two-instruction chains, which can then be executed in parallel if the processor allows out-of-order execution. In general, register renaming is of more benefit on out-of-order processors than on in-order processors, because out-of-order processors can reorder instructions once register renaming has broken the name dependencies.

EXAMPLE

On an out-of-order superscalar processor with 8 execution units, what is the execution time of the following sequence with and without register renaming if any execution unit can execute any instruction and the latency of all instructions is one cycle? Assume that the hardware register file contains enough registers to remap each destination register to a different hardware register and that the pipeline depth is 5 stages.

```
LD  r7,  (r8)
MUL r1,  r7,  r2
SUB r7,  r4,  r5
ADD r9,  r7,  r8
LD  r8,  (r12)
DIV r10, r8,  r10
```

Solution

In this example, WAR dependencies are a significant limitation on parallelism, forcing the DIV to issue 3 cycles after the first LD, for a total execution time of 8 cycles (the MUL and the SUB can execute in parallel, as can the ADD and the second LD). After register renaming, the program becomes

```
LD  hw7,  (hw8)
MUL hw1,  hw7,  hw2
SUB hw17, hw4,  hw5
ADD hw9,  hw17, hw8
LD  hw18, (hw 12)
DIV hw10, hw18, hw10
```

(Again, all of the renaming register choices are arbitrary.)

With register renaming, the program has been broken into three sets of two dependent instructions (LD and MUL, SUB and ADD, LD and DIV). The SUB and the second LD instruction can now issue in the same cycle as the first LD. The MUL, ADD, and DIV instructions all issue in the next cycle, for a total execution time of 6 cycles.

Adding register renaming to a processor generally gives less of an improvement than changing the instruction set architecture to make the new registers part of the architectural registers, because the compiler cannot use the new registers to store temporary values. However, register renaming allows new processors to remain compatible with programs compiled for older versions of the processor because it does not require changing the ISA. In addition, increasing the number of architectural registers in a processor increases the number of bits required for each instruction, as a larger number of bits is required to encode the operands and destination register.

7.8 VLIW Processors

The superscalar processors that we have discussed so far in this chapter use hardware to exploit ILP by locating instructions that can execute in parallel from within sequential programs. Their ability to achieve performance improvements on old programs and maintain compatibility between generations of a processor family has made them tremendously successful commercially, but achieving good performance on superscalar processors requires a great deal of hardware. Very long instruction word (VLIW) processors take a different approach to instruction-level parallelism, relying on the compiler to determine which instructions may be executed in parallel and provide that information to the hardware.

In a VLIW processor, each instruction specifies several independent operations that are executed in parallel by the hardware, as shown in Figs. 7-5 and 7-6. Each

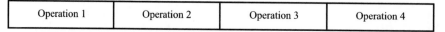

| Operation 1 | Operation 2 | Operation 3 | Operation 4 |

Fig. 7-5. VLIW instruction.

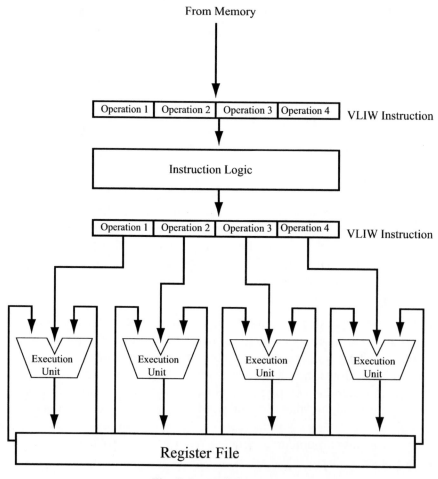

Fig. 7-6. VLIW processor.

operation in a VLIW instruction is equivalent to one instruction in a superscalar or purely sequential processor. The number of operations in a VLIW instruction is equal to the number of execution units in the processor, and each operation specifies the instruction that will be executed on the corresponding execution unit in the cycle that the VLIW instruction is issued. There is no need for the hardware to examine the instruction stream to determine which instructions may be executed in parallel, as the compiler is responsible for ensuring that all of the operations in an instruction can be executed simultaneously. Because of this, the instruction issue logic on a VLIW processor is much simpler than the instruction issue logic on a superscalar processor with the same number of execution units.

Most VLIW processors do not have scoreboards on their register files. Instead, the compiler is responsible for ensuring that an operation is not issued before its operands are ready. Each cycle, the instruction logic fetches a VLIW instruction from the memory and issues it to the execution units for execution. Thus, the compiler can predict exactly how many cycles will elapse between the execution of two operations by counting the number of VLIW instructions between them. In addition, the compiler can schedule instructions with a WAR dependency out of order so long as the instruction that reads the register issues before the instruction that writes the register completes, because the old value in the register is not overwritten until the writing instruction completes. For example, on a VLIW processor with a two-cycle load latency, the sequence ADD r1, r2, r3, LD r2, (r4) could be scheduled so that the ADD operation appeared in the instruction after the load, since the load will not overwrite r2 until two cycles have elapsed.

7.8.1 PROS AND CONS OF VLIW

The main advantages of VLIW architectures are that their simpler instruction logic often allows them to be implemented with shorter clock cycles than superscalar processors and that the compiler has complete control over when operations are executed. The compiler generally has a larger-scale view of the program than the instruction logic in a superscalar processor and is therefore generally better than the issue logic at finding instructions to execute in parallel. Their simpler instruction issue logic also often allows VLIW processors to fit more execution units onto a given amount of chip space than superscalar processors.

The most significant disadvantage of VLIW processors is that VLIW programs only work correctly when executed on a processor with the same number of execution units and the same instruction latencies as the processor they were compiled for, which makes it virtually impossible to maintain compatibility between generations of a processor family. If the number of execution units in a processor increases between generations, the new processor will try to combine operations from multiple instructions in each cycle, potentially causing dependent instructions to execute in the same cycle. Changing instruction latencies between generations of a processor family can cause operations to execute before their inputs are ready or after their inputs have been overwritten, resulting in incorrect behavior. In addition, if the compiler cannot find enough parallel operations to fill all of the slots in an instruction, it must place explicit NOP (no-operation) operations into the corresponding operation slots. This causes VLIW programs to take more memory than equivalent programs for superscalar processors.

Because of their advantages and disadvantages, VLIW processors are often used in digital signal-processing (DSP) applications, where high performance and low cost are critical. They have been less successful in general-purpose computers such as workstations and PCs, because customers demand software compatibility between generations of a processor.

EXAMPLE

Show how a compiler would schedule the following sequence of operations for execution on a VLIW processor with 3 execution units. Assume that all operations have a latency of two cycles, and that any execution unit can execute any operation.

```
ADD r1, r2, r3
SUB r16, r14, r7
LD r2, (r4)
LD r14, (r15)
MUL r5, r1, r9
ADD r9, r10, r11
SUB r12, r2, r14
```

Solution

Figure 7-7 shows how these operations would be scheduled. Note that the LD r14, (r15) is scheduled in the instruction before the SUB r16, r14, r7 operation despite the fact that the SUB instruction appears earlier in the original program and reads the destination register of the LD. Because VLIW operations do not overwrite their register values until they complete, the previous value of r14 remains available until 2 cycles after the instruction containing the LD issues, allowing the SUB to see the old value of r14 and generate the correct result. Scheduling these operations out-of-order in this way allows the program to be scheduled into fewer instructions than would be possible otherwise. Similarly the ADD r9, r10, r11 operation is scheduled ahead of the MUL r5, r1, r9 operation, although these operations could have been placed in the same instruction without increasing the number of instructions required by the program.

Instruction 1	*ADD r1, r2, r3*	*LD r2, (r4)*	*LD r14, (r15)*
Instruction 2	*SUB r16, r14, r7*	*ADD r9, r10, r11*	*NOP*
Instruction 3	*MUL r5, r1, r9*	*SUB r12, r2, r14*	*NOP*

Fig. 7-7. VLIW scheduling example.

7.9   Compilation Techniques for Instruction-Level Parallelism

Compilers use a wide variety of techniques to improve the performance of compiled programs, including constant propagation, dead code elimination, and register allocation. A general discussion of compiler optimizations is beyond the scope of this book, but this section will cover loop unrolling, an optimization that significantly increases instruction-level parallelism, in detail and will briefly describe software pipelining, another compilation technique used to improve performance.

7.9.1   LOOP UNROLLING

Individual loop iterations tend to have relatively low instruction-level parallelism because they often contain chains of dependent instructions, and because of the limited number of instructions between branches. Loop unrolling addresses this limitation by transforming a loop with N iterations into a loop with N/M iterations, where each iteration in the new loop does the work of M iterations of the old loop. This increases the number of instructions between branches, giving the compiler and the hardware more opportunity to find instruction-level parallelism. In addition, if the iterations of the original loop are independent or contain only a few dependent computations, loop unrolling can create multiple chains of dependent instructions where only one chain existed before unrolling, also increasing the ability of the system to exploit instruction-level parallelism.

Figure 7-8 shows a C-language example of loop unrolling. The original loop iterates through the source arrays one element at a time, computing the sum of corresponding elements in the source arrays and storing the result in the destination array. The unrolled loop steps through the arrays at two elements per iteration, performing the work of two iterations of the original loop in each iteration of the unrolled loop. In this example, the loop has been unrolled two times.[2] The original loop could have been unrolled four times by adding 4 to the loop index i in each iteration and performing the work of four original iterations in each iteration of the unrolled loop.

Original Loop

```
for (i = 0; i < 100; i++){
    a[i] = b[i] + c[i];
}
```

Unrolled Loop

```
for (i = 0; i < 100; i += 2) {
    a[i] = b[i] + c[i];
    a[i + 1] = b[i + 1] + c[i + 1];
}
```

Fig. 7-8.   C-language loop unrolling example.

This example also illustrates another advantage of loop unrolling: reduction in loop overhead. By unrolling the original loop two times, we reduce the number of iterations of the loop from 100 to 50. This halves the number of conditional branch

---

[2] A loop is said to have been unrolled n times if each iteration of the unrolled loop performs the work of n iterations of the original loop.

instructions that must be executed at the end of loop iterations, reducing the total number of instructions that the system needs to execute during the loop in addition to exposing more instruction-level parallelism. Thus, loop unrolling can be of some benefit even on purely sequential processors, although its benefits are most significant on ILP processors.

Figure 7-9 shows how the loop from Fig. 7-8 might be implemented in assembly language, and how a compiler might unroll the loop and schedule it for fast execution on a superscalar processor with 32-bit data types. Even in the original loop, the compiler has scheduled the code to expose as much ILP as possible by placing both of the initial loads ahead of either of the ADDs that increment pointers, and by performing the pointer increments ahead of the ADD that implements $a[i] = b[i] + c[i]$. Arranging instructions such that independent instructions are close together in the program makes it easier for the hardware in a superscalar processor to locate instruction-level parallelism, while placing the pointer increments between the loads and the computation of $a[i]$ increases the number of operations between the loads and the use of their results, making it more likely that the loads will complete before their results are needed.

The unrolled loop begins with three adds to generate pointers to $a[i + 1]$, $b[i + 1]$, and $c[i + 1]$. Keeping these pointers in separate registers from the pointers to $a[i]$, $b[i]$, and $c[i]$ allows the loads and stores to the ith and $i + 1$th elements of each array to be done in parallel, rather than having to increment each pointer between memory references. This initial block of setup instructions for the unrolled loop is called the *preamble* to the loop. In the body of the loop, the compiler has placed all of the loads in one block, followed by all of the pointer increments, then the computation of $a[i]$ and $a[i + 1]$, and finally the stores and loopback branch. This maximizes both parallelism and the time for the loads to complete.

In the example we have studied so far, the number of iterations of the original loop was evenly divisible by the degree of loop unrolling, making it easy to unroll the loop. In many cases, however, the number of loop iterations is not divisible by the degree of unrolling, or it is not known at compile time, making it harder to unroll the loop. For example, the compiler might want to unroll the loop of Fig. 7-8 eight times, or the number of iterations might be an input parameter to the procedure containing the loop.

In these cases, the compiler generates two loops. The first loop is an unrolled version of the original loop, and it executes until the number of iterations remaining is less than the degree of loop unrolling. The second loop then executes the remaining iterations one at a time. In loops where the number of iterations is not known at the start of the loop, such as a loop that iterates through a string looking for the end-of-string character, it becomes much harder to unroll the loop and more sophisticated techniques are required.

Figure 7-10 shows how the loop of Fig. 7-8 would be unrolled eight times. The first loop steps through the iterations eight at a time, until there are fewer than eight iterations remaining (detected when $i + 8 >= 100$). The second loop starts at the next iteration and steps through the remaining iterations one at a time. Because i is an integer variable, the computation $i = ((100/8) \times 8)$ does not set i to 100. The integer computation $100/8$ generates only the integer portion of the quotient

Original Loop

```
     MOV r31, #0    /* initialize i */
loop: LD r1, (r2);    /* r2 contains pointer to b[i] */
     LD r3, (r4);    /* r4 contains pointer to c[i] */
     ADD r2, #4, r2;    /* Increment to b[i + 1] */
     ADD r4, #4, r4;    /* Increment to c[i + 1] */
     ADD r6, r1, r3;
     ST (r7), r6;    /* r7 contains pointer to a[i] */
     ADD r7, #4, r7;    /* Increment to a[i + 1] */
     ADD r31, #1, r31;    /* Increment i */
     BNE loop, r31, #100; /* Jump to next iteration if not done */
```

Unrolled Loop

```
     MOV r31, #0
     ADD r8, #4, r2;    /* r8 contains pointer to b[i +1] */
     ADD r10, #4, r4;    /* r10 contains pointer to c[i + 1] */
     ADD r13, #4, r6;    /* r13 contains pointer to a[i + 1] */
loop: LD r1, (r2);
     LD r9, (r8);
     LD r3, (r4);
     LD r11, (r10);
     ADD r2, #8, r2;    /* Note: increment by 2×32 bits */
     ADD r4, #8, r4;
     ADD r8, #8, r8;
     ADD r10, #8, r10;
     ADD r6, r1, r3;
     ADD r12, r9, r11;
     ST (r7), r6;
     ST (r13), r12;
     ADD r7, #8, r7;
     ADD r13, #8, r13;
     ADD r31, #2, r31;    /* r31 gets incremented by 2 instead of 1 */
     BNE loop, r31, #100;
```

Fig. 7-9. Assembly-language loop unrolling example.

Unrolled Loop

```
for (i = 0; i < 100; i += 8) {
    a[i] = b[i] + c[i];
    a[i + 1] = b[i + 1] + c[i + 1];
    a[i + 2] = b[i + 2] + c[i + 2];
    a[i + 3] = b[i + 3] + c[i + 3];
    a[i + 4] = b[i + 4] + c[i + 4];
    a[i + 5] = b[i + 5] + c[i + 5];
    a[i + 6] = b[i + 6] + c[i + 6];
    a[i + 7] = b[i + 7] + c[i + 7];
}
for (i = ((100 / 8)×8); i < 100; i++){
    a[i] = b[i] + c[i];
}
```

Original Loop

```
for (i = 0; i < 100; i++){
    a[i] = b[i] + c[i];
}
```

➡

Fig. 7-10. Uneven loop unrolling.

(dropping the remainder), and multiplying that result by 8 gives the largest multiple of 8 that is less than 100 (96), which is where the second loop should begin its iterations.

7.9.2 SOFTWARE PIPELINING

Loop unrolling improves performance by increasing the number of independent operations within a loop iteration. Another optimization, *software pipelining*, improves performance by distributing each iteration of the original loop over multiple iterations of the pipelined loop, so that each iteration of the new loop performs some of the work of multiple iterations of the original loop. For example, a loop that fetched $b[i]$ and $c[i]$ from memory, added them together to generate $a[i]$, and wrote $a[i]$ back to memory might be transformed so that each interaction first wrote $a[i-1]$ back to memory, then computed $a[i]$ based on the values of $b[i]$ and $c[i]$ that were fetched in the last iteration, and finally fetched $b[i+1]$ and $c[i+1]$ from memory to prepare for the next iteration. Thus, the work of computing a given element of the $a[\ ]$ array is distributed across three iterations of the new loop.

Interleaving portions of different loop iterations in this way increases instruction-level parallelism in much the same way that loop unrolling does. It also increases the number of instructions between the computation of a value and its use, making it more likely that the value will be ready before it is needed. Many compilers combine software pipelining and loop unrolling to increase instruction-level parallelism further than is possible by applying either optimization individually.

7.10   Summary

Exploiting instruction-level parallelism can greatly improve the performance of a processor by allowing independent instructions to execute at the same time. The performance of an ILP processor on a given program is limited by several factors. The number of execution units in the processor determines the maximum number of instructions that the processor can execute simultaneously. Instruction dependencies limit the amount of instruction-level parallelism available in the program. This limitation is particularly significant for in-order superscalar processors, because one pair of dependent instructions can stall all of the remaining instructions in the program. Finally, instruction-level parallelism can be limited by restrictions on the window of instructions that the system can examine to find instructions that can execute in parallel.

In this chapter, we have covered the two most common architectures for instruction-level parallelism: superscalar processors and very long instruction word processors. VLIW processors rely on the compiler to schedule instructions for parallel execution by placing multiple operations in a single long instruction word. All of the operations in a VLIW instruction execute in the same cycle, allowing the compiler to control which instructions execute in any given cycle. VLIW processors can be relatively simple, allowing them to be implemented at high clock speeds, but they are generally unable to maintain compatibility between generations because any change to the processor implementation requires that programs be recompiled if they are to execute correctly.

Superscalar processors, on the other hand, contain hardware that examines a sequential program to locate instructions that can be executed in parallel. This allows them to maintain compatibility between generations and to achieve speedups on programs that were compiled for sequential processors, but they have a limited window of instructions that the hardware examines to select instructions that can be executed in parallel, which can reduce performance.

Two hardware techniques to improve the performance of superscalar processors were discussed. Out-of-order execution allows the processor to execute instructions in any order that does not change the result of the program. This improves performance by preventing dependent instructions from holding up the execution of later independent instructions. Register renaming breaks WAW and WAR hazards by mapping the architectural register set of the processor onto a larger hardware register set, allowing more instructions to be executed in parallel.

Finally, compiler techniques for ILP processors were briefly discussed. In particular, the loop unrolling optimization, which fuses several iterations of an original loop into one iteration to improve instruction-level parallelism, was discussed in detail. Good compilers are crucial to the performance of both VLIW and superscalar processors.

Instruction-level parallelism will continue to be an important technique for improving performance in the future. As fabrication technologies advance, the amount of time required for each execution unit to communicate with the processor's register file and instruction issue logic may limit performance, requiring more advanced architectures that distribute these resources into several smaller modules that are located close to the individual execution units. This style of processor architecture is an active area of research, and the next decade should see substantial changes in the way instruction-level processors are built.

Solved Problems

Instruction-Level Parallelism

7.1 What is instruction-level parallelism? How do processors exploit it to improve performance?

Solution

Instruction-level parallelism refers to the fact that many of the instructions in a sequential program are independent, meaning that it is not necessary to execute them in the order that they appear in the program to produce the correct result. Processors exploit this by executing these instructions in parallel rather than sequentially, reducing the amount of time that they take to execute programs.

Dependent Operations

7.2 What is the longest chain of dependent operations (include name dependencies) in the following program fragment?

```
LD  r7, (r8)
SUB r10, r11, r12
MUL r13, r7, r11
ST  (r9), r13
ADD r13, r2, r1
LD  r5, (r6)
SUB r3, r4, r5
```

Solution

The longest chain of dependencies is four instructions long.

```
LD  r7, (r8)
MUL r13, r7, r11
ST  (r9), r13
ADD r13, r2, r1
```

Note that the dependency between the ST and the ADD instructions is a WAR dependency.

Limits of Parallelism

7.3 If the code fragment from Problem 7.2 was executed on a superscalar processor with an infinite number of execution units and one-cycle latencies for all operations, how long would it take to issue? (In other words, what limitations do the dependencies in the program fragment place on the issue time?)

Solution

With an infinite number of execution units, the processor's ability to issue instructions in parallel is limited only by the depth of the chains of dependent instructions in the program.

The longest chain of dependent instructions was identified in the last exercise, and the next-longest chain is only two instructions.

If all of the dependencies in the longest chain were RAW dependencies, the instructions in the chain would have to be issued in sequence, making the issue time four cycles. However, one of the dependencies is a WAR dependency, and instructions with a WAR dependency can be issued in the same cycle. This allows the ST (r9), r13 and ADD r13, r2, r1 instructions to be issued in the same cycle, reducing the issue time to 3 cycles.

In-Order Execution (I)

7.4 How long will the following code fragment take to issue on an in-order superscalar processor with two execution units, where all instructions have latencies of 1 cycle and any execution unit can execute any instruction?

```
LD  r1, (r2)
SUB r4, r5, r6
ADD r3, r1, r7
MUL r8, r3, r3
ST  (r11), r4
ST  (r12), r8
ADD r15, r14, r13
SUB r10, r15, r10
ST  (r9), r10
```

Solution

This code fragment takes 6 cycles to issue, as shown below. Note that there are several instructions in the fragment whose data dependencies would allow them to be executed earlier, but that the processor cannot move up any earlier because of the in-order execution requirement.

```
Cycle 1: LD r1, (r2)        SUB r4, r5, r6
Cycle 2: ADD r3, r1, r7
Cycle 3: MUL r8, r3, r3     ST (r11), r4
Cycle 4: ST (r12) r8        ADD r15, r14, r13
Cycle 5: SUB r10, r15, r10
Cycle 6: ST (r9), r10
```

In-Order Execution (II)

7.5 How long will the following code sequence take to issue on an in-order superscalar processor with 4 execution units, where any execution unit can execute any operation, load operations have a 2-cycle latency, and all other operations have a 1-cycle latency?

```
ADD r1, r2, r3
SUB r5, r4, r5
LD  r4, (r7)
MUL r4, r4, r4
ST  (r7), r4
```

```
LD r9, (r10)
LD r11, (r12)
ADD r11, r11, r12
MUL r11, r11, r11
ST (r12), r11
```

Solution

The code sequence will take 8 cycles to issue, as shown in the following:

```
Cycle 1: ADD r1, r2, r3    SUB r5, r4, r5  LD r4, (r7)
Cycle 2: (nothing)
Cycle 3: MUL r4, r4, r4
Cycle 4: ST (r7), r4        LD r9, (r10)    LD r11, (r12)
Cycle 5: (nothing)
Cycle 6: ADD r11, r11, r12
Cycle 7: MUL r11, r11, r11
Cycle 8: ST (r12), r11
```

In-Order Execution (III)

7.6 How long would the following instructions take to execute on an in-order superscalar processor with two execution units, where each execution unit can execute any operation, load operations have a latency of 3 cycles, and all other operations have a latency of 2 cycles? Assume the processor has a 6-stage pipeline.

```
LD r4, (r5)
LD r7, (r8)
ADD r9, r4, r7
LD r10, (r11)
MUL r12, r13, r14
SUB r2, r3, r1
ST (r2), r15
MUL r21, r4, r7
ST (r22), r23
ST (r24), r21
```

Solution

The pipeline latency is 6 cycles, and it takes 9 cycles to issue all of the instructions, as shown in the following:

```
Cycle 1: LD r4, (r5)        LD r7, (r8)
Cycle 2: (nothing)
Cycle 3: (nothing)
Cycle 4: ADD r9, r4, r7     LD r10, (r11)
Cycle 5: MUL r12, r13, r14 SUB r2, r3, r1
Cycle 6: (nothing)
Cycle 7: ST (r2), r15       MUL r21, r4, r7
Cycle 8: ST (r22), r23
Cycle 9: ST (r24), r21
```

Therefore, the total execution time is $6 + 9 - 1 = 14$ cycles

Restricted Execution Units

7.7 How long would the program from Problem 7.6 take to issue if the processor was limited so that at most one of the instructions issued in a cycle could be a memory (load or store) operation, and at most one of the instructions could be a non-memory operation (i.e., if one of the execution units executed only memory instructions and one of the execution units executed only non-memory instructions?) All other parameters of the processor are the same as in Problem 7.6.

Solution:

The program would take 11 cycles to issue:

```
Cycle 1: LD r4, (r5)
Cycle 2: LD r7, (r8)
Cycle 3: (nothing)
Cycle 4: (nothing)
Cycle 5: ADD r9, r4, r7     LD r10, (r11)
Cycle 6: MUL r12, r13, r14
Cycle 7: SUB r2, r3, r1
Cycle 8: (nothing)
Cycle 9: ST (r2), r15        MUL r21, r4, r7
Cycle 10: ST (r22), r23
Cycle 11: ST (r24), r21
```

Out-of-Order Execution (I)

7.8 How long would the code fragment from Problem 7.4 take to issue on an out-of-order superscalar processor with all other parameters the same as the original exercise? Assume that the instruction window of the processor is large enough to cover the entire code fragment and that the processor takes the greedy approach to issuing instructions discussed in the chapter.

Solution

It would take 5 cycles, as shown in the following:

```
Cycle 1: LD r1, (r2)      SUB r4, r5, r6
Cycle 2: ADD r3, r1, r7   ST (r11), r4
Cycle 3: MUL r8, r3, r3   ADD r15, r14, r13
Cycle 4: ST (r12), r8     SUB r10, r15, r10
Cycle 5: ST (r9), r10
```

Out-of-Order Execution (II)

7.9 How long will the code fragment from Problem 7.5 take to issue on an out-of-order processor whose other parameters are the same as the one in the original exercise? Use the greedy scheduling assumption, and assume that the instruction window of the processor is large enough to cover the entire program fragment.

Solution

It would take 6 cycles to issue. Note that the time to issue these instructions could have been reduced by placing the LD r11, (r12) in cycle 1 instead of the LD r9, (r10), but this would have violated our greedy scheduling assumption.

```
Cycle 1: ADD r1, r2, r3    SUB r5, r4, r5    LD r4, (r7) LD r9, (r10)
Cycle 2: LD r11, (r12)
Cycle 3: MUL r4, r4, r4
Cycle 4: ST (r7), r4        ADD r11, r11, r12
Cycle 5: MUL r11, r11, r11
Cycle 6: ST (r12), r11
```

Out-of-Order Execution (III)

7.10　How long would the instructions from Problem 7.6 take to issue on an out-of-order superscalar processor with 2 execution units, where all operation latencies are the same as in Problem 7.6? Use the greedy scheduling assumption, and assume that the processor's instruction window is large enough to cover the entire program fragment.

Solution

They would take 6 cycles to issue:

```
Cycle 1: LD r4, (r5)       LD r7, (r8)
Cycle 2: LD r10, (r11)     MUL r12, r13, r14
Cycle 3: SUB r2, r3, r1    ST (r22), r23
Cycle 4: ADD r9, r4, r7    MUL r21, r4, r7
Cycle 5: ST (r2), r15
Cycle 6: ST (r24), r21
```

Out-of-Order Execution with Restricted Execution Units

7.11　Suppose the processor from Problem 7.10 had 1 execution unit that executed memory instructions and 1 execution unit that executed non-memory instructions. If all other parameters of the processor remain the same, how long would the code fragment take to issue?

Solution

It would take 8 cycles to issue:

```
Cycle 1: LD r4, (r5)       MUL, r12, r13, r14
Cycle 2: LD r7, (r8)       SUB r2, r3, r1
Cycle 3: LD r10, (r11)
Cycle 4: ST (r2), r15
Cycle 5: ADD r9, r4, r7    ST (r22), r23
Cycle 6: MUL r21, r4, r7
Cycle 7: (nothing)
Cycle 8: ST (r24), r21
```

Register Renaming (I)

7.12   How many hardware registers are required to allow register renaming to break all of the WAR and WAW dependencies in the following set of instructions?

```
LD r1, (r2)
ADD r3, r4, r1
SUB r4, r5, r6
MUL r7, r4, r8
ASH r8, r9, r10
SUB r11, r8, r12
DIV r12, r13, r14
ST (r15), r12
```

Solution

The code fragment uses 15 architectural registers. In addition, there are three WAR dependencies: ADD r3, r4, r1 → SUB r4, r5, r6, MUL r7, r4, r8 → ASH r8, r9, r10, and SUB r11, r8, r12 → DIV r12, r13, r14. There are no WAW dependencies in the code. Therefore, a total of 18 hardware registers are required if register renaming is to break all of the name dependencies in the program (15 for the 15 architectural registers, plus 3 to rename each of the registers involved in the WAR dependencies).

Register Renaming (II)

7.13   Show how register renaming hardware would transform the code fragment from the previous exercise. Assume that the processor has sufficient hardware registers to perform the required renaming.

Solution

(Hardware register numbers are the same as architectural register numbers except when renaming is required to break dependencies.)

```
LD hw1, (hw2)
ADD hw3, hw4, hw1
SUB hw16, hw5, hw6
MUL hw7, hw16, hw8
ASH hw17, hw9, hw10
SUB hw11, hw17, hw12
DIV hw18, hw13, hw14
ST (hw15), hw18
```

Register Renaming (III)

7.14   How long would the original code sequence from Problem 7.12 and the renamed code sequence from the previous exercise take to issue on an out-of-order superscalar processor with 4 execution units, each of which can execute any operation? Assume all instructions have latencies of 1 cycle, use the greedy scheduling assumption, and assume that the processor's instruction window is large enough to cover the entire code sequence.

Solution

Without register renaming the sequence takes 5 cycles to issue, because instructions with a WAR dependency can issue in the same cycle, but not out of order:

```
Cycle 1: LD r1, (r2)
Cycle 2: ADD r3, r4, r1    SUB r4, r5, r6
Cycle 3: MUL r7, r4, r8    ASH r8, r9, r10
Cycle 4: SUB r11, r8, r12  DIV r12, r13, r14
Cycle 5: ST (r15), r12
```

With register renaming, the sequence can be issued in 2 cycles, because we can issue instructions that originally had WAR dependencies out of order:

```
Cycle 1: LD hw1, (hw2)      SUB hw16, hw5, hw6   ASH hw17, hw9, hw10   DIV hw18, hw13, hw14
Cycle 2: ADD hw3, hw4, hw1  MUL hw7, hw16, hw8   SUB hw11, hw17, hw12  ST(hw15), hw18
```

VLIW Scheduling (I)

7.15 Show how a compiler would schedule the code from Problem 7.5 for execution on a VLIW processor with the same number of execution units and instruction latencies as specified in the original exercise. Unlike the out-of-order execution problems, you should assume that the compiler examines all possible instruction orderings to find the best schedule. (This reflects the fact that the compiler can devote greater effort to finding the best schedule than is usually possible in hardware.) Be sure to include the NOPs (no operation instruction) for unused operations.

Solution

The code can be scheduled in 5 instructions. One example of a correct schedule is shown in the following, although other schedules that use the same number of instructions exist:

```
Instruction 1: SUB r4, r5, r5   LD r4, (r7)         LD r9, (r10)   LD r11, (r12)
Instruction 2: ADD r1, r2, r3   NOP                 NOP            NOP
Instruction 3: MUL r4, r4, r4   ADD r11, r11, r12   NOP            NOP
Instruction 4: ST (r7), r4      MUL r11, r11, r11   NOP            NOP
Instruction 5: ST (r12), r11    NOP                 NOP            NOP
```

VLIW Scheduling (II)

7.16 Show how a compiler would schedule the following program for execution on a VLIW with 4 execution units, each of which can execute any instruction type. Load instructions have a latency of 3 cycles, and all other instructions have a latency of 1 cycle. Keep in mind that, in a VLIW, the old value of an operation's destination register remains available to be read until the operation completes.

```
SUB r4,  r7,  r8
MUL r10, r11, r12
DIV r14, r13, r15
```

```
ADD r9, r3, r2
LD r7, (r20)
LD r8, (r21)
LD r11, (r22)
LD r12, (r23)
LD r13, (r24)
LD r15, (r25)
LD r3, (r30)
LD r2, (r31)
ST (r26), r4
ST (r27), r10
ST (r28), r14
ST (r29), r9
```

Solution

Taking advantage of the fact that old register contents are not overwritten in a VLIW processor until the writing instruction completes, this sequence can be scheduled into 4 instructions. Here, we are deliberately scheduling the SUB r4, r7, r8 after instructions that load r7 and r8, but before those instructions complete. The subtract will see the old value of r7 and r8, which is what we want, since the subtract appears before the loads in the original program. The MUL, DIV and ADD instructions are similarly scheduled during the latencies of instructions that overwrite their input operands so that they see the old values of those registers.

Instruction 1: LD r7, (r20)   LD r8, (r21)   LD r11, (r22)   LD r12, (r23)
Instruction 2: LD r13, (r24)   LD r15, (r25)   LD r3, (r30)   LD r2, (r31)
Instruction 3: SUB r4, r7, r8 MUL r10, r11, r12 DIV r14, r13, r15 ADD r9, r3, r2
Instruction 4: ST (r26), r4   ST (r27), r10   ST (r28), r14   ST (r29), r9

(Note that the load instructions can be placed in the first two instructions in any order without changing the number of instructions that are required.)

Loop Unrolling (I)

7.17 Why does unrolling a loop often improve performance?

Solution

Loop unrolling improves performance because iterations of loops are often independent, or at least contain some operations that do not depend on the previous iteration of the loop. However, the control hazard created by the branch back to the start of the loop makes it hard for processors to issue instructions from multiple loop iterations simultaneously. Unrolling a loop merges several iterations into one straight-line section of code that the processor or compiler can examine to locate independent instructions. This generally increases the amount of instruction-level parallelism in the program (number of instructions that can be executed per cycle), improving performance. Loop unrolling also reduces the number of conditional branch instructions executed during the execution of the loop, further improving performance.

Loop Unrolling (II)

7.18 Show how a compiler would unroll the following infinite loop 4 times. Be sure to include the preamble code (the code that computes all of the pointers required for the operations within each iteration of the unrolled loop). Assume that the processor has as many architectural registers as required.

```
loop:
    LD r1, (r2)
    LD r3, (r4)
    LD r5, (r6)
    ADD r1, r1, r3
    ADD r1, r1, r5
    DIV r1, r1, r7
    ST (r0), r1
    ADD r2, #4, r2
    ADD r4, #4, r4
    ADD r6, #4, r6
    ADD r0, #4, r0
    BR loop
```

Solution

Here is an example of how the compiler might unroll the loop. The key elements in the loop unrolling are the preamble, to generate the pointers required by the unrolled loop, incrementing all of the pointers by 16 instead of 4 in each unrolled iteration because the unrolled iteration contains 4 of the original iterations, and realizing that r7 does not change from iteration to iteration of the original loop, so we do not need multiple registers to hold the value in r7 during different iterations of the original loop. There are many different ways in which this loop could be unrolled. Any solution that incorporates the key elements described above and performs the work of 4 iterations of the old loop in each iteration of the unrolled one is correct.

In addition to the basic unrolling, this example moves all of the loads in the unrolled loop to the beginning of the loop, and it schedules as many operations as possible between the divides and the stores that write the results of the divides to memory. These reorderings will improve the performance of the loop by giving the loads and divides, which are often long-latency operations, more time to complete before their results are needed.

```
preamble:
    ADD r8,  #4,  r0
    ADD r10, #4,  r2
    ADD r12, #4,  r4
    ADD r14, #4,  r6
    ADD r16, #8,  r0
    ADD r18, #8,  r2
    ADD r20, #8,  r4
    ADD r22, #8,  r6
    ADD r24, #12, r0
    ADD r26, #12, r2
    ADD r28, #12, r4
    ADD r30, #12, r6
```

```
loop:
    LD  r1,  (r2)
    LD  r3,  (r4)
    LD  r5,  (r6)
    LD  r9,  (r10)
    LD  r11, (r12)
    LD  r13, (r14)
    LD  r17, (r18)
    LD  r19, (r20)
    LD  r21, (r22)
    LD  r25, (r26)
    LD  r27, (r28)
    LD  r29, (r30)
    ADD r1,  r1,  r3
    ADD r1,  r1,  r5
    DIV r1,  r1,  r7
    ADD r9,  r9,  r11
    ADD r9,  r9,  r13
    DIV r9,  r9,  r7
    ADD r17, r17, r19
    ADD r17, r17, r21
    DIV r17, r17, r7
    ADD r25, r25, r27
    ADD r25, r25, r29
    DIV r25, r25, r7
    ADD r2,  #16, r2
    ADD r4,  #16, r4
    ADD r6,  #16, r6
    ADD r10, #16, r10
    ADD r12, #16, r12
    ADD r14, #16, r14
    ADD r18, #16, r18
    ADD r20, #16, r20
    ADD r22, #16, r22
    ADD r26, #16, r26
    ADD r28, #16, r28
    ADD r30, #16, r30
    ST  (r0), r1
    ADD r0,  #16, r0
    ST  (r8), r9
    ADD r8,  #16, r8
    ST  (r16), r17
    ADD r16, #16, r16
    ST  (r24), r25
    ADD r24, #16, r24
    BR  loop
```

Impact of Loop Unrolling on Execution Time

7.19 Show how a compiler would schedule the original and unrolled versions of the loop from the previous exercise for execution on a 4-wide VLIW processor that can execute an instruction on any execution unit. Assume latencies of 3 cycles for LD operations, and 2 cycles for DIVs and ADDs. Assume that the branch delay of the processor is long enough that all operations in one iteration complete before the next iteration starts. As in the other VLIW problems, assume that the compiler examines all possible operation orderings to find one that fits into the fewest number of instructions. For the unrolled loop, schedule only the loop body, not the preamble.

Solution

In both parts of this problem, there are many ways to convert the loop for execution on the VLIW in the minimum number of instructions. Here, we present examples of how the loop could be placed in the minimum number of instructions, but any solution that achieves this number of instructions without violating the loop's data dependencies is correct.

Original loop: 10 instructions.

Instruction	op1	op2	op3	op4
1	LD r1, (r2)	LD r3, (r4)	LD r5, (r6)	ADD r2, #4, r2
2	ADD r4, #4, r4	ADD r6, #4, r6	NOP	NOP
3	NOP	NOP	NOP	NOP
4	ADD r1, r1, r3	NOP	NOP	NOP
5	NOP	NOP	NOP	NOP
6	ADD r1, r1, r5	NOP	NOP	NOP
7	NOP	NOP	NOP	NOP
8	DIV r1, r1, r7	NOP	NOP	NOP
9	NOP	NOP	NOP	NOP
10	ST (r0), r1	BR loop	ADD r0, #4, r0	NOP

Unrolled loop: 12 instructions. By unrolling the loop, we have managed to do 4 times as much work in each iteration, with only a 20 percent decrease in the execution time of an iteration.

Instruction	op1	op2	op3	op4
1	LD r1, (r2)	LD r3, (r4)	LD r9, (r10)	LD r11, (r12)
2	LD r17, (r18)	LD r19, (r20)	LD r25, (r26)	LD r27, (r28)
3	LD r5, (r6)	LD r13, (r14)	LD r21, (r22)	LD r29, (r30)
4	ADD r1, r1, r3	ADD r9, r9, r11	ADD r2, #16, r2	ADD r4, #16, r4
5	ADD r17, r17, r19	ADD r25, r25, r27	ADD r10, #16, r10	ADD r12, #16, r12
6	ADD r1, r1, r5	ADD r9, r9, r13	ADD r18, #16, r18	ADD r20, #16, r20
7	ADD r17, r17, r21	ADD r25, r25, r29	ADD r26, #16, r26	ADD r28, #16, r28
8	DIV r1, r1, r7	DIV r9, r9, r7	ADD r6, #16, r6	ADD r14, #16, r14
9	DIV r17, r17, r7	DIV r25, r25, r7	ADD r22, #16, r22	ADD r30, #16, r30
10	ST (r0), r1	ST (r8), r9	ADD r0, #16, r0	ADD r8, #16, r8
11	ST (r16), r17	ST (r24), r25	ADD r16, #16, r16	ADD r24, #16, r24
12	BR loop	NOP	NOP	NOP

CHAPTER 8

Memory Systems

8.1 Objectives

The last several chapters have dealt with various elements of processor design, including register file organization, instruction set architecture, pipelining, and instruction-level parallelism. In this chapter, we begin our discussion of memory systems, which will be continued in the next two chapters. By the end of this chapter you should

1. Understand the concepts of latency and bandwidth and how they relate to memory systems
2. Understand the concept of memory hierarchy and be able to compute average memory access times for memory hierarchies
3. Understand the difference between DRAM and SRAM memory technologies and be able to explain how common access modes such as page mode affect average access times

8.2   Introduction

Until now, we have treated the memory system as a "black box" that the processor could place data into for retrieval later. We have assumed that all memory operations take the same amount of time to complete, and that each memory operation had to finish before the next one could begin. Starting with this chapter, we will delve into that black box to explore how memory systems are implemented in modern computer systems.

This chapter begins with a discussion of latency, throughput, and bandwidth, the three quantities that are used to measure memory system performance. Next, we discuss memory hierarchies, explaining why and how multiple memory technologies are used to implement a single memory system. Finally, we cover memory technologies, explaining how memory chips are implemented, the difference between SRAM and DRAM, and how the different access modes found in DRAMs are implemented.

8.3 Latency, Throughput, and Bandwidth

In discussing processor pipelines, we used the terms *latency* and *throughput* to describe the time taken to complete an individual operation and the rate at which operations can be completed. These terms are also used in discussing memory systems and have the same meaning as in our discussion of processors. An additional term that is used in discussing memory systems is *bandwidth*, which describes the total rate at which data can be moved between the processor and the memory system. Bandwidth can be thought of as the product of the throughput and the amount of data referenced by each memory operation.

EXAMPLE

If a memory system has a latency of 10 ns per operation and a data width of 32 bits, what is the throughput and bandwidth of the memory system, assuming only one operation can be performed at a time and there is no delay between operations?

Solution

As we saw in Chapter 6, throughput = 1/(latency) when operations execute sequentially. Therefore, the throughput of this memory system is 100 million operations/s. Since each operation references 32 bits of data, the bandwidth is 3.2 billion bits/s, or 400 million bytes/s.

8.3.1 PIPELINING, PARALLELISM, AND PRECHARGING

If all memory operations were executed sequentially, computing the latency and bandwidth of a memory system would be simple. However, many memory systems are designed in ways that make the relationship between latency and bandwidth more complex. Memory systems can be *pipelined* in the same way that processors are pipelined, allowing operations to overlap execution to improve throughput. Also, many memory technologies require that a certain amount of idle time elapse between memory accesses. This time is used to prepare, or *precharge*, the circuitry for the next access. Precharging the circuitry does some of the work of accessing the memory before the address arrives. This reduces the delay from the time that an address is sent to the memory system until a memory operation completes. If the memory system is idle much of the time, doing the precharge at the end of each memory operation improves performance because there usually isn't another operation waiting to use the memory system. If the memory system is being used most of the time, the rate at which operations can be completed is determined by the sum of the memory latency and the precharge time.

EXAMPLE
What is the bandwidth of a memory system with a latency of 40 ns, that transfers 1 byte per operation, and is pipelined to allow 4 operations to overlap execution (assume no pipeline overhead)?

Solution

Dividing the latency of 40 ns by the number of overlapped operations (4) gives a rate of 1 operation per 10 ns as the throughput of the memory system. At 1 byte of data per operation, this gives a bandwidth of 10^8 bytes/s.

EXAMPLE
What is the bandwidth of a memory system that has a latency of 20 ns, a precharge time of 5 ns, and transfers 2 bytes of data per access?

Solution

The latency of 20 ns and precharge time of 5 ns combine to allow a new memory reference to be started every 25 ns. This gives a throughput of 4×10^7 operations/s. Multiplying by 2 bytes/operation gives a bandwidth of 8×10^7 bytes/s.

Another way that designers improve the performance of memory systems is to design them to support multiple memory references in parallel. This is most commonly done by attaching multiple memories to the processor's memory bus, as shown in Fig. 8-1. Because a single memory bus is used, it is not possible for more than one memory reference to begin or finish at the same time, since only one request may use the bus at any one time. However, the processor can send memory requests to idle memories while it is waiting for other requests to complete. Since memory requests often take several clock cycles to complete, this arrangement increases the rate at which memory requests can be handled without increasing the number of I/O pins required on the processor chip, which would increase the cost of the processor.

Systems that support parallel memory requests are divided into two types. *Replicated* memory systems provide multiple copies of the entire memory. This means that each copy of the memory can handle any memory request, but it increases the amount of memory required by a factor equal to the number of copies. To keep the contents of each memory the same, all store operations must be sent to each copy of the memory, making stores much more expensive than loads in terms of the amount of bandwidth they consume.

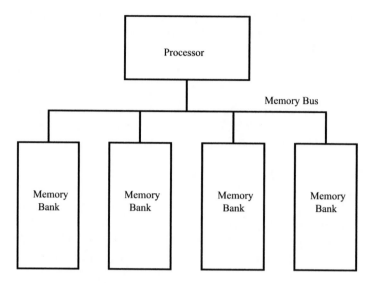

Fig. 8-1. Banked/replicated memory system.

The more common type of parallel memory system is a *banked* memory system. In a banked memory system, the data is divided, or *interleaved*, across the memories so that each memory contains only a fraction of the data. Typically, some of the bits of the address are used to select which memory bank a given datum resides in. For example, in the system illustrated in Fig. 8-1, bytes whose low two address bits are 0b00 might be placed in the leftmost bank, bytes whose low two address bits are 0b01 might go in the next bank, and so on. Alternately, two other address bits could be used to select a bank. Generally, relatively low-order address bits are used to select the bank, so that references to sequential memory addresses go to different banks.

Banked memory systems have the advantage that they don't require any more memory than an equivalent memory system with only one memory, and it is only necessary to send store operations to the bank containing the data to be written. However, they suffer from the problem that some pairs of memory references will target the same bank, requiring one of the operations to wait until the other completes. In most cases, the additional memory required to implement a replicated memory system is a bigger disadvantage than the bandwidth lost because of conflicts for memory banks, so banked memory systems are more common than replicated memory systems.

EXAMPLE
What is the memory bandwidth of a replicated memory system with 4 memories, where each memory provides a bandwidth of 10 MB/s? How much memory is required if the system needs to be able to store 32 MB of data? Also, what is the bandwidth and total memory required of a banked memory system with 4 banks and all other parameters the same as the first system?

Solution

In both cases, the memory bandwidth will be 40 MB/s, the sum of the bandwidths of the banks/copies. For the replicated memory system, a total of 128 MB of memory will be required while the banked system will only require 32 MB of storage.

The example above illustrates a common hazard when analyzing memory systems. We calculated the bandwidth of the banked memory system by multiplying the bandwidth of each bank by the number of banks, but we know that requests will sometimes be sent to banks that are already busy, so they will have to wait before they can proceed. When this happens, the actual rate at which data is transferred to or from the memory system will be lower than the calculated bandwidth. In the extreme case where all memory requests go to the same bank, the system described above could have a bandwidth as low as 10 MB/s. For this reason, the term *peak bandwidth* is often used to describe the result of calculations, such as the example above, that determine the maximum bandwidth of a system. In practice, the actual bandwidth achievable when running programs on a computer is generally much less than the peak bandwidth, because there are times when there are no requests going to the memory system, conflicts for memory banks, and other factors.

8.4   Memory Hierarchies

So far, we have treated memory systems as single-level structures, similar to the left half of Fig. 8-2. In reality, the memory systems of modern computers are multilevel memory hierarchies, as illustrated in the right half of the figure. The figure shows a three-level memory hierarchy, consisting of a cache, a main memory, and a virtual memory.

The primary reason that memory systems are constructed as hierarchies is that the cost per bit of a memory technology is generally proportional to the speed of the technology. Fast memories, such as static RAMs (SRAMs), tend to have a high cost per bit (in both dollars and chip area), making it prohibitively expensive to construct a computer's memory entirely out of these devices. Slower technologies, such as dynamic RAM (DRAM), are less expensive, making it practical to construct larger memories using these technologies.

In a memory hierarchy, the levels closest to the processor, such as the cache shown in the figure, contain a relatively small amount of memory that is implemented in a fast memory technology to give a low access time. Proceeding down the hierarchy, each level contains more storage and takes longer to access than the level above it. The goal of a memory hierarchy is to keep the data that will be referenced most by a program in the top levels of the hierarchy, so that most memory requests can be handled by the top level or levels. This results in a memory system that has an average access time similar to the access time of the fastest level, but with an average cost per bit similar to that of the slowest level.

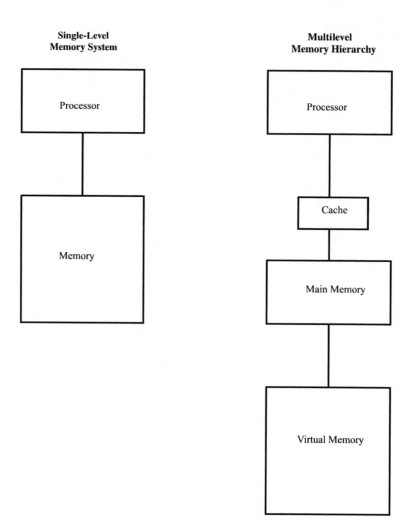

Fig. 8-2. Memory hierarchies.

In general, it is not possible to predict which memory locations will be accessed most frequently, so computers use a demand-based system for determining which data to keep in the top levels of the hierarchy. When a memory request is sent to the hierarchy, the top level is checked to see if it contains the address. If so, the request completes. If not, the next-lower level is checked, with the process repeating until either the data is found or the bottom level of the hierarchy is reached, which is guaranteed to contain the data.

If a memory request cannot be handled by the top level in the hierarchy, a *block* of sequential locations containing the referenced address is copied from the first level that contains the address into every level above that. This is done for two reasons. The first is that many storage technologies, such as the page-mode DRAMs that will be discussed later in this chapter and hard disks, allow multiple sequential words of data to be read or written in less time than an equal number of randomly located words, making it faster to bring a multibyte block of data into the top levels of the hierarchy than to fetch each byte in the block from the lower levels of the hierarchy individually. Second, most programs display *locality of reference*—memory references that occur close together in time tend to have addresses that are close to each other, making it likely that the other addresses within a block will be referenced soon after the first reference to an address in the block.

As long as the probability that each address within the block will be referenced is sufficiently high, using multibyte blocks reduces the average access time, because fetching the block takes less time than fetching each word within the block separately. Different levels in the memory hierarchy will often have different block sizes, depending on the characteristics of the levels below them in the hierarchy. For example, caches tend to have block sizes of approximately 64 bytes, while main memories generally have block sizes of around 4 kB, because the time to fetch a large block of data from the virtual memory is only slightly longer than the time to fetch 1 byte, while the time to fetch a block of data into the cache from the main memory is much closer to the time to fetch each byte individually.

8.4.1 LEVELS IN THE HIERARCHY

In the memory hierarchy shown in Fig. 8-2, the different levels of the hierarchy had specific names. This results from the fact that different levels of a memory hierarchy tend to be implemented very differently, so computer architects use different terms to describe them. The top level or levels of the hierarchy are typically referred to as the *cache*. Caches are generally implemented using SRAM, and most modern computers have at least two levels of cache memory in their memory hierarchy. Caches have hardware to keep track of the addresses that are stored in them, tend to be relatively small, and have small block sizes, usually 32 to 128 bytes. The main memory of a computer is generally constructed out of DRAM, relies on software to keep track of the addresses that are contained in it, and has a large block size, often several kilobytes. Finally, virtual memory is usually implemented using disks and contains all of the data in the memory system. Chapter 9 discusses caches in more detail, while Chapter 10 covers virtual memory systems.

8.4.2 TERMINOLOGY

A set of terminology has been developed to describe memory hierarchies. When the address that an operation references is found in a level of the memory hierarchy, a *hit* is said to have occurred in that level. Otherwise, a *miss* is said to have occurred. Similarly, the *hit rate* of a level is the percentage of references that reach the level that result in hits, and the *miss rate* is the percentage of references that reach the level that result in misses. The hit rate and the miss rate of a level in the hierarchy always sum to 100 percent. It is important to note that neither the hit rate nor the miss rate count references that are handled by higher levels in the hierarchy. For example, requests that hit in the cache of our example memory hierarchy do not count in the hit rate or miss rate of the main memory.

As described above, when a miss occurs in a level of the hierarchy, a block of data containing the address of the miss is brought into the level. As a program runs, the level will fill up with data and run out of free space to put blocks in. When this happens, a block must be removed from the level to make room for the new block.

This is called an *eviction* or *replacement*, and the method by which the system selects a block to be removed is called the *replacement policy*. Common replacement policies are described in the next chapter. To simplify evicting data blocks from a level, many memory systems maintain a property called *inclusion*, in which the presence of an address in a given level of the memory system guarantees that the address is present in all lower levels of the memory system.

Another set of terminology describes how memory hierarchies handle writes (stores). In *write-back* systems, data that is written is placed only in the top level of the hierarchy. When the block containing the data is evicted from that level, the written data is copied into the next level down in the hierarchy, and so on. Blocks containing data that has been written are called *dirty*, to distinguish them from *clean* blocks, which have not been modified. Implementing write-back systems is much easier if they maintain inclusion, because it is never necessary to evict a block from a level to make room for data being written back from a higher level.

In contrast, *write-through* memory systems copy written data into each level of the memory hierarchy when a write occurs. Many systems have different write policies for different levels in the hierarchy. For example, it is not uncommon for computers to have write-through caches and write-back main memories. The decision about whether to make a level in the hierarchy write back or write through is based on a tradeoff between bandwidth and complexity—write-back systems can have higher bandwidth because they don't require each level of the hierarchy to be accessed on every write, but they are more complex than write-through systems because it is necessary to keep track of which blocks in a level have been written since they were brought into the level.

8.4.3   AVERAGE ACCESS TIMES

If we know the hit rate and access time (time to complete a request that hits) for each level in the memory hierarchy, we can compute the average access time of the memory hierarchy. For each level in the hierarchy, the average access time is $(T_{hit} \times P_{hit}) + (T_{miss} \times P_{miss})$, where T_{hit} is the time to resolve requests that hit in the level, P_{hit} is the hit rate of the level (expressed as a probability), T_{miss} is the average access time of the levels below this one in the hierarchy, and P_{miss} is the miss rate of the level. Since the hit rate of the lowest level in the hierarchy is 100 percent (all requests that reach the bottom level are handled by the bottom level), we can start at the bottom level and work up to compute the average access time of each level in the hierarchy.

EXAMPLE

If a level of the memory hierarchy has a hit rate of 75 percent, memory requests take 12 ns to complete if they hit in the level, and memory requests that miss in the level take 100 ns to complete, what is the average access time of the level?

Solution

Using the formula given above, the average access time is $(12\,ns \times 0.75) + (100\,ns \times 0.25) = 34\,ns$.

EXAMPLE

A memory system contains a cache, a main memory, and a virtual memory. The access time of the cache is 5 ns, and it has an 80 percent hit rate. The access time of the main memory is 100 ns, and it has a 99.5 percent hit rate. The access time of the virtual memory is 10 milliseconds (ms). What is the average access time of the hierarchy?

Solution

To solve this sort of problem, we start at the bottom of the hierarchy and work up. Since the hit rate of the virtual memory is 100 percent, we can compute the average access time for requests that reach the main memory as $(100 \text{ ns} \times 0.995) + (10 \text{ ms} \times 0.005) = 50{,}099.5 \text{ ns}$. Given this, the average access time for requests that reach the cache (which is all requests) is $(5 \text{ ns} \times 0.80) + (50{,}099.5 \text{ ns} \times 0.20) = 10{,}024 \text{ ns}$.

8.5   Memory Technologies

Three different technologies are used to implement the memory systems of modern computers: static RAM (SRAM), dynamic RAM (DRAM), and hard disks. Hard disks are by far the slowest of these technologies and are reserved for the lowest level of the memory system, the virtual memory. Virtual memory is discussed in more detail in Chapter 10. SRAM and DRAM are up to a factor of 1,000,000 faster than disk-based memory and are the technologies used to implement the caches and main memories of almost all computers.

8.5.1   MEMORY CHIP ORGANIZATION

SRAM and DRAM memory chips have the same basic structure, which is shown in Fig. 8-3. Data is stored in a rectangular array of *bit cells*, each of which holds 1 bit of data. To read data from the array, half of the address to be read (generally the high-order bits) is fed into a decoder. The decoder asserts (drives high) the *word line* corresponding to the value of its input bits, which causes all of the bit cells in the corresponding row to drive their values onto the *bit lines* that they are connected to. The other half of the address is then used as the input to a multiplexer that selects the appropriate bit line and drives its output onto the output pins of the chip. To store data on the chip, the same process is used, except the value to be written is driven on the appropriate bit line and written into the selected bit cell.

Most memory chips generate more than 1 bit of output. This is done either by building several arrays of bit cells, each of which produces one bit of output, or by designing a multiplexer that selects the outputs of several of the bit lines and drives them on the chip's outputs.

The speed of a memory chip is determined by a number of factors, including the length of the bit and word lines and how the bit cells are constructed. Longer bit and

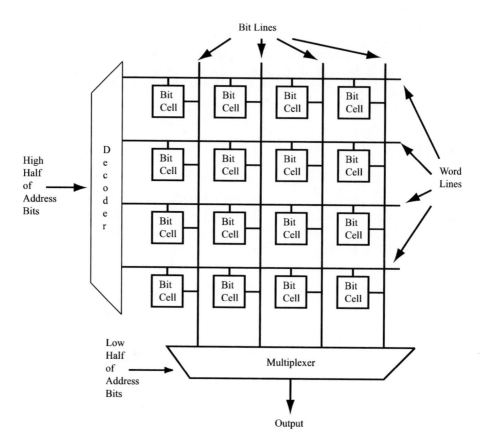

Fig. 8-3. Memory chip organization.

word lines have higher capacitances and resistances, so it takes longer to drive a signal on these wires as their lengths increase. For this reason, many modern memory chips are constructed out of many small arrays of bit cells to keep the word and bit lines short.

The techniques used in constructing the bit cells affect the speed of the memory chip because they affect how much current is available to drive the output of the bit cell onto the bit lines, which determines how long it takes to propagate the bit cell's output to the multiplexer. As we will see in the next two sections, SRAM bit cells can drive much more current than DRAM bit cells, which is one of the main reasons why SRAMs tend to be much faster than DRAMs.

8.5.2 SRAMS

The main difference between SRAMs and DRAMs is how their bit cells are constructed. As shown in Fig. 8-4, the core of an SRAM bit cell consists of two inverters connected in a back-to-back configuration. Once a value has been placed in the bit cell, the ring structure of the two inverters will maintain the value indefinitely, because each inverter's input is the opposite of the other's. This is the reason why

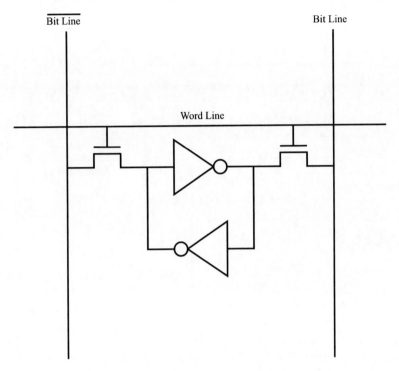

Fig. 8-4.   SRAM bit cell.

SRAMs are called *static* RAMs; values stored in the RAM remain there as long as power is applied to the device. DRAMs, on the other hand, will lose their stored values over time, which is why they are known as *dynamic* RAMs.

To read a value from the bit cell, the word line is driven high, which causes the two transistors to connect the outputs of the inverters to the bit line and the inverted bit line. These signals can then be read by the multiplexer and sent to the output of the chip. Writing an SRAM bit cell is accomplished by asserting the word line and driving the appropriate values on the bit line and inverted bit line. As long as the device driving the bit line is stronger than the inverter, the values on the bit line will dominate the value originally stored in the bit cell, and will be stored in the bit cell when the word line is de-asserted.

Figure 8-5 shows the timing of a read and write access to a typical SRAM. To read the device, the address to be read is placed on the address pins of the device, and the chip enable signal is asserted.[1] After a delay, the memory chip places the contents of the address on its data outputs. Write operations are similar, except that the processor places the data to be written on the data pins at the same time as the address is sent to the chip, and the write control signal is used to indicate that a write is being done.

---

[1] In practice, many of the input signals to SRAMs and DRAMs are active-low. For simplicity, we will ignore this in this book and treat all signals as active-high.

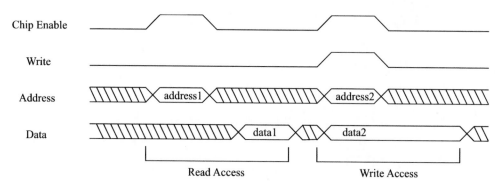

Fig. 8-5.   SRAM access.

8.5.3 DRAMS

Figure 8-6 shows a DRAM bit cell. Instead of a pair of inverters, a capacitor is used to store the bit cell's data. When the word line is asserted, the capacitor is connected to the bit line, allowing the value stored in the cell to be read by examining the voltage stored on the capacitor or written by placing a new voltage on the capacitor. This figure illustrates why DRAMs generally have much larger capacities than SRAMs constructed in the same fabrication technology: SRAMs require many more devices to implement a bit cell. Each inverter typically requires two transistors, for a total of six transistors in the bit cell (some implementations use somewhat more or fewer transistors). In contrast, a DRAM bit cell requires only one transistor and one capacitor, which takes up much less space on the chip.

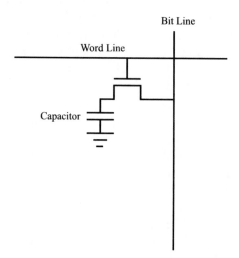

Fig. 8-6.   DRAM bit cell.

Figures 8-4 and 8-6 also show why SRAMs are typically much faster than DRAMs. In SRAMs, an active device (the inverter) drives the value stored in the bit cell onto the bit line and inverted bit line. In DRAMs, the capacitor is connected to the bit line when the word line is asserted, which is a much weaker signal than the one produced by the inverters in an SRAM bit cell. Thus, it takes much longer for the output of a DRAM bit cell to be driven onto its bit line than it takes for an SRAM bit cell to drive an equivalent bit line.

8.5.4 DRAM REFRESH

DRAMs are called dynamic RAMs because the values stored in each bit cell are not stable. Over time, leakage currents will cause the charge stored on the capacitor to drain away and be lost. To prevent the contents of a DRAM from being lost, the DRAM must be refreshed. Essentially, a refresh operation reads the contents of each bit cell in a row of the bit cell array, and then it writes the same values back into the bit cells, restoring them to their original value. As long as each row in a DRAM is refreshed sufficiently frequently that none of its capacitors' charges decay low enough that the hardware misinterprets the values stored in the row, the DRAM can hold its contents indefinitely. One of the specifications on a DRAM chip is its *refresh time*, which is how often a row can go without being refreshed before it is in danger of losing its contents.

EXAMPLE
If a DRAM has 512 rows, and its refresh time is 10 ms, how often (on average) does a row refresh operation need to be done?

Solution

Because the refresh time is 10 ms, each row needs to be refreshed at least once every 10 ms. Since there are 512 rows, we have to do 512 row refresh operations in each 10-ms period, or an average of 1 row refresh every 1.95×10^{-5} s. Note that it is up to the designer to decide how those row refreshes are distributed across the 10-ms period—they can be distributed evenly, done as a block of row refreshes at the start of each period, or anything in between.

8.5.5 DRAM ACCESS TIMINGS

Figure 8-7 shows the timing of a read operation on a typical DRAM. Unlike SRAMs, the address input to a DRAM is divided into two parts, the row address and the column address, which are sent to the DRAM in separate operations. Typically, the high bits of a memory address are used for the row address, and the low bits are used for the column address. As might be expected from the name, the row address selects the row of the DRAM array that is being referenced, while the column address selects a bit or set of bits out of that row.

The RAS (row address strobe) signal indicates that a row address is being sent, and the CAS (column address strobe) signal indicates that a column address is being sent. The total time to read the DRAM is the sum of the RAS-CAS delay and the

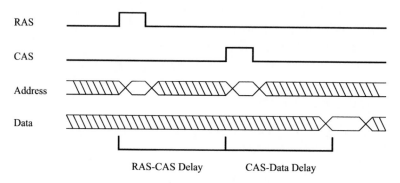

RAS-CAS Delay   CAS-Data Delay

Fig. 8-7.   DRAM read access.

CAS-data delay. Write operations have similar timings, but the data to be written is generally driven on the data pins at the same time as the column address.

Sending the address to the DRAM in two parts reduces the number of address pins required on the DRAM, because the same pins can be used for the row and column addresses. Dividing the address into these two parts doesn't significantly increase the access time of the DRAM, because the row address selects the row of the bit cell array whose contents are driven on the bit lines, while the column address selects which bit line is driven to the output. Therefore, the column address isn't needed by the DRAM until the bit cells have driven their outputs onto the bit lines, so sending it to the DRAM after the row address doesn't increase the access time.

8.5.6   PAGE MODE AND NEWER DRAMS

One weakness of the memory chip design shown in Fig. 8-3 is that an entire row's contents are sent to the multiplexer during each operation, but only 1 bit out of the row is actually sent to the output. If the contents of the row could be kept in or near the multiplexer, it would be possible to read other bits within the same row by just sending a different column address to the DRAM, rather than doing a full RAS-CAS cycle. DRAMs that do this are called *page-mode* DRAMs, and use an organization such as the one shown in Fig. 8-8.

Page-mode DRAMs add a latch between the outputs of the bit cells and the multiplexer. Whenever a row address is sent to the DRAM, the entire contents of the row are stored in the latch. This allows subsequent accesses that reference a column within the same row to simply send a second column address to the DRAM, as shown in Fig. 8-9, greatly reducing the time required to fetch a contiguous block of data from the DRAM.

EXAMPLE
If page-mode DRAMs are used to implement the main memory of a system whose cache uses 8-word blocks, how many RAS-CAS delays are saved each time a block of memory is fetched into the cache? (Assume that blocks are

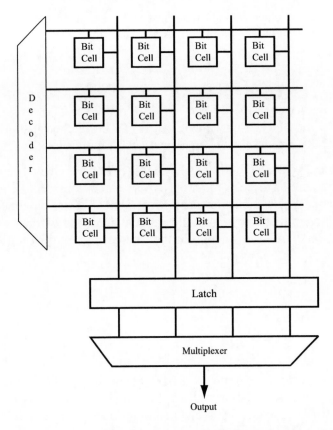

Fig. 8-8. Page mode DRAM.

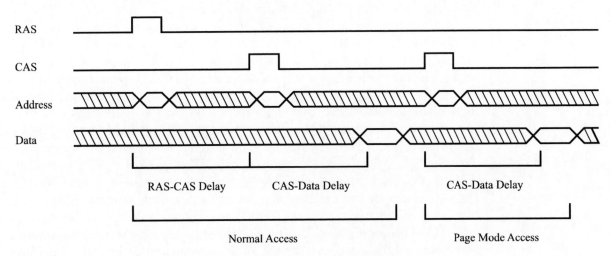

Fig. 8-9. Page mode access.

aligned such that a block's data always lies within the same row of the DRAM and that the memory returns one word of data per access.)

Solution

Using page mode, we only need to do a full RAS-CAS cycle to fetch the first word of the block. Subsequent words can be fetched using only a CAS. Therefore, 7 RAS-CAS delays are saved each time a block is fetched.

In the last several years, synchronous DRAMs (SDRAMs) have been introduced. These devices are similar to page-mode DRAMs, except they require a clock input (other DRAMs are asynchronous devices). Most SDRAMs are pipelined, and many provide access modes that allow multiple sequential words of data to be read or written with just one RAS-CAS cycle, further increasing bandwidth.

8.6   Summary

In this chapter, we began to explore the details of memory system design, breaking down the random-access memory abstraction that we have used in previous chapters. The initial sections of this chapter introduced hierarchy and parallelism in memory systems. Memory hierarchies provide a compromise between system cost and performance by providing a small amount of fast memory and a larger amount of slower memory. The goal of the memory hierarchy is to keep frequently used data in the faster levels of the hierarchy so that the majority of memory references can be completed quickly, providing the illusion of a large memory whose average speed is close to that of the fastest devices in the memory hierarchy. Levels of a memory hierarchy may also be banked or replicated to allow multiple simultaneous accesses to the memory system.

Most memory hierarchies consist of three different types of storage. Caches, which form the top levels of the hierarchy, are constructed out of SRAM memory, making them fast but giving them a high cost per bit of storage. Main memory, the middle level of the hierarchy, is constructed out of DRAM memory, which is slower than SRAM but much cheaper per bit. Finally, the bottom level of the hierarchy is the virtual memory, which uses magnetic media such as hard disks, to store data. Virtual memory is much slower than either DRAM or SRAM, but it is also much cheaper. Caches and virtual memory are covered in more detail in the next two chapters.

After the discussion of memory hierarchies, we described how SRAM and DRAM devices are implemented at a circuit level, starting with the array of bit cells that forms the core of both types of memory. The main difference between SRAM and DRAM is how the bit cells are implemented, with SRAM using an implementation optimized for speed and DRAM an implementation optimized for density. The RAS-CAS addressing cycle of DRAM memories was described, along with more advanced addressing schemes, such as page mode, that allow accesses to sequential locations to be completed more quickly than is possible for random accesses to the device.

In the next two chapters, we will expand our discussion of memory systems by describing the details of cache memories and virtual memory. These two techniques are the core of most modern memory system implementations. Cache memories greatly improve memory system performance at a relatively low cost, while virtual memory provides both large amounts of storage for programs that need to access a great deal of data and protection between programs, allowing multiple programs to safely share a single processor.

 ## Solved Problems

Latency versus Bandwidth (I)

8.1 What is the bandwidth of a memory system that transfers 64 bits of data per request, has a latency of 25 ns per operation, and has a precharge time of 5 ns between operations?

Solution

Given the latency of 25 ns and precharge time of 5 ns, we can initiate one memory reference every 30 ns, and each memory reference fetches 64 bits (8 bytes) of data. Therefore, the bandwidth of the system is 8 bytes/30 ns $= 2.7 \times 10^8$ bytes/s.

Latency versus Bandwidth (II)

8.2 If a memory system has a bandwidth of 120,000,000 bytes/s, transfers 2 bytes of data per access, and has a precharge time of 5 ns between accesses, what is the memory system's latency? (Assume no pipelining and that the memory system does not have multiple banks.)

Solution

To get a bandwidth of 120,000,000 bytes/s at 2 bytes/access, the memory system must have a throughput of 60,000,000 accesses/s, or one access every 16.7 ns. Since the time between accesses is the sum of the memory latency and the precharge time, the memory latency must be 16.7 ns $-$ 5 ns $=$ 11.7 ns.

Latency versus Bandwidth (III)

8.3 Suppose a memory system is constructed out of devices with a latency of 10 ns and no precharge delay. How many banks does the memory system need to provide a peak bandwidth of at least 1.5×10^{10} bytes/s, if each bank transfers 4 bytes per access? (Another way to phrase this question is to ask how many operations the memory system needs to be able to handle in parallel to achieve the specified bandwidth.)

Solution

The easiest way to solve this is to compute the bandwidth of each memory bank first, and then divide the total bandwidth by that to get the number of banks required. At 10 ns per access and 4 bytes transferred per access, a bank has a bandwidth of 4×10^8 bytes/s. Dividing 1.5×10^{10} by that value gives 38 as the required number of banks, since the number of banks must be rounded up to the next integer.

Banked Memory Systems (I)

8.4   Suppose a memory system has four banks, each of which has a latency of 100 ns and is pipelined to allow 8 operations to overlap execution. If each bank returns 4 bytes of data in response to a memory request, what is the peak throughput and peak bandwidth of this system?

Solution

Each bank has a latency of 100 ns and can pipeline 8 operations. Therefore, the throughput of each bank is 1 operation every $100 \, \text{ns}/8 = 12.5 \, \text{ns}$, or 80,000,000 operarations/s. Since there are 4 banks, the peak throughput of the memory system is $4 \times 80,000,000 = 320,000,000$ operations/s. With each memory operation returning 4 bytes of data, this gives a peak bandwidth of $4 \times 320,000,000 = 1,280,000,000$ bytes/s.

Peak versus Actual Bandwidth (I)

8.5   Why is it important to differentiate between the peak bandwidth of a memory system and the actual bandwidth achieved during program execution?

Solution

The peak bandwidth figure for a memory system assumes that memory operations are perfectly distributed for the memory system, avoiding conflicts for banks and the memory bus. It also assumes that there are always memory references waiting for the memory system. In practice, there are times during most programs when the memory system is idle waiting for the processor to make memory requests, and conflicts do occur for the memory bus or memory banks. Thus, the actual bandwidth achieved by the memory system will typically be significantly less than the peak bandwidth.

Peak versus Actual Bandwidth (II)

8.6   For this problem, assume a memory system with two banks, one of which stores even-addressed words and one of which stores odd-addressed words. Assume that the banks have independent connections to the processor, so that there are no conflicts for the memory bus, and that the processor can execute up to 2 memory operations in a given cycle, but that memory operations must be executed in order. Also make the simplifying assumption that the latency of each memory bank is one processor cycle, so the banks are never busy handling requests from previous cycles. Finally, assume that the processor always has 2 memory operations that it would like to execute on a given cycle.

a.   What is the peak throughput of the memory system (in operations per cycle)?

b. If the addresses of each memory request are random (a very unrealistic assumption), how many memory operations will the processor be able to execute each cycle on average?

c. If each memory bank returns 8 bytes of data per request, and processor cycles are 10 ns long, what is the peak bandwidth (in bytes/s) of this memory system, and what is the bandwidth that it will achieve on average?

Solution

a. Each bank can handle one operation/cycle, so the peak throughput is 2 operations/cycle.

b. At the start of each cycle, both banks are ready to accept requests. Therefore, the processor will always be able to execute at least one memory request per cycle. Since memory addresses are random 50 percent of the time, the second operation that the processor could execute will target the same bank as the first, and it will have to wait for the next cycle. The other 50 percent of the time, the two operations will target different banks, and they will be able to execute simultaneously. Therefore, the processor will be able to execute an average of 1.5 memory operations per cycle.

c. Each memory bank can execute 1 operation every 10 ns (100,000,000 operations/s), and each returns 8 bytes of data per operation. Therefore, the peak bandwidth of one memory bank is 800,000,000 bytes/s. Since there are two banks, the peak bandwidth of the memory system will be 1,600,000,000 bytes/s.

On average the system will be able to execute 1.5 memory operations per cycle. Therefore, the average bandwidth of the memory system is 1.5*800,000,000 bytes/s = 1,200,000,000 bytes/s.

Memory Hierarchies (I)

8.7 Why are computers' memory systems typically built as hierarchies?

Solution

The faster a memory technology is, the more it tends to cost per bit of storage. Using a memory hierarchy allows the computer to provide a large memory capacity, fast average access time, and low memory cost. The lower levels of the memory hierarchy, which contain the most storage, are implemented using slow but cheap memory technologies. The higher levels, which contain smaller amounts of storage, are implemented in fast but expensive memory technologies. As data is referenced, it is moved into the higher levels of the memory hierarchy so that most memory references are handled by the top levels of the hierarchy. If enough references are handled by the top levels of the hierarchy, the memory system gives an average access time similar to that of the fastest level of the hierarchy, with a cost per bit similar to that of the lowest level of the hierarchy

Memory Hierarchies (II)

8.8 Suppose that SRAM costs $25 per MB for an access time of 5 ns, DRAM costs $1 per MB with an access time of 60 ns, and disk space costs $10 per GB with an access time of 7 ms.

a. For a memory system with 256 KB of cache SRAM, 128 MB of main memory DRAM, and 1 GB of virtual memory (implemented as disk), what is the total cost of the memory system and the cost per byte?

b. If the hit rate at each level in the memory hierarchy is 80 percent (expect the last), what is the average memory access time?

c. What is the average memory access time if the hit rate at each level except the last is 90 percent?

d. How about if the hit rate is 99 percent at each level except the last?

Solution

a. SRAM costs $25 per MB, so the 256 KB (1/4 MB) of SRAM in the system costs $6.25. DRAM costs $1/MB, so 128 MB of DRAM costs $128. Disk space costs $10 per GB, for a total of $10. Adding these values together gives a total cost of $144.25 for the storage in the memory system. To get the cost per byte, we divide by the total storage of 256 KB + 128 MB + 1 GB = 256 KB + 128 × 1024 KB + 1 × 1024 × 1024 KB = 1,179,904 KB = 1,208,221,696 B. This gives a cost of 1.19 × 10^{-7} $/B.

b. For each level, average access time = (hit rate × access time for that level) + (1-hit rate) × (average access time for next level). Therefore, for this memory system, the average access time = (0.80 × 5 ns) + 0.20 × (0.80 × 60 ns) + 0.20 × 7 ms) = 280,013.6 ns.

c. Changing the hit rates from the above equation, we get an average access time of 70,009.9 ns.

d. With these hit rates, the average access time is 705.5 ns.

These examples illustrate the importance of having a high hit rate when there is a large gap between the access times of different levels of the memory hierarchy. Otherwise, the long access time of the disks used to implement the lowest level of the hierarchy dominates the average access time, even though only a small fraction of the memory references reach this level of the hierarchy.

Memory Hierarchies (III)

8.9 In a two-level memory hierarchy, if the top level has an access time of 8 ns and the bottom level has an access time of 60 ns, what is the hit rate in the top level required to give an average access time of 10 ns?

Solution

To solve this problem, we use the formula for average access time in a memory with the hit rate as the variable instead of the average access time, and solve for the hit rate. Plugging values into the formula gives 10 ns = (hit rate × 8 ns) + (miss rate × 60 ns) = (hit rate × 8 ns) + ((1-hit rate) × 60 ns).

Solving for the hit rate, we get a required hit rate of 96.2 percent.

Memory Hierarchies (IV)

8.10 A two-level memory system has an average access time of 12 ns. The top level of the memory system has a hit rate of 90 percent and an access time of 5 ns. What is the access time of the lower level of the memory system?

Solution

Use the formula for average access time and solve for T_{miss} of the first level of the memory hierarchy, which is equal to the access time of the second level of the hierarchy in a two-level hierarchy. This gives $12\,ns = (0.90 \times 5\,ns) + (0.10 \times T_{miss})$. Solving for T_{miss}, we get an access time of 75 ns for the second level of the hierarchy.

Inclusion

8.11 Explain why maintaining inclusion between different levels of the memory hierarchy makes implementing write-back memory hierarchies easier.

Solution

Maintaining inclusion between levels in the memory hierarchy (ensuring that all data in a level is also contained in all of the levels below it) makes it easier to implement write-back memory hierarchies because it guarantees that, when a block of data is removed from a level of the hierarchy, there is space on the next-lower level to write the data if it has been modified. If the levels of a hierarchy did not maintain inclusion, then there might not be space in the next-lower level to write the block, requiring that a block be removed from that level to make space, which would make removing blocks more complicated.

Hit and Miss Rates

8.12 Given a memory hierarchy like the one shown in Fig. 8-2, what are the hit and miss rates in the cache and the main memory if the processor executes a total of 1,000,000 memory references, 945,000 of which hit in the cache and 45,000 of which hit in the main memory.

Solution

The hit rate is the ratio of the number of hits at a given level in the hierarchy to the number of references that reach that level of the hierarchy, and the miss rate is the ratio of the number of misses at the level to the number of references that reach the level. All 1,000,000 memory references reach the cache, so the hit rate in the cache is $945,000/1,000,000 = 94.5$ percent. The miss rate is then $55,000/1,000,000 = 5.5$ percent. (The hit and miss rates at a given level should always sum to 100 percent.)

Because 55,000 memory references (all the references that miss in the cache) reach the main memory, its hit rate is $45,000/55,000 = 81.8$ percent, and its miss rate is $10,000/55,000 = 18.2$ percent.

SRAMs versus DRAMs (I)

8.13 Why do DRAMs generally have much larger capacities than SRAMs constructed in the same fabrication technology?

Solution

DRAM bit cells require only two devices—a capacitor and a transistor—while SRAM bit cells typically require six transistors. This makes the bit cells of the DRAM much smaller than the bit cells of the SRAM, allowing the DRAM to store more data in the same amount of chip space.

SRAMs versus DRAMs (II)

8.14 For each of the following cases, state whether SRAMs or DRAMs would be more appropriate building blocks for the memory system, and explain why. Assume that there is only one level in the memory hierarchy.

a. A memory system where performance was the most important goal

b. A memory system where cost was the most important factor

c. A design where it is important for data to be stored for long periods of time without any action on the processor's part

Solution

a. SRAMs generally have lower latencies than DRAMs, so SRAMs would be a better choice for this system.

b. DRAMs have lower cost/bit than SRAMs, so they would be better here.

c. DRAMs have to have their contents refreshed in order to store data for long periods of time, while SRAMS do not. Since the goal here is to store data for extended periods without processor intervention, SRAMs would be better than DRAMs.

DRAM Bandwidth

8.15 Suppose a DRAM has a RAS-CAS delay of 45 ns, has a CAS-data delay of 35 ns, and requires a precharge time of 20 ns. If the DRAM does not support page mode and returns 4 bits of data from each memory reference, what is its latency for read operations, throughput (assume reads and writes take the same amount of time), and bandwidth?

Solution

The latency is the sum of the RAS-CAS delay and the CAS-data delay (80 ns). To find the throughput, we add the precharge time to the latency to get the rate at which operations can be initiated (1 operation every 100 ns = 10,000,000 operations/s). Bandwidth is the product of throughput and the amount of data returned on each operation = 40,000,000 bits/s = 5,000,000 bytes/s.

DRAM Refresh

8.16 If a DRAM has 1024 rows in its array of bit cells and a refresh time of 8 ms, how often must a row refresh operation be performed on average? Also, what fraction of the DRAM's time is spent performing refreshes if each row refresh operation takes 100 ns?

Solution

Each row must be refreshed once every refresh time, so 1024 row refresh operations must be done every 8 ms, or 1 row refresh every 7.8 microseconds on average. Each row refresh takes 100 ns, so the fraction of the DRAM's time taken by row refreshes is 100 ns/7.8 microseconds = 1.28 percent.

Page Mode

8.17 Suppose that a processor's memory is constructed out of page-mode DRAMs whose RAS-CAS delay and CAS-data delay are 50 ns each. The main memory returns 1 word of data for each request from the processor. If the block size of the processor's cache is 16 words, what fraction of the memory requests from the processor will be able to use page mode, and what will be the reduction in the time to transfer a block from the main memory because of the use of page mode? Assume that blocks are aligned so that they always lie completely within one row of the DRAM, and that successive blocks lie in different rows of the DRAM. Also assume that the DRAM does not require any precharge time between requests.

Solution

Since the main memory returns 1 word per request from the cache, 16 requests are required to fetch each block. Successive blocks lie in different rows of the DRAM, but each block is completely contained within a DRAM row, so the first request for each block will be unable to use page mode, but the rest will be able to use page mode. Therefore, 15/16 = 93.8 percent of the requests will use page mode.

If the DRAM did not support page mode, each request would take 100 ns (50 ns RAS-CAS delay + 50 ns CAS-data delay), so transferring a block into the cache would take 1600 ns. With page mode, the first request still takes 100 ns, but the next 15 take only 50 ns (just the CAS-data delay), so the total time to transfer a block is 850 ns, a saving of 47 percent.

CHAPTER 9

Caches

9.1 Objectives

This chapter continues our discussion of memory systems by describing *caches*—small, fast memories that are located close to a processor. After reading this chapter and completing the exercises, you should

1. Understand how caches are organized and implemented, and be able to determine how much memory is required for a cache of a given size and organization
2. Be familiar with the difference between instruction and data caches, and be able to explain why most processors incorporate both of these structures
3. Be able to define and describe cache terminology

9.2 Introduction

Caches are generally the top level or levels of the memory hierarchy and are almost always constructed out of SRAM. The main structural difference between a cache and other levels in the memory hierarchy is that caches contain hardware to track the memory addresses that are contained in the cache and to move data into and out of the cache as necessary. Lower levels in the hierarchy generally rely on software or a combination of hardware and software to perform this function.

Cache memories generally contain a *tag array* and a *data array*, as shown in Fig. 9-1. The tag array contains the addresses of the data contained in the cache, while the data array contains the data itself. Dividing the cache into separate tag and data arrays reduces the access time of the cache, because the tag array typically contains many fewer bits than the data array and can therefore be accessed more quickly than either the data array or a single combined tag/data array. Once the tag array has been accessed, its output must be compared to the address of the memory reference to

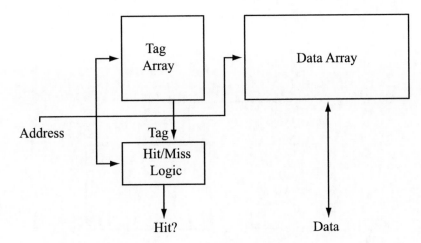

Fig. 9-1.   Cache block diagram.

determine if a hit has occurred. Separating the cache into tag and data arrays allows the hit/miss determination to be done in parallel with some of the data array lookup time, reducing the overall access time.

9.3   Data Caches, Instruction Caches, and Unified Caches

In our discussions of memory systems, we have generally acted as if instructions and data share space within each level of the memory hierarchy. For the main memory and the virtual memory, this is generally true. However, for caches, data and instructions are often stored in separate data and instruction caches, as shown in Fig. 9-2. This arrangement, which is sometimes called a *Harvard cache or Harvard architecture*, is used because it allows the processor to fetch instructions from the instruction cache and data from the data cache simultaneously. When a cache contains both instructions and data, it is called a *unified* cache.

Another advantage of separating the instruction and data caches is that programs do not in general modify their own instructions. Thus, instruction caches can be designed as read-only devices that do not allow modification of the instructions they contain. This means that an instruction cache can simply discard any blocks that have to be evicted from it without writing them back to the main memory, since the data they contain is guaranteed not to have changed since it was brought into the cache. Finally, keeping the instruction and data caches separate prevents conflicts between blocks of instructions and data that might map into the same storage locations in a unified cache.

One disadvantage of using separate instruction and data caches is that it makes writing self-modifying programs more difficult. When a program modifies its own instructions, those instructions are treated as data and are stored in the data cache,

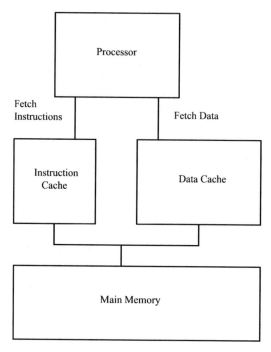

Fig. 9-2.　Harvard cache architecture.

not the instruction cache. For the modified instructions to be executed, the program must use special cache flush operations to ensure that the original versions of the instructions are not present in the instruction cache, forcing the program to fetch the modified versions from main memory before they can be executed. If the data cache is write-back, additional cache flush operations may be required to ensure that the modified instructions have been written out to the main memory before they are read into the instruction cache. The additional overhead imposed by these cache flush operations reduces the performance benefit of self-modifying code, making it less useful.

Often, a system's instruction cache will be significantly smaller (two to four times) than its data cache. This is because the instructions for a program generally take up much less memory than the program's data. Also, most programs spend the majority of their time in loops that reuse the same instructions multiple times. As a result of this, a system's instruction cache can be significantly smaller than its data cache and have the same hit rate, so designers often choose to devote more chip area to the data cache than the instruction cache.

9.4　Describing Caches

To compare caches, designers discuss their capacity, line length, associativity (number of places a given address can reside), replacement policy, and whether the cache is write-back or write-through.

9.5   Capacity

The *capacity* of a cache is simply the amount of data that can be stored in the cache, so a cache with a capacity of 32 KB can store 32 kilobytes of data. Such a cache will require more than 32 KB of memory to implement, because the storage in the tag array is not included in the capacity.

9.6   Line Length

The *line length* of a cache is the cache's block size—the size of the chunks of data that are brought into and thrown out of the cache in response to a cache miss. For example, when a cache with 32-byte cache lines has a cache miss, it brings a 32-byte block of data containing the address of the miss into the cache, evicting a 32-byte block of data beforehand if necessary to make room for the new data. Cache lines are *aligned*—the address of the first byte in a cache line is always a multiple of the line length. This simplifies the process of determining whether or not a cache hit has occurred, because the low bits of the address determine which byte an address refers to within the line that contains it, and only the higher bits in the address need to be sent to the tag array to determine if a hit has occurred. The exact number of bits that need to be compared to detect cache hits is determined by the size of the cache, the length of the cache lines, and the associativity of the cache. This will be discussed in more detail later in the chapter.

EXAMPLE
In a cache with 64-byte cache lines, how many bits are used to determine which byte within a cache line an address points to?

Solution

The $\log_2$ of 64 is 6, so the low 6 bits of the address determine an address's byte within a cache line.

EXAMPLE
In a cache with 64-byte cache lines, what is the address of the first word in the cache line containing the address 0xbee3de72?

Solution

Cache lines are aligned on a multiple of their size, so the address of the first word in a line can be found by setting all of the bits that determine the byte within the line to 0. In this case, 6 bits are used to select a byte within the line, so we can find the starting address of the line by setting the low 6 bits of the address to 0, giving 0xbee3de40 as the address of the first word in the line.

Designers have to take a number of factors into account when selecting the line length of a cache. In general, increasing the length of a cache's lines increases the hit rate, due to the property of locality. Increasing the line length increases the amount of data that is brought into the cache when a cache miss occurs. Since addresses close to the address of a miss are likely to be referenced soon after a miss, using long cache lines means that each miss brings more data that is likely to be referenced soon into the cache, preventing misses if that data is referenced.

However, increasing the length of a system's cache lines too much often increases the amount of time programs take to execute, even if it results in lower miss rates than using shorter lines. This occurs because of the amount of time it takes to bring longer cache lines into the cache, and because the probability that a given byte of data will be needed in the near future goes down as the address of the byte gets further from the address of the cache miss. As a cache's line length increases, the increase in the line fetch time becomes a more significant factor than the decrease in the miss rate. For this reason, most modern caches have lines in the 32-byte to 128-byte range, which is a good trade-off between hit rate and line fetch time.

EXAMPLE

If a cache has 64-byte cache lines, how long does it take to fetch a cache line if the main memory takes 20 cycles to respond to each memory request and returns 2 bytes of data in response to each request?

Solution

Since the main memory returns 2 bytes of data in response to each request, 32 memory requests are required to fetch the line. At 20 cycles per request, fetching a cache line will take 640 cycles.

EXAMPLE

How does the line fetch time of the above system change if page-mode DRAMs that have a CAS-data delay of 10 cycles are used to implement the main memory? (Assume cache lines always lie within a single row of the DRAM, but that each line lies in a different row than the last line fetched.)

Solution

The system still requires 32 memory requests to fetch each cache line. Using page mode, only the first request takes the full 20 cycles, and the other 31 take only 10 cycles. Therefore, the time to fetch a cache line is $20 + (31 \times 10) = 330$ cycles. Page-mode DRAMs significantly reduce the time to fetch longer cache lines, which can increase the line length that gives the best performance.

9.7   Associativity

The *associativity* of a cache determines how many locations within the cache may contain a given memory address. Caches with high associativity allow each address to be stored in many locations in the cache, which reduces cache misses caused by conflicts between lines that must be stored in the same set of locations. Caches with low associativity restrict the number of locations an address can be placed in, which increases the number of cache misses but simplifies the cache's hardware, reducing the amount of space taken up by the cache and often reducing the access time.

9.7.1   FULLY ASSOCIATIVE CACHES

Fully associative caches, as illustrated in Fig 9.3, allow any address to be stored in any line in the cache. When a memory operation is sent to the cache, the address of the request must be compared to each entry in the tag array to determine whether the data referenced by the operation is contained in the cache. Note that fully associative caches are generally still implemented with separate tag and data arrays. The diagram attaches the tag entry and data line to make it clearer which line is associated with each tag.

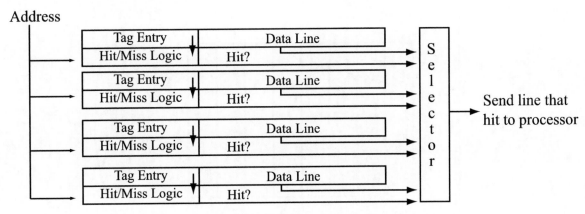

Fig. 9-3.   Fully-associative cache.

9.7.2   DIRECT-MAPPED CACHES

Direct-mapped caches are the opposite extreme from fully associative caches. In a direct-mapped cache, each memory address can only be stored in one location in the cache. As shown in Fig. 9-4, when a memory operation is sent to a direct-mapped cache, a subset of the bits in the address is used to select the line in the cache that may contain the address, and another subset of the bits is used to select the byte within a cache line that the address points to. In general, the n lowest-order bits in the address are used to determine the position of the address within its cache line, where n is the base-2 logarithm of the number of bytes in the line. The m next-higher-order bits, where m is the base-2 logarithm of the number of lines in the

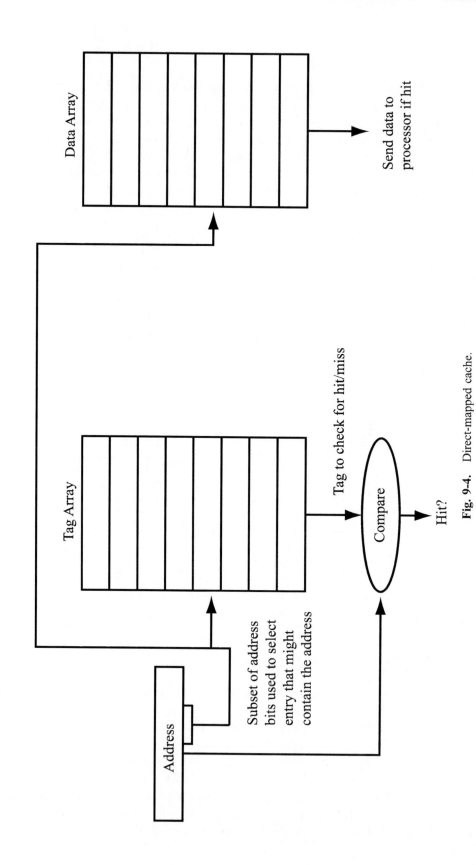

Fig. 9-4. Direct-mapped cache.

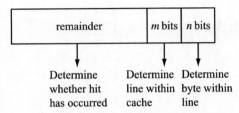

$n = \log_2$ of number of bytes in line

$m = \log_2$ of number of lines in cache

| remainder | m bits | n bits |

Determine whether hit has occurred

Determine line within cache

Determine byte within line

Fig. 9-5. Address breakdown.

cache, are used to select the line in which the address may be stored, as shown in Fig. 9-5.

EXAMPLE

In a direct-mapped cache with a capacity of 16 KB and a line length of 32 bytes, how many bits are used to determine the byte that a memory operation references within a cache line, and how many bits are used to select the line in the cache that may contain the data?

Solution

Log$_2$ of 32 is 5, so 5 bits are required to determine which byte within a cache line is being referenced. With 32-byte lines, there are 512 lines in the 16-KB cache, so 9 bits are required to select the line that may contain the address ($\log_2$ of 512 = 9).

Direct-mapped caches have the advantage of requiring significantly less chip space to implement than fully associative caches because they only require one comparator to determine if a hit has occurred, while fully associative caches require one comparator for each line in the cache. In addition, direct-mapped caches usually have lower access times because there is only one comparison to examine to determine if a hit has occurred, while a fully associative cache must examine each of the comparisons and select the appropriate word of data to send to the processor.

However, direct-mapped caches tend to have lower hit rates than fully associative caches, due to conflicts between lines that map into the same space in the cache. Each address can only be placed in one location in the cache, which is determined by the m address bits illustrated in Fig. 9-5. If two addresses have the same value in those bits, they map onto the same line in the cache and cannot reside in the cache at the same time. A program that alternated between references to these two addresses would never hit in the cache, since the line containing each address would always have been evicted before the next reference to the address. Thus, the cache could achieve a 0 percent hit rate, even though the program only referenced two addresses. In practice, direct-mapped caches, particularly large direct-mapped caches, can achieve good hit rates, although their hit rates tend to be lower than those caches that provide multiple possible locations for each cache line.

9.7.3 SET-ASSOCIATIVE CACHES

Set-associative caches are a compromise between fully associative caches and direct-mapped caches. In a set-associative cache, there are a fixed number of locations (called a *set*) that a given address may be stored in. The number of locations in each set is the associativity of the cache.

Figure 9-6 shows how a two-way set-associative cache, in which there are two possible locations in the cache for an address, handles a memory request. Like a direct-mapped cache, a subset of the address bits are used to select the set that might contain the address. Because the cache is two-way set-associative, there are two tags that must be compared to the address of the memory reference to determine if a hit has occurred. If either of the tags matches the address, a hit has occurred and the corresponding line from the data array is selected. Caches with higher associativity have similar structures, with more comparators to determine if a hit has occurred.

A set-associative cache will have fewer sets than a direct-mapped cache that contains the same number of lines and will therefore use fewer bits of an address to select the set that the address will be stored in. The number of sets in a cache can be found by computing the number of lines in the cache and dividing by the associativity.

> **EXAMPLE**
>
> How many sets are there in a two-way set-associative cache with 32-KB capacity and 64-byte lines, and how many bits of the address are used to select a set in this cache? What about an eight-way set-associative cache with the same capacity and line length?

Solution

A 32-KB cache with 64-byte lines contains 512 lines of data. In a two-way set-associative cache, each set contains 2 lines, so there are 256 sets in the cache. $\text{Log}_2(256) = 8$, so 8 bits of an address are used to select a set that the address maps to. The eight-way set-associative cache has 64 lines and uses 6 bits of the address to select a set.

In general, set-associative caches have better hit rates than direct-mapped caches but worse hit rates than fully associative caches of the same size, because allowing each address to be stored in multiple locations eliminates some, but not all, of the conflicts between cache lines that occur in a direct-mapped cache. The difference in hit rate is a function of the capacity of the cache, the degree of associativity, and the data referenced by a given program. Some programs reference large blocks of contiguous data, leading to few conflicts, while others reference many disjoint data objects, which can lead to conflicts if the objects map to the same sets in the cache.

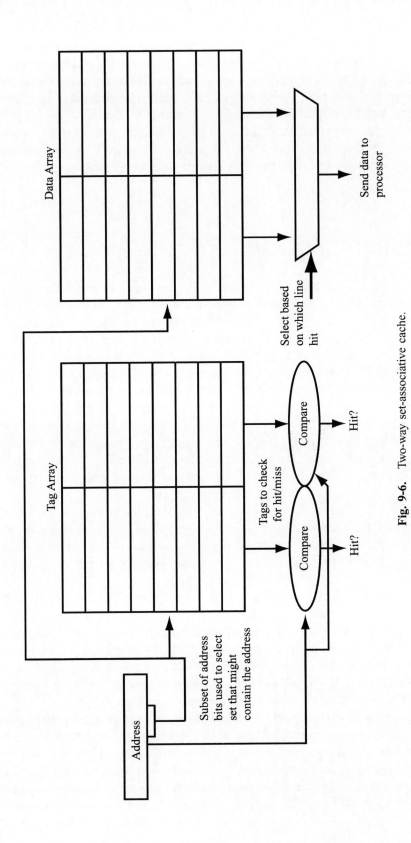

Fig. 9-6. Two-way set-associative cache.

The larger a cache is, the less benefit it tends to see from associativity, since there is a lower probability that any two addresses will map onto the same space in the cache. Finally, successive increases in associativity have diminishing returns. Going from a direct-mapped cache to two-way set-associative usually causes significant reductions in the miss rate. Increasing to four-way set-associative (associativity is usually a power of 2 to simplify the hardware, but other associativities are possible) has a less significant effect, and increasing beyond that tends to have very little effect, except for extremely small caches. For this reason two-way and four-way set-associative caches are most common in current microprocessors.

9.8   Replacement Policy

When a line must be evicted from a cache to make room for incoming data, either because the cache is full or because of conflicts for a set, the replacement policy determines which line is evicted. In direct-mapped caches, there is no choice about which line to evict, since the incoming line can only be placed in one location in the cache, but set-associative and fully associative caches contain multiple lines that could be evicted to make room for the incoming line. In these caches, the general goal of the replacement policy is to minimize future cache misses by evicting a line that will not be referenced often in the future. Designers of replacement policies must also take into account the cost of their replacement policy; if a replacement policy reduces future misses slightly but requires so much hardware that the capacity of the cache must be reduced to accommodate the replacement policy, the additional cache misses that result from the reduced capacity may overwhelm the savings from the improved replacement policy.

The perfect replacement policy would examine the future behavior of the program being run and evict the line that results in the fewest cache misses. Since computers don't know what their programs will do in the future, replacement policies must guess which line should be evicted based on what the program has done in the past.

One common replacement policy is *least-recently used* (LRU). In LRU replacement, the cache ranks each of the lines in a set according to how recently they have been accessed and evicts the least-recently used line from a set when an eviction is necessary. This is based on the observation that lines that have not been referenced in the recent past are unlikely to be referenced in the near future. Another policy that has been studied is *random replacement*, in which a randomly selected line from the appropriate set is evicted to make room for incoming data.

Studies have shown that LRU replacement generally gives slightly higher hit rates than random replacement, but that the differences are very small for caches of reasonable size. However, LRU replacement is relatively complex to implement. Whenever a line in a set is referenced, the information on how recently all of the lines in the set have been referenced must be updated, leading to relatively complicated hardware. For this reason, some caches use a *not-most-recently used* replacement policy. In this policy, the cache keeps track of the line in each set that

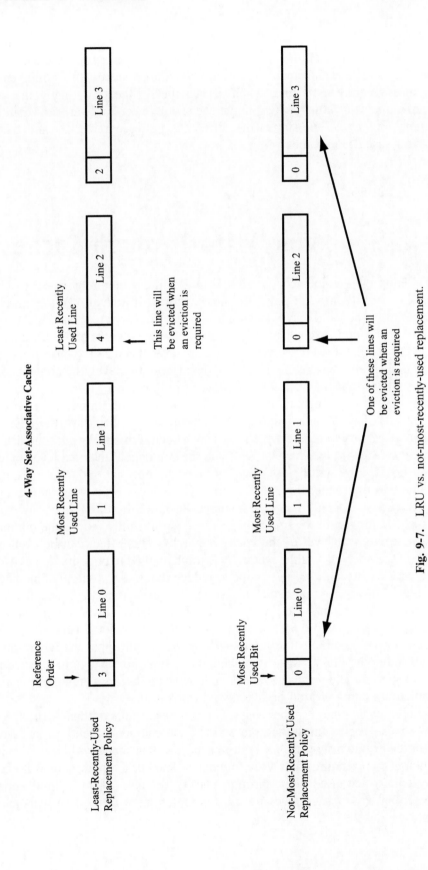

Fig. 9-7. LRU vs. not-most-recently-used replacement.

has been referenced most recently and evicts one of the other lines (often selected at random) whenever an eviction is necessary. For two-way set-associative caches, this is equivalent to LRU replacement. For more-associative caches, this policy ensures that the most-recently used line, which is statistically the most likely line to be referenced in the near future, is kept in the cache at a lower hardware cost than LRU replacement. Figure 9-7 illustrates the difference between the LRU and the not-most-recently-used replacement policies.

9.9   Write-Back versus Write-Through Caches

As discussed in the previous chapter, levels in a memory hierarchy can use either a write-back or a write-through policy to handle stores. If a level of the hierarchy is write-through, stored values are written into the level and sent to the next level down as the store operation is executed. This ensures that the contents of the level and the next level down are always the same. Write-back levels keep stored data in the level, and when a block that has been written is evicted from the level, the contents of the block are written back (copied) into the next level down.

Caches may be implemented as either write-back or write-through systems, and both approaches have their advantages. Write-through caches have the advantage that it is not necessary to record which lines have been written. Because the data in a write-through cache is always consistent with the contents of the next level, evicting a line can be done by writing the new line over the old one, reducing the time to bring a line into the cache. In contrast, write-back caches only write their contents back when a line is evicted. If a given line receives multiple store requests while it is in the cache, waiting until the line is evicted can significantly reduce the number of writes sent to the next level of the cache hierarchy. This effect can be even more significant if the next level of the hierarchy is implemented in page-mode DRAM, as the write-back cache can use page mode to reduce the time to write the line back to the next level. However, write-back caches require hardware to track whether or not each line has been written since it was fetched. Also, when a dirty line (one that has been written since it was brought into the cache) must be evicted from the cache to make room for an incoming line, write-back caches require that the incoming line wait for the outgoing line to be written back, increasing the delay until the incoming line is available. Some write-back caches include *write buffers* as temporary storage for lines that are being written back to avoid this delay.

In general, write-back caches have higher performance than write-through caches, because cache lines that are written at least once tend to be written enough times to make writing the entire cache line back once when it is evicted more efficient than sending each write to the next level of the hierarchy as it occurs. Older systems often used write-through caches because of their lower control complexity, but write-back caches have become dominant in modern workstations and PCs.

EXAMPLE

The level below a cache in the memory hierarchy is implemented out of non-page-mode DRAM that requires 60 ns to read or write a word of data. If cache lines are 8 lines long, how many times does the average line have to be written (counting only lines that are written at least once) before a write-back cache is more efficient than a write-through cache?

Solution

In a write-back cache, each dirty 8-word line is written back once for every time it is brought into the cache, taking 480 ns (8×60 ns). In a write-through cache, each store operation requires that its data be written through to the next level, taking 60 ns. Therefore, if the average line that gets written at least once gets written more than 8 times, the write-back cache will be more efficient.

EXAMPLE

How does the answer to the previous example change if the next level of the hierarchy is implemented using page-mode DRAM that has a first-word access time of 60 ns, and then 10 ns/word thereafter?

Solution

In this system, writing back a line takes $60 \text{ ns} + 7 \times 10 \text{ ns} = 130 \text{ ns}$, enough time for 2.17 single-word memory operations. Therefore, if the average line that is written at least once is written more than 2.17 times, the write-back cache will be more efficient.

EXAMPLE

In the above system (with page-mode DRAM), what is the average time to fetch a line into the cache if 40 percent of all evicted cache lines have been written at least once? (The answers will be different for write-through and write-back caches.)

Solution

In the write-through cache, the time to fetch a line into the cache is simply the time to read the line into memory (130 ns), since all writes are copied out to the next level of the hierarchy when they occur. In the write-back cache, 40 percent of the lines will be dirty and will have to be written back before the incoming line can be fetched. Thus, the average line fetch time is 130 ns (time to read the line) + 0.40 × 130 ns (time to write a line times the percentage of lines that need to be written) = 182 ns. This illustrates why many write-back caches incorporate write buffers to allow line fetches to go ahead of write-backs.

9.10   Cache Implementations

So far, we have discussed how caches are structured, without paying much attention to the details of how they are implemented. Figure 9-1 shows a basic diagram of how most caches are implemented out of a tag array, hit/miss detection logic, and data array. In the next few sections of this chapter, we will discuss how these three components are implemented.

9.11   Tag Arrays

In general, the tag array is organized as a two-dimensional structure containing a row of tag entries for each set in the cache, with the number of tag entries in each row equal to the associativity of the cache. Figure 9-8 shows the structure of the tag array for a four-way set-associative cache.

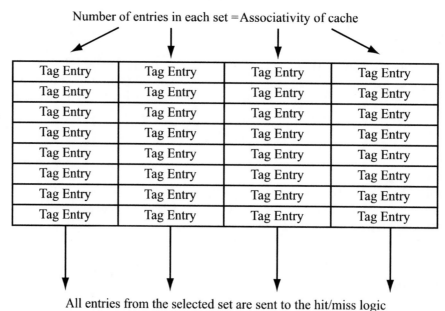

Fig. 9-8.   Tag array for 4-way set-associative cache.

A tag entry contains the information necessary to record which line of data is stored in the line of the data cache that is associated with the entry. Each entry describes one cache line of data. As shown in Fig. 9-9, a tag entry consists of a tag field that contains the portion of the address of the line that is not used to select a set (the "remainder" field from Fig. 9-5), a valid bit that records whether or not the line associated with this tag array entry contains valid data, and a dirty bit (for write-

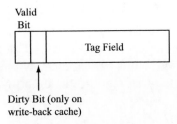

Fig. 9-9.   Tag array entry.

back caches). Depending on the replacement policy of the cache, the tag entry might also contain one or more additional bits. For example, in a cache that implements LRU replacement, each tag entry must be able to record how many of the other lines in the set have been referenced since the last time that the line it corresponds to was referenced, so that the replacement policy can locate the least recently used line when a replacement is required. This requires $\log_2$ (cache associativity) bits of data in each tag entry.

When a computer is first powered up, all of the valid bits in the tag array are set to 0, to record the fact that there is no data in the cache. Whenever a line is brought into the cache, the valid bit in the corresponding entry of the tag array is set to 1, recording that the line now contains valid data. In general, once a line becomes full, it remains full, because the data that was loaded into it remains in the cache until it is replaced with another line of data. The exception to this is when a program deliberately removes a line of data from the cache (most processors provide instructions to do this), in which case the line becomes empty and its valid bit is set to 0.

The amount of storage required for the tag array is determined by the number of lines in the cache, the number of tag bits required for each entry, and whether any additional bits are required to record whether the line is dirty and how recently it has been referenced. Using the terminology of Fig. 9-5, the n bits used to indicate which byte within a cache line is being referenced and the m bits used to select a set within the cache do not need to be included in the tag field, so the number of bits in each tag field is equal to the width of the addresses used by the machine, minus $(n + m)$. Adding in the valid bit and any dirty or recently used bits gives the width of the tag entry, which can then be multiplied by the number of lines in the cache to find the amount of storage required for the tag array.

EXAMPLE
How many bits of storage are required for the tag array of a 32-KB cache with 256-byte cache lines and four-way set-associativity if the cache is write-back but does not require any additional bits of data in the tag array to implement the write-back policy? Assume that the system containing the cache uses 32-bit addresses.

Solution

A 32-KB cache with 256-byte lines contains 128 lines. Since the cache is four-way set-associative, it has 32 sets, so $m = 5$ bits. Lines that are 256 bytes long mean that $n = 8$, so 13 bits of the address are used to select a set and determine the byte within the line that an address points to. Therefore, the tag field of each tag array entry is $32 - 13 = 19$ bits long. Adding 2 bits for the dirty and valid bits, we get 21 bits per tag entry. Multiplying by the 128 lines in the cache gives 2688 bits of storage in the tag array.

9.12   Hit/Miss Logic

The hit/miss logic compares the "remainder" bits of the address of a memory reference to the contents of the tag field in each tag entry in the set. If these bit fields match, and the valid bit of the tag entry is set, then a hit has occurred, as shown in Fig. 9-10.

9.13   Data Arrays

The structure of a cache's data array is similar to that of the tag array. The data array is a two-dimensional array of cache lines, with one row for each set in the cache and

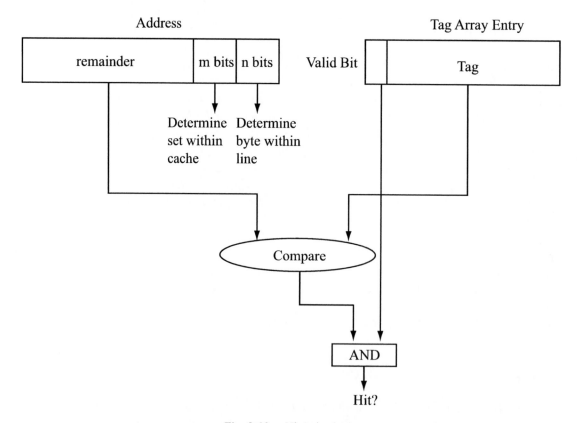

Fig. 9-10. Hit/miss logic.

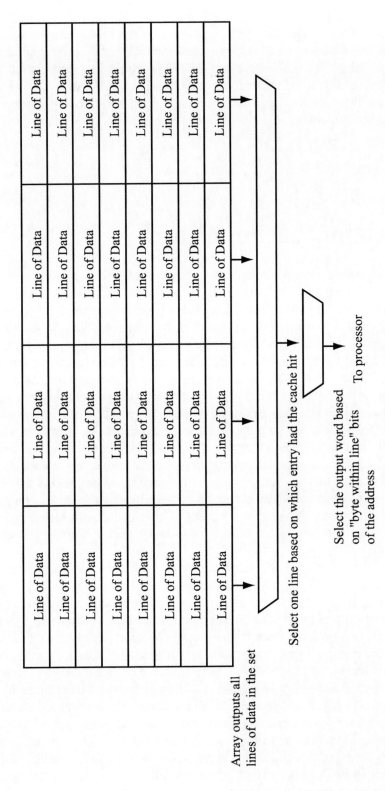

Fig. 9-11. Data array organization.

a number of columns equal to the associativity of the cache. Figure 9-11 shows how the data array that goes with the tag array of Fig. 9-8 would be laid out. When an address is sent to the cache, the array outputs all of the cache lines in the set that might contain the address. If a cache hit occurs, the line of data corresponding to the tag entry that had the hit is selected, and the "byte within line" bits of the address are used to select the word of data to be sent to the processor. During a store operation, data flows in the opposite direction, and the data being written by the store is routed to the correct location within the set.

9.14 Categorizing Cache Misses

To better understand how to reduce the number of cache misses seen by an application, architects divide them into three categories: *compulsory* misses, *capacity* misses, and *conflict* misses. Compulsory misses are cache misses caused by the first reference to a line, which causes it to be brought into the cache for the first time. Capacity misses occur when the amount of data referenced by a program exceeds the capacity of the cache, requiring that some data be evicted to make room for new data. If the evicted data is referenced again by the program, a cache miss occurs, which is termed a capacity miss. Conflict misses occur when a program references more lines of data that map to the same set in the cache than the associativity of the cache, forcing the cache to evict one of the lines to make room. If the evicted line is referenced again, the miss that results is a conflict miss. Capacity and conflict misses both occur because data must be evicted from the cache to make room for new data, but the difference between them is that conflict misses can occur even when there is free space elsewhere in the cache. If a program references multiple lines that map to the same set in the cache, it may be necessary to evict some of them to make room for new data, even if every other set in the cache is empty.

Understanding why a cache miss occurs helps determine what improvements to the cache are necessary to prevent that miss from occurring the next time the program is run. Compulsory misses are hard to eliminate, because data is not copied into the cache until it is referenced for the first time. Some systems use a technique called *prefetching* to reduce compulsory misses by predicting which data will be referenced and bringing it into the cache before it is needed. Capacity misses can be reduced by increasing the size of the cache so that more of the data referenced by the program fits in the cache simultaneously. Conflict misses can be reduced by either increasing associativity, so that more lines that map to the same set can be stored in the cache, or by increasing capacity, which can cause lines that mapped to the same set to map onto different sets. In general, increasing the associativity of a cache is the less hardware-expensive of the two approaches, as it requires building additional hit/miss detection logic and restructuring the layout of the tag and data arrays, rather than adding more capacity to the array.

EXAMPLE

A program accesses two cache lines, one that begins at address 0x1000, and one that begins at address 0x2000. Memory accesses alternate between the two lines, and each line is accessed 100 times. If the program is run on a system with a 1-KB direct-mapped data cache with 32-byte lines, how many data cache misses will occur? How many of these misses will be compulsory, capacity, and conflict misses?

Solution

A 1-KB cache with 32-byte lines contains 32 lines and uses bits 5 through 9 of the address to select the cache line that a line of data maps into (bits 0 through 4 determine the byte within the line). Since the addresses of each of these lines have 0s in bits 5 through 9, they will map into the same set.

Since the program alternates between references to each line, the line being referenced will never be in the cache, as it will have been evicted to make room for the other line. Therefore, all 200 memory references (100 to each line) will result in cache misses. The first 2 of these will be compulsory misses, and the other 198 will be conflict misses. Since the total amount of data referenced by the program is less than the capacity of the cache, no capacity misses will occur.

9.15   Multilevel Caches

In many systems, more than one level of the memory hierarchy is implemented as a cache, as shown in Fig. 9-12. When this is done, it is most common for the first-level cache (the one closest to the processor) to be implemented as separate instruction and data caches, while other levels are implemented as unified caches. This gives the processor the additional bandwidth provided by a Harvard architecture at the top level of the memory system, while simplifying the design of the lower levels. For a multilevel cache to significantly improve the average memory access time of a system, each level must have a significantly larger capacity than the level above it in the hierarchy, because the locality of reference seen by each level decreases as one gets deeper in the hierarchy. (Requests to recently referenced data are handled by the upper levels of the memory system, so requests that make it to the lower levels tend to be more widely distributed across the address space.) Caches with larger capacities tend to be slower, so the speed benefit of separate instruction and data caches is not as significant in lower levels of the memory hierarchy, another argument in favor of using unified caches for these levels.

In the early 1990s, the most common hierarchy for personal computers and desktop workstations was for the first-level (L1) cache to be relatively small and located on the same chip as the processor. Lower-level caches were implemented off-chip out of discrete SRAM chips. Capacities of 4 to 16 KB were not unusual in L1 caches, with L2 caches reaching 64 to 256 KB. As the number of transistors that

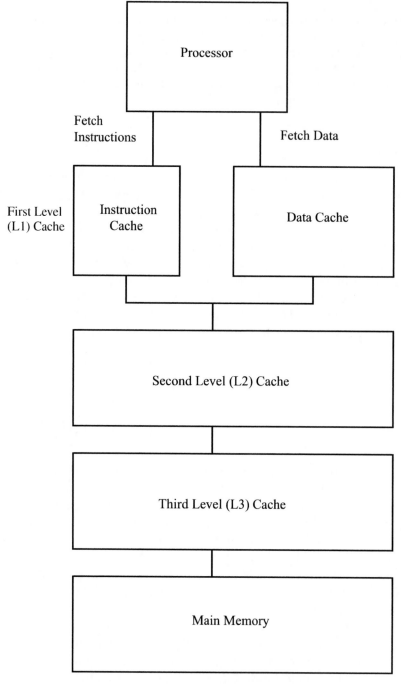

Fig. 9-12. Multilevel cache hierarchy.

can be fabricated on a chip has increased, additional levels of cache have been moved onto the processor chip. Many current systems have both their first-level and second-level caches on the same chip as the processor, or at least in the same package. Third-level caches are often implemented off-chip, can be multiple megabytes in size, and can be expected to be integrated onto the processor die in the next few years.

9.16 Summary

Cache memories are one of the most effective techniques that computer architects have for reducing average memory latency. By storing frequently accessed data in small, fast memories located physically close to the processor, the latency of most memory references can be greatly reduced.

The capacity of a cache is simply the amount of data that can be stored in the cache, while the line length describes the size of the units of data that the cache operates on. Long cache lines tend to increase the hit rate of the cache by fetching more data into the cache on each cache miss, but they can increase the total execution time of programs by increasing the amount of unneeded data that gets fetched.

The associativity of a cache determines how many legal locations there are for a given line of data in the cache. Direct-mapped caches allow each line to be mapped in exactly one place, which simplifies implementation of the cache and results in lower cache hit latencies but increases the miss rate caused by conflicts between lines that must be stored in the same location. Fully associative caches allow any line to be stored in any location in the cache, eliminating conflicts between lines but increasing the complexity of the cache hardware and the cache hit latency. Set-associative caches allow each line to be stored in a limited number of locations, providing hit rates and cache latencies between those of direct-mapped and fully associative caches.

Write-back caches store modified data in the cache, writing it out to the next level of the memory hierarchy only when the line is evicted, while write-through caches send each write to the next level of the hierarchy when it occurs. In general, write-back caches give higher performance, because most lines that are written at all are written multiple times before they are evicted from the cache. Write-through caches are somewhat simpler to design and are sometimes used when another device is allowed to access the next level of the memory hierarchy, because they keep the contents of the next level of the hierarchy consistent with the cache at all times.

Multiple levels of the memory hierarchy can be implemented as cache memories. These systems are known as multilevel caches and are very common in current workstations and PCs. Most current systems have at least two levels of cache memory, with three-level caches becoming increasingly common as fabrication technology advances.

 Solved Problems

Cache Size

9.1 Why does increasing the capacity of a cache tend to increase its hit rate?

Solution

Increasing the capacity of a cache allows more data to be stored in the cache. If a program references more data than the capacity of a cache, increasing the cache's capacity will increase the fraction of a program's data that can be kept in the cache. This will usually increase the bit rate of the cache. If a program references less data than the capacity of a cache, increasing the capacity of the cache generally does not affect the hit rate unless this change causes two or more lines that conflicted for space in the cache to not conflict, since the program does not need the extra space.

Associativity

9.2 Why does increasing the associativity of a cache generally increase its hit rate?

Solution

Increasing the associativity of a cache can increase its hit rate by reducing the number of conflict misses—misses that occur because more lines compete for a set in the cache than can fit in the set. Increasing the associativity increases the number of lines that can fit in the set and therefore can reduce the number of conflict misses.

Line Length

9.3 **a.** Why does increasing the line length of a cache often increase its hit rate?

b. Why does increasing the line length of a cache sometimes reduce the performance of the system containing the cache, even if the hit rate of the cache increases?

c. Why could increasing the length of a cache's lines decrease the hit rate?

Solution

a. Increasing the line length of a cache can increase the hit rate because of the property of locality of reference; addresses close to an address that has just been referenced are likely to be referenced in the near future. Increasing the line length increases the amount of data near the address that caused the miss that is brought into the cache on a cache miss. Since some or all of this data is likely to be accessed in the near future, bringing it into the cache eliminates the cache misses that would have occurred when the data was referenced.

b. Increasing a cache's line length often increases the hit rate by increasing the amount of data brought into the cache on a miss. However, the probability that a given address will be used soon after a memory reference to another address decreases as the distance between the addresses increases. This means that, as the cache line length increases, the chance that the additional data brought into the cache by the larger line length will be used goes down. At some point, the amount of time spent fetching data that is not used into the cache becomes greater than the time saved through increases in the hit rate, and overall performance goes down.

c. Assuming the cache size stays the same, increasing the length of each line decreases the number of lines that can be stored in the cache. This can increase the number of conflict misses, because there are fewer spaces for lines to be placed in the cache, so it is more likely that two lines will compete for the same space in the cache.

Alignment

9.4 For a cache with 128-byte cache lines, give the address of the first word in the line containing the following addresses:

a. 0xa23847ef
b. 0x7245e824
c. 0xeefabcd2

Solution

For 128-byte cache lines, the low 7 bits of the address indicate which byte within the line an address refers to. Since lines are aligned, the address of the first word in the line can be found by setting the bits of the address that determine the byte within the line to 0. Therefore, the addresses of the first bytes in the lines containing the above addresses are as follows:

a. 0xa2384780
b. 0x7245e800
c. 0xeefabc80

Lines versus Line Length

9.5 For a cache with a capacity of 32 KB, how many lines does the cache hold for line lengths of 32, 64, or 128 bytes?

Solution

The number of lines in a cache is simply the capacity divided by the line length, so the cache has 1024 lines with 32-byte lines, 512 lines with 64-byte lines, and 256 lines with 128-byte lines.

DRAM Technology and Line Load Time

9.6 Suppose a non-page-mode DRAM has a latency of 10 processor cycles per reference, and a competing page-mode DRAM has a latency of 10 cycles for the first reference to a row of the DRAM and 5 cycles for each subsequent reference. You are trying to decide which DRAM to use to implement the main memory of a system that has a cache with 64-byte cache lines.

a. If the main memory transfers one 4-byte word into the cache in response to each memory reference, how long does it take to fetch a cache line with each DRAM type? Assume lines always lie within a single row of the DRAM, but that each line fetched lies in a different row of the DRAM from the previous one.

b. Given your answer to **a**, how much data would a memory using non-page-mode DRAMs have to transfer into the cache in response to each request for the non-page-mode memory to have a cache line fetch time equal to or less than the line fetch time of the page-mode DRAM memory from part a? Your answer must involve an integer number of memory requests to fetch each cache line.

c. How do your answers to **a.** and **b.** change if the cache has 256-byte lines?

Solution

a. To fetch a 64-byte line, we need to make 16 memory requests with either type of DRAM. For the non-page-mode DRAM, each request takes 10 cycles, so fetching a line into the cache takes 160 cycles. For the page-mode DRAM, the first memory request takes 10 cycles, and the remaining 15 take 5 cycles, for a total of 85 cycles.

b. The page-mode DRAM takes 85 cycles to fetch a cache line, which is sufficient time for a non-page-mode DRAM to handle 8.5 requests, which rounds down to 8, because we can't do half a memory request. Given this, the non-page-mode DRAM would have to return 64 bytes/8 requests = 8 bytes (two words) per request to match the page-mode DRAM's line fetch time.

c. With 256-byte lines, 64 fetches are required to bring a line into the cache. Therefore, the non-page-mode DRAM will require 640 cycles to fetch a line, and the page-mode DRAM will require 325 cycles. 325 cycles is enough time to allow the non-page-mode DRAM to perform 32 fetches, so the non-page-mode DRAM would have to return 2 words of data per request to have the same line fetch time as the page-mode DRAM

Sets versus Associativity

9.7 If a cache has a capacity of 16 KB and a line length of 128 bytes, how many sets does the cache have if it is 2-way, 4-way, or 8-way set-associative?

Solution

With 128-byte lines, the cache contains a total of 128 lines. The number of sets in the cache is the number of lines divided by the associativity so the cache has 64 sets if it is 2-way set-associative, 32 sets if 4-way set-associative, and 16 sets if 8-way set-associative.

Tag Array Sizes

9.8 A cache has 64-KB capacity, 128-byte lines, and is 4-way set-associative. The system containing the cache uses 32-bit addresses.
    a. How many lines and sets does the cache have?
    b. How many entries are required in the tag array?
    c. How many bits of tag are required in each entry in the tag array?
    d. If the cache is write-through, how many bits are required for each entry in the tag array, and how much total storage is required for the tag array if an LRU replacement policy is used? What if the cache is write-back?

Solution

a. 64 KB/128 B = 512, so the cache has 512 lines. Since it is 4-way set-associative, the cache has 512/4 = 128 sets.

b. One tag array entry is required for each line, so the tag array needs 512 entries.

c. Since there are 128 sets, 7 bits of the address will be used to select a set out of the array. An additional 7 bits will be used to select a byte within each line, because lines are 128 bytes long. Therefore, 18 (32-14) bits of tag are required in each entry in the tag array.

d. Because the cache uses LRU replacement and is 4-way set-associative, 2 bits are required in each tag array entry to hold the age of the line. Write-through caches require a valid bit in each tag array entry but no dirty bit, bringing the size of each tag array entry to 21 bits (18 + 2 + 1). Since there are 512 lines in the cache, the size of the tag array is 10,752 bits. Write-back caches require a dirty bit in each tag array entry in addition to the bits required in a similar write-through cache, so each entry in the tag array would require 22 bits, for a total array size of 11,264 bits.

Addressing

9.9   For a cache with the same parameters as the one in Problem 9.8, give the number of the set that will be searched to determine if each of the following addresses are contained in the cache, and the byte within the cache line that each of these addresses references. Assume that the bits used to select a byte within the line are the lowest-order bits in the address, and that the bits used to select the set are the next-lowest-order bits.

a.   0xabc89987

b.   0x32651987

c.   0x228945db

d.   0x48569cac

Solution

In Problem 9.8, we determined that 7 bits were required to select a byte within the cache line, so the lowest 7 bits of the address will determine the byte of the reference. Seven bits are also required to select the set, which will be mapped to bits 7 through 13 of the address. Given this, the answers to this exercise are as follows:

a.   Byte within line = 0x7, set = 0x33 (51)

b.   The low 14 bits of this address are the same as the low 14 bits of the address for part a, so the byte within line and set will be the same (7 and 51).

c.   Byte within line = 0x5b (91), set = 0xb (11)

d.   Byte within line = 0x2c (44), set = 0x39 (57)

Cache Access Time

9.10   Suppose it takes 2.5 ns access the tag array of a set-associative cache, 4 ns to access the data array, 1 ns to perform the hit/miss comparison, and 1 ns to return the selected data to the processor in the case of a hit.

a.   Is the time to determine if a hit has occurred or the data array access the critical path in a cache hit?

b.   What is the cache hit latency of the system?

c.   What would the cache hit latency of the system be if both the tag and data array access time were 3 ns?

Solution

a.   Determining if a hit has occurred requires accessing the tag array, which takes 2.5 ns, and then doing the hit/miss comparison, which takes 1 ns. Therefore, it takes 3.5 ns to determine if a hit has occurred. This is less than the 4 ns to access the data array, so the data array is the critical path.

b.   Since the data array is the critical path, the cache hit latency is equal to the data array access time plus the time to return the selected data to the processor, or 5 ns.

c.   In this case, the hit/miss computation is the critical path during a cache hit, so the cache hit latency is equal to the tag array access time plus the hit/miss comparison time plus the time to return the data to the processor, or 5 ns. Note that some direct-mapped caches overlap the return of data to the processor with the hit/miss computation, since there is only one possible word of data to be returned on a cache hit. In this case, the hit latency would be 4 ns, since we could do the hit/miss comparison and the data return simultaneously.

Hit Rate versus Access Time

9.11 Suppose a given cache has an access time (cache hit latency) of 10 ns and a miss rate of 5 percent. A given change to the cache will decrease the miss rate to 3 percent, but it will increase the cache hit latency to 15 ns. Under what conditions does this change result in greater performance (lower average memory access time)?

Solution

Average memory access time $= (T_{hit} \times P_{hit}) + T_{miss} \times P_{miss})$. For this change to reduce access time, we need $(15 \text{ ns} \times 0.97) + (T_{miss} \times 0.03) < (10 \text{ ns} \times 0.95) + (T_{miss} \times 0.05)$. Solving this gives $T_{miss} > 252.5$ ns. As long as the cache miss time is greater than this value, the reduction in cache miss frequency will be more significant than the increase in cache hit time.

Intuitively, this makes sense — as the cache miss time becomes larger, we become more willing to increase the cache hit time in order to reduce the cache miss rate, because each cache miss becomes more and more expensive.

Hit Rate versus Line Fetch Time

9.12 A cache has a hit rate of 95 percent, 128-byte lines, and a cache hit latency of 5 ns. The main memory takes 100 ns to return the first word (32 bits) of a line, and 10 ns to return each subsequent word.

   a. What is T_{miss} for this cache? (Assume that the cache waits until the line has been fetched into the cache and then reexecutes the memory operation, resulting in a cache hit. Neglect the time required to write the line into the cache once it has been fetched from the main memory. Also assume that the cache takes the same amount of time to detect that a miss has occurred as to handle a cache hit.)

   b. If doubling the cache line length reduces the miss rate to 3 percent, does it reduce the average memory access time?

Solution

   a. The cache has 128-byte lines, which is 32 words. Using the specified memory timings, the cache spends 5 ns detecting that a miss has occurred, and 100 ns + 31(10 ns) = 410 ns fetching a line from the main memory into the cache. The cache then reexecutes the operation that caused the miss, taking 5 ns. This gives a cache miss time of 420 ns.

   b. For the base cache, the average memory access time is $(0.95 \times 5 \text{ ns}) + (0.05 \times 420 \text{ ns}) = 25.75$ ns. If we double the cache line length, cache lines become 64 words long and take 730 ns to fetch from memory, so the cache miss latency becomes 740 ns. Average memory access time becomes $(0.97 \times 5 \text{ ns}) + (0.03 \times 740 \text{ ns}) = 27.1$ ns, so the average memory access time increases if we make this change.

Compulsory, Capacity, and Conflict Misses

9.13   A program executes 1,000,000 memory references. When run on a system containing a particular cache, the cache has a miss rate of 7 percent, of which 1/4 are compulsory misses, 1/4 are capacity misses, and 1/2 are conflict misses.

    a.   If the only change you're allowed to make to the cache is to increase the associativity, what is the maximum number of misses that you can hope to eliminate?

    b.   If you're allowed to both increase the cache size and increase the associativity, what is the maximum number of misses that you can hope to eliminate?

Solution

    a.   Increasing the associativity will reduce the number of conflict misses (misses that occur because cache lines compete for a limited number of spaces in the cache) but will not affect the number of compulsory misses (misses that occur the first time a line is accessed) or the number of capacity misses (misses that occur because a program references more data than will fit in the cache). Therefore, the best we can hope to do by increasing the associativity is to eliminate all of the conflict misses. Since the miss rate is 7 percent and the program makes 1,000,000 memory references, the total number of misses is 70,000. Half of those are conflict misses, so the maximum number of misses that you can eliminate by increasing the associativity of the cache is 35,000.

    b.   Increasing both the size and the associativity of the cache will eliminate both capacity and conflict misses. Together, these compose 3/4 of the total misses, so the maximum number of misses that can be eliminated is 52,500.

Write-Back versus Write-Through Caches

9.14   A given cache has 4-word cache lines, and the next level down in the memory hierarchy is implemented out of page-mode DRAMs with a latency to first word of 100 ns, and a latency of 10 ns for each additional sequential word accessed. Assume that 25 percent of all cache lines are dirty when they are evicted from the cache, and that the average dirty line was written to 5 times before it is evicted.

    a.   What is the average time to fetch a line into the cache if it is write-through? Write-back?

    b.   Would a write-back or write-through cache spend more time writing data to the next level of the memory?

    c.   How many times would the average cache line that is stored to have to be written before your answer to **b.** would change?

Solution

    a.   For a write-through cache, the time to fetch a line is $100\,\text{ns} + 3 \times 10\,\text{ns} = 130\,\text{ns}$. For the write-back cache, we have to account for the times that data has to be written back before a line can be loaded, so the average fetch time is $130\,\text{ns} + 0.25 \times (130\,\text{ns}) = 162.5\,\text{ns}$.

    b.   Both caches sustain the same number of writes. In the write-through cache, each write takes 100 ns to resolve (one-word access to the next level of the memory system). Since each line that is written sustains an average of 5 writes, the average line that is written will require 500 ns to write data into the next level. In the write-back cache, it takes

130 ns to write back each line that is written, regardless of the number of times it is written, so the write-back cache will spend less time writing data.

c. Regardless of the number of writes to a line, the write-back cache spends 130 ns writing it back, which is enough time for 1.3 single-word accesses to memory. Therefore, if the average number of writes per line that is written is less than 1.3, the write-through cache will spend less time writing data to the next level of the memory

Unified versus Harvard Caches

9.15   A system initially has separate instruction and data caches, each of which have capacities of 16 KB. These caches are replaced with a unified cache that has a total capacity of 48 KB, 50 percent more than the total capacity of the two caches, but a given program sustains more total cache misses (counting both instruction and data references) after the change than before.

a. If the program takes up 10 KB of memory and references 64 KB of data, what is the most likely explanation for the increase in misses?

b. Suppose the program takes up 10 KB of memory and references 15 KB of data. What would the most likely explanation for the increase in cache misses be?

Solution

a. With separate instruction and data caches, the instruction cache would be expected to sustain very few misses other than the compulsory misses to fetch the program into the cache, since the program is significantly smaller than the cache capacity (this assumes few conflict misses). However, the program references much more data than fits in the data cache, so it would be expected that the data cache would have a significant number of cache misses.

When the separate caches are replaced with a unified cache, the sum of the space taken up by the program's instructions and data is greater than the capacity of the cache. Now, not only does the program's data compete with itself for space in the cache, it also competes with the instructions. Thus, the program will start to see cache misses when referencing instructions as well as when referencing data, so the miss rate might go up.

b. In this case, the program's instructions and data both fit within their respective caches, and the sum of the space taken up by instructions and data is less than the capacity of the unified cache. Given this, the most likely explanation is that the program's instructions and data are located in memory such that they compete for the same lines in the unified cache, causing conflict misses.

Data Alignment

9.16   Consider the following program:

```
main(){
  int a[128], b[128],c[128], i;
  for (i=0;  i<128;i++){
   a[i]=b[i]+c[i];
  }
}
```

Suppose the program is running on a system with a 32-KB data cache and a 16-KB instruction cache. Each cache is direct-mapped and has 128-byte cache lines, and integers are 32-bit (4-byte) quantities on the machine in question.

a. Does the system's choice of where to place the instructions of the program in memory affect the hit rate of either cache? (Assume the program is the only one running on the machine, and neglect the operating system.)

b. Is it possible to place the arrays a, b, and c in memory such that there are no conflict or capacity misses in the data cache (ignore the single integer i in this and following questions)? If so, what are the constraints on how the three arrays are placed in memory that allow the elimination of conflict and capacity misses?

c. Suppose the associativity of the data cache were increased. What is the highest associativity that we can have in the data cache and still have conflict misses?

d. Suppose the separate instruction and data caches were replaced with a single, unified cache with a 48-KB capacity. How would your answers to parts **a.** and **c.** change?

Solution

a. Since the instruction and data caches are separate, the choice of where the program is placed in memory does not in general affect the hit rate of the caches. If we take the operating system into account (which this question did not require), then the placement of the program in memory can affect the cache hit rate by causing conflicts between the program code and the operating system code.

b. Each of the three arrays takes up 512 bytes of storage (128 integers $\times$ 4 bytes/integer), for a total of 1.5 KB of storage. This is much less than the capacity of the data cache, so it is possible to place the arrays in memory so that there are no capacity or conflict misses.

To eliminate conflicts, we need to make sure that each of the three arrays maps to a different group of sets in the cache. A 32-kilobyte direct-mapped cache with 128-byte lines has 256 lines and 256 sets. It will use bits 0 through 6 of each address to select the word being referenced within the line, and bits 7 through 14 to select a set within the cache to place each line in. To eliminate conflict misses, we need to make sure that the lines that make up each array map to different sets in the cache, meaning that they have different values in bits 7 through 14 of their addresses.

c. The easiest way to approach this is to think about what the worst-possible placement of the arrays in memory would be (i.e., the one that would cause the most conflict misses). In this case, that would be a placement that caused all three arrays to map onto the same sets in the cache. This would cause conflict misses in a cache that did not have three-way or greater associativity. Therefore, the highest cache associativity that could possibly have conflict misses from this program would be two-way set-associative (assuming that each array is laid out in a contiguous block of memory).

Note that, as the associativity of the cache becomes very high, different lines within each array start to map onto the same sets. However, in this case, the associativity is high enough that all of the potentially conflicting lines can reside in the same set without conflicts.

d. If the data and instruction caches are replaced with a unified cache, then it becomes possible for the program's code and data to conflict in the cache. In this case, the placement of the program in memory can affect the hit rate of the cache, so the answer to **a.** changes. Also, we now have four data objects that can possibly conflict, so it becomes possible to have conflict misses in a cache that is three-way or lower set-associative. (This assumes that the program is not so large that parts of the program can conflict with each other in the cache. For a short program like the one in this problem, this is a reasonable assumption.)

CHAPTER 10

Virtual Memory

10.1   Objectives

Virtual memory is a technique that is used to both allow magnetic storage, such as hard disks, to serve as a level in the memory system and to provide protection between programs running on the same system, so that one program cannot modify another's data.

After completing this chapter, you should

1. Understand virtual memory, virtual addresses, and physical addresses
2. Be able to solve problems involving virtual memory and address translation
3. Understand translation lookaside buffers (TLBs), and be able to solve problems relating to them
4. Understand and be able to reason about the way in which virtual memory provides protection in modern computer systems

10.2   Introduction

The cost of memory was a significant limitation in early computer systems. Before the development of semiconductor DRAMs, the most prevalent memory technology was *core memory*, in which a doughnut-shaped ring of magnetic material was used to store each bit of data. The expense of producing these magnetic rings and the cost involved in assembling them into memory devices led to limited memory capacities on many machines, often less than that required by programs.

To address this problem, virtual memory was developed. In a virtual memory system, hard disks or other magnetic media form the bottom layer of the memory hierarchy, with DRAMs or core memory forming the main memory level of the hierarchy. Programs cannot directly access data stored on the magnetic media. Instead, the address space of a program is divided into *pages*, contiguous blocks of data that are stored on the magnetic media. In modern systems, pages are typically 2 to 8 KB in size, although some systems provide support for pages of multiple sizes. When a page of data is referenced, the system copies it into the main memory, allowing it to be accessed. This may require that another page of data be copied from the main memory to the magnetic media in order to make room for the incoming page.

Figure 10-1 illustrates many of the key concepts in virtual memory. Each program has its own *virtual address space*, which is the set of addresses that programs use for load and store operations. The *physical address space* is the set of addresses used to reference locations in the main memory, and the terms *virtual address* and *physical address* are used to describe addresses in the virtual and physical address spaces. The virtual address space is divided into pages, some of which have been copied into *page frames* (slots in the main memory where a page of data can be stored) because they have been referenced recently, and some of which are resident only on the disk. Pages are always aligned on a multiple of the page length, so they never overlap. The terms *virtual page* and *physical page* are used to describe a page of data in the virtual and physical address spaces, respectively. Pages that have been loaded into the main memory from disk are said to have been *mapped* into the main memory.

Virtual memory allows a computer to act as if its main memory were much larger than it actually is. When a program references a virtual address, it cannot tell, except by timing the latency of the operation, whether the virtual address was resident in the main memory of the computer or whether it had to be fetched from the magnetic media. Thus, the computer can shuffle pages into and out of the main memory as needed, similar to the way that cache lines are brought into and out of the cache as required, allowing programs to reference more data than can be stored in the main memory at any one time.

10.3   Address Translation

Programs running on a system with virtual memory use virtual addresses as the arguments to load and store instructions, but the main memory uses physical addresses to record the locations where data is actually stored. Whenever a program performs a memory reference, the virtual address it uses must be converted into the equivalent physical address, a process known as *address translation*. Figure 10-2 shows a flowchart of address translation.

When a user program executes an instruction that references memory, the operating system accesses the *page table*, a data structure in memory that holds the mapping of virtual to physical addresses, to determine whether or not the virtual page containing the address referenced by the operation is currently mapped onto a physical page. If so, the operating system determines the physical address that corresponds to the virtual address from the page table, and the operation proceeds, using the physical address to access the main memory. If the virtual page containing the referenced address is not currently mapped onto a physical page, a *page fault* occurs, and the operating system fetches the page containing the requested data from memory, loading it into a page frame and updating the page table with the new

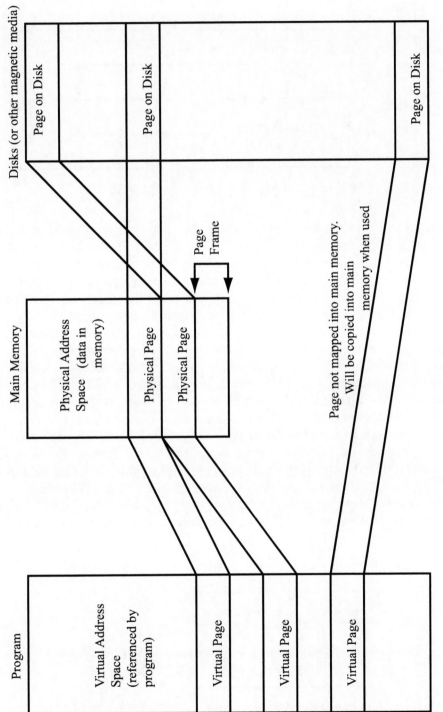

Fig. 10-1.   Virtual memory.

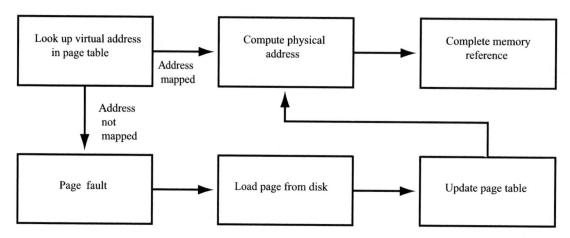

Fig. 10-2. Address translation.

translation. Once the page has been read into the main memory from disk and the page table updated, the physical address of the page can be determined and the memory reference completed. If all of the page frames in the system already contain data, one of them must be evicted to the magnetic media to make room for the incoming page. The replacement policies used to select the page that is evicted are similar to the ones discussed in the previous chapter for set-associative caches.

Because both virtual and physical pages are always aligned on a multiple of their size, the page table does not need to keep track of the full virtual or physical address of a page that is mapped in the main memory. Instead, virtual addresses are divided into a virtual page identifier called the *virtual page number*, or VPN, and a set of bits that describes the offset from the start of the virtual page to the virtual address. Physical pages are similarly divided into a *physical page number* (PPN) and an offset from the start of the physical page to the physical address, as shown in Fig. 10-3. The virtual and physical pages in a given system are generally the same size, so the number of bits ($\log_2$ of the page size) required to hold the offset field of the virtual and physical addresses are the same, although the VPN and PPN may well be different lengths. Many systems, particularly 64-bit systems, have longer virtual addresses than physical addresses, given the current impracticality of building a system with 2^{64} bytes of DRAM memory.

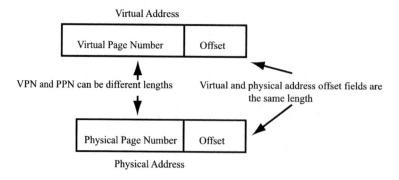

Fig. 10-3. Virtual and physical addresses.

When a virtual address is translated, the operating system looks up the entry corresponding to the VPN in the page table and returns the corresponding PPN. The offset bits of the virtual address are then concatenated onto the PPN to generate the physical address, as shown in Fig. 10-4.

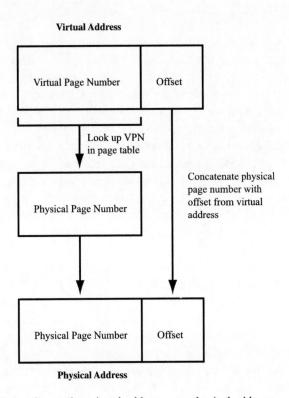

Fig. 10-4.   Converting virtual addresses to physical addresses.

EXAMPLE
In a system with 64-bit virtual addresses and 43-bit physical addresses (similar to some of the first 64-bit processors), how many bits are required for the VPN and PPN if pages are 8 KB in size?

Solution

$\log_2(8\,\text{KB}) = 13$, so 13 bits are required for the offset field of both the virtual and physical address. Therefore, 51 ($64 - 13$) bits are required for the virtual page number, and 30 bits are required for the physical page number.

10.4   Demand Paging versus Swapping

The virtual memory system described above is an example of *demand paging*, the type of virtual memory most commonly used today. In demand paging, pages of data are only brought into the main memory when a program accesses them. When a context switch occurs, the operating system does not copy any of the old program's pages out to the disk or any of the new program's pages into the main memory. Instead, it just begins executing the new program and fetches that program's pages as they are referenced.

Swapping is a related technique that uses magnetic media to store the state of programs that are not currently running on the processor. In a system that uses swapping, the operating system treats all of a program's data as an atomic unit and moves all of the data into or out of the main memory at one time. When the operating system on a computer that uses swapping selects a program to run on the processor, it loads all of the program's data into the main memory, evicting other programs from the main memory if necessary.

If all of the programs being executed on a computer fit into the main memory (counting both their instructions and data), both demand paging and swapping allow the computer to operate in a multiprogrammed mode without having to fetch data from disk. Swapping systems have the advantage that, once a program has been fetched from disk, all of the program's data is mapped in the main memory. This makes the execution time of the program more predictable, since page faults never occur during a program's use of the CPU.

Demand-paging systems have the advantage that they only fetch the pages of data that a program actually uses from the disk. If a program only needs to reference a fraction of its data during each timeslice of execution, this can significantly reduce the amount of time spent copying data to and from the disk. Also, systems that use swapping typically cannot use their magnetic storage to allow a single program to reference more data than fits in the main memory, because all of a program's data must be swapped into or out of the main memory as a unit. In a demand-paging system, individual pages of a program's data can be brought into the memory as needed, making the limit on the maximum amount of data a program can reference the amount of space available on the disk, not the amount of main memory. For most applications, the advantages of demand paging outweigh the disadvantages, making demand paging the choice for most current workstation/PC operating systems.

10.5   Page Tables

As discussed earlier in the chapter, the operating system uses a data structure known as the *page table* to keep track of how virtual addresses map to physical addresses. Because each program has its own virtual-physical address mapping, separate page tables are required for each program on the system. The simplest page table implementation is just an array of page table entries, one entry per virtual page, and is known as a single-level page table to distinguish it from the multilevel page tables that we will describe later. To perform an address translation, the operating system uses the virtual page number of the address as an index into the array of page table entries to locate the physical page number corresponding to the virtual page. This is shown in Fig. 10-5, which shows a page table for a system whose virtual address space is only eight pages long.

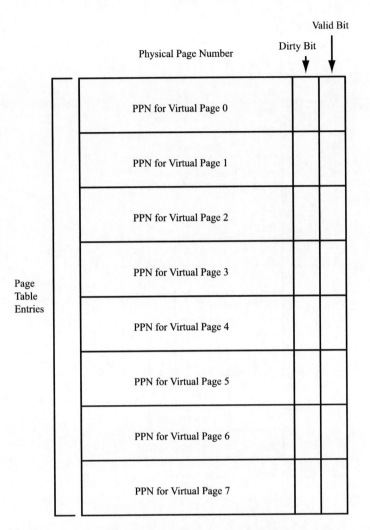

Fig. 10-5.   Single-level page table.

As illustrated in Fig. 10-5, page table entries generally contain a physical page number, a *valid bit*, and a *dirty bit*. The valid bit encodes whether the virtual page corresponding to the entry is currently mapped into physical memory. If the valid bit is set, then the physical page number field contains the physical page number of the page frame that contains the virtual page's data. The dirty bit records whether or not the page has been written since it was brought into the main memory. This is used to determine whether the contents of the page must be written back to the disk when the page is evicted from main memory, similar to the dirty bit in a write-back cache. (Because of the time required to access the magnetic media, all virtual memory systems are write-back instead of write-through.)

Figure 10-6 diagrams the use of a page table to translate a virtual address. Systems with single-level page tables generally require that the entire page table be kept in physical memory at all times, so that the operating system can access the table for address translations.

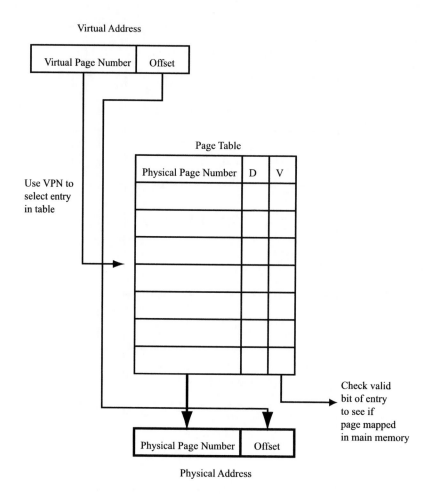

Fig. 10-6.   Address translation using a page table.

10.5.1 MULTILEVEL PAGE TABLES

Page tables can require a great deal of storage. For example, a single-level page table for a system with a 32-bit address space (both virtual and physical) and 4-KB pages would require 2^{20} entries. If each entry required 3 bytes of storage, the total storage required for the page table would be 3 MB. On a system with 64 MB of main memory, this would require that almost 5 percent of the main memory be dedicated to the page table, a sizable overhead. On systems with less memory, the overhead would be even higher, and it would not be possible to implement virtual memory at all on a system with less than 3 MB of storage.

To address this problem, designers use *multilevel page tables*, which allow much of the page table to be stored in virtual memory and kept on disk when not in use. In a multilevel page table, the page table itself is broken into pages and arranged into a hierarchy. Entries in the bottom level of the hierarchy are similar to entries in a single-level page table, containing the PPN of the appropriate page along with valid and dirty bits. Entries in the other levels of the page table identify the page in memory that contains the next level of the hierarchy for the address being translated.

Using this system, only the page containing the top level of the page table needs to be kept in memory at all times. Other pages in the page table can be copied to and from the hard disk as needed.[1]

To perform an address translation, the VPN of an address is divided into groups of bits, where each group contains a number of bits equal to the base-2 logarithm of the number of page table entries in a page of data, as shown in Fig. 10-7. If the number of bits in the VPN does not divide evenly by the base-2 logarithm of the number of page table entries in a page of data, it is necessary to round the number of groups up to the next integer.

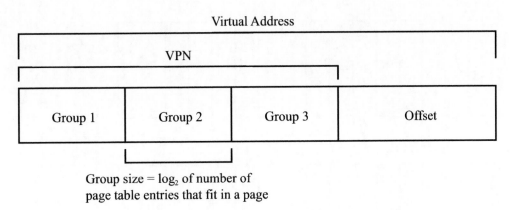

Group size = $\log_2$ of number of
page table entries that fit in a page

Fig. 10-7.   Address division for multilevel page tables.

The highest-order group of bits is then used to select an entry in the top-level page of the page table. (If one group of bits contains fewer bits than the others, it is best to use this group to index the first level of the page table, as this results in less wasted memory than using the odd-sized group of bits to index a lower level in the page table.) This entry contains the address of the page of data containing the next set of entries to be searched. The next-lower-order group is then used to index into the page pointed to by the entry in the top level of the page table, and the process is repeated until the lowest level of the page table, which contains the PPN for the desired page, is found. Figure 10-8 shows this process on a system with 6-bit VPNs and four entries in each page. If any of the pages in the page table that are required during the address translation are not mapped in the main memory, the system simply fetches them from disk and continues with the translation.

EXAMPLE
On a system with 32-bit addresses and 4-KB pages, how many levels are required in a multilevel page table? Assume that each entry in the page table takes 4 bytes of storage.

---

[1] This is something of an oversimplification, because the system must be able to determine the physical address of each page in the page table in order to access the page table. Some systems handle this by requiring that address translation information for the pages that make up the page table always be kept in the main memory.

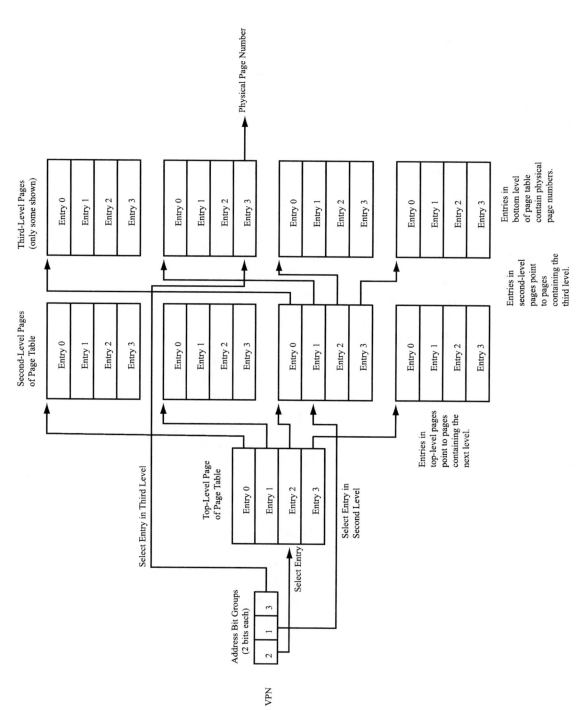

Fig. 10-8.   Address translation with multilevel page table.

Solution

With 4-KB pages and 4-byte page table entries, each page can contain 2^{10} entries, so each group of bits in the VPN is 10 bits long. The offset field for 4-KB pages is 12 bits, so the VPN required for this system is 20 bits long. Therefore, there are 2 groups of bits in each VPN, and 2 levels in the page table.

10.5.2 INVERTED PAGE TABLES

Even with multilevel page tables, the amount of storage required to hold page tables that can map the entire address space of a modern processor is enormous. For example, on a system with 64-bit addresses and 4-KB pages, 2^{52} page table entries are required. If each entry requires 7 bytes of storage to hold a 52-bit PPN, the valid bit, and the dirty bit, 7×2^{52} bytes of storage (about 30,000,000 GB) would be required to hold the page table for a single program. Given that hard disks only hold about 75 GB of data at the time this book is being written, it is clearly impractical to implement such a page table, even if its organization allows much of it not to be mapped onto the main memory at a given time.

The root cause of the problem is that the amount of storage required for the page table grows with the size of the virtual address space, not the amount of storage on the system. *Inverted page tables* are a technique that greatly reduces the amount of storage required for page tables in systems with large address spaces. A thorough discussion of inverted page tables is beyond the scope of this book, but the basic idea is that an inverted page table consists of a set of entries, one for each physical page frame in the system. Each entry in the inverted page table contains the VPN of the virtual page mapped into that page frame. Thus, the amount of storage required for the page table depends on the amount of main memory in the system, not the size of the virtual address space. Because inverted page table entries are organized by physical address, not virtual address, they are harder to search than conventional page tables, since the virtual address cannot be used to determine the appropriate entry in the page table. Typically, data structures such as hash tables are used to reduce the time to search the inverted page table.

Another approach to this problem is to allow the page table to map a subset of the virtual address space instead of the entire address space. In systems that use this approach, the page table contains an additional field that indicates the range of addresses mapped by the page table. This approach requires page table entries for the entire range of virtual addresses between the lowest and highest addresses used by the program, so its efficiency depends on whether a program allocates data densely or sparsely.

10.6 Translation Lookaside Buffers

A major disadvantage of using page tables for address translation is that the page table must be accessed on each memory reference. On a system with a single-level page table, this doubles the number of memory accesses required, since each load or store operation requires one memory reference to access the appropriate page table entry and one to perform the actual load or store. This greatly increases the latency of a memory reference, and the problem is even greater on systems that have multilevel page tables, because multiple memory references are required to traverse the page table.

To reduce this penalty, processors that are intended to use virtual memory incorporate *translation lookaside buffers* (TLBs) that act as caches for the page table. Whenever a program performs a memory reference, the virtual address is sent to the TLB to determine if it contains a translation for the address. If so, the TLB returns the physical address of the data, and the memory reference continues. If not, a *TLB miss* occurs, and the system searches the page table for a translation. Some systems provide hardware to perform the page table access on a TLB miss, while others require the operating system to access the page table in software. Figure 10-9 shows the address translation process in a system containing a TLB.

10.6.1 TLB MISSES VERSUS PAGE FAULTS

In a system that contains a TLB, there are three possible scenarios for handling a memory reference:

1. *Hit in the TLB*—In this case, the TLB contains a translation for the virtual address and the physical address of the reference can be used to complete the memory reference in hardware without software involvement. When a page is evicted from the main memory, translations for the page are evicted from the TLB as well, so a TLB hit means that the physical page containing the address is mapped in memory.

2. *TLB miss, but the page is mapped*—In this case, the system accesses the page table to find the translation for the virtual address, copies that translation into the TLB, and the memory reference proceeds.

3. *TLB miss, and the page is not mapped*—In this case, the system accesses the page table, determines that the address is not mapped, and a page fault occurs. The operating system then loads the page's data from the disk in the same manner as a virtual memory system that does not contain a TLB.

TLB misses and page faults are handled very differently by the operating system because of the difference in the amount of time it takes to resolve each event. TLB misses generally take a relatively short time to resolve, because the system just has to access the page table. Assuming no page faults occur while accessing the page table, TLB misses can usually be resolved in a few hundred cycles, so the user program just waits until the TLB miss has been resolved.

Page faults, on the other hand, require accessing the disk to fetch the page. Accessing a hard disk typically takes several milliseconds, an amount of time that is comparable to the amount of time that the operating system lets a program run before giving another program access to the processor. (Many operating systems switch programs 60–100 times per second, allowing each program to execute for 16.7 to 10 ms between context switches.) Given how long it takes to handle a page

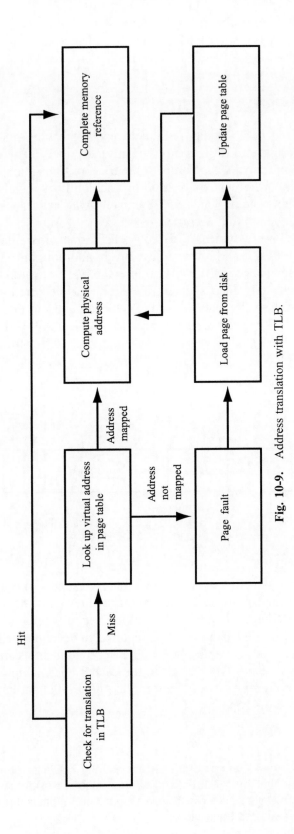

Fig. 10-9. Address translation with TLB.

fault, it is not uncommon for the operating system to do a context switch when a page fault occurs, giving some other program a chance to execute while the page fault is being resolved.

10.6.2 TLB ORGANIZATION

TLBs are organized in a similar fashion to caches, having an associativity and number of sets. While cache sizes are typically described in bytes, TLB sizes are usually described in terms of the number of entries, or translations, contained in the TLB, since the amount of space taken up by each entry is mostly irrelevant to the performance of the system. Thus, a 128-entry, 4-way set-associative TLB would have 32 sets, each containing 4 entries.

Figure 10-10 shows a typical TLB entry. Its format is similar to a page table entry, containing a PPN, valid bit, and dirty bit. In addition, the TLB entry contains the VPN of the page that it is a translation for, which is compared to the VPN of the address of a memory reference to determine if a hit has occurred. Like a cache's tag array entry, bits of the VPN that are used to select an entry in the TLB are typically omitted from the VPN stored in the entry to save space. All of the bits of the PPN must be stored in the TLB, however, because they may differ from the corresponding bits in the VPN.

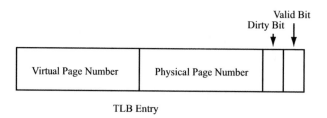

TLB Entry

Fig. 10-10.   TLB entry.

TLBs are typically much smaller than a system's cache(s), because each entry in a TLB refers to much more data than a cache line, allowing a relatively small number of TLB entries to describe the working set of a program. TLBs typically contain many more entries than would be required to describe the data contained in the cache, because it is desirable for the TLB to contain translations for data that resides in the main memory as well as in the cache. For example, TLBs with 128 entries were common in processors built in the mid-1990s that had 32 to 64 KB of first-level cache and 4 KB pages.

EXAMPLE
Suppose a TLB has a hit rate of 95 percent and the TLB miss penalty is 150 cycles. Assume that, on a TLB hit, address translation takes zero time. (Section 10.8 will explain why this is a reasonable assumption.) What is the average time required for an address translation?

Solution

As with caches, the average time for an address translation is $T_{hit} \times P_{hit} + T_{miss} \times P_{miss}$. Plugging in the probabilities and delay numbers, we get an average address translation time of 7.5 cycles, a reduction of 20x over the translation time without the TLB.

10.6.3 SUPERPAGES (PAGE BLOCKS)

One problem with TLBs is that the amount of data referenced by programs is growing quickly over time, but the size of pages is growing fairly slowly. This is because of the trade-off between the number of page table and TLB entries required, which decreases as page size increases, and the amount of memory wasted because fractions of a page cannot be assigned to a program, which increases as the page size increases. Because of this trend, the number of pages of data referenced by a program is growing over time, meaning that a TLB of a given size is able to contain translations for less and less of the data referenced by a program, reducing the TLB hit rate. For example, a processor with 128 TLB entries and 4-KB pages can cache translations for 512 KB of data in the TLB. If the system containing the processor has 128 MB of main memory, the translations in the TLB cover less than 0.5 percent of the main memory.

To address this problem, some processors now provide the ability to map larger blocks of data, called *superpages* or *page blocks*, in each TLB entry. Some systems allow each TLB entry to contain the translation for a variable-sized block of data, while others provide two sizes—one equal to the page size and one much larger, often more than a megabyte in size. When an application references large blocks of contiguous data, these improvements can greatly increase the TLB hit rate.

10.7   Protection

In addition to allowing systems to treat magnetic media as a level of the memory hierarchy, virtual memory is also very useful on multiprogrammed computer systems because it provides memory protection, preventing one program from accessing the data of another. Figure 10-11 illustrates how this works. Each program has its own virtual address space, but the physical address space is shared between all of the programs running on the system. The address translation system ensures that the virtual pages used by each program map onto different physical pages and different locations on the magnetic media.

This has two benefits. First, it prevents programs from accessing each other's data, because any virtual address that a program references will be translated into a physical address belonging to it. There is no way for a program to create a virtual address that maps onto a physical address belonging to another program, and thus no way for a program to access another program's data. If programs want to share

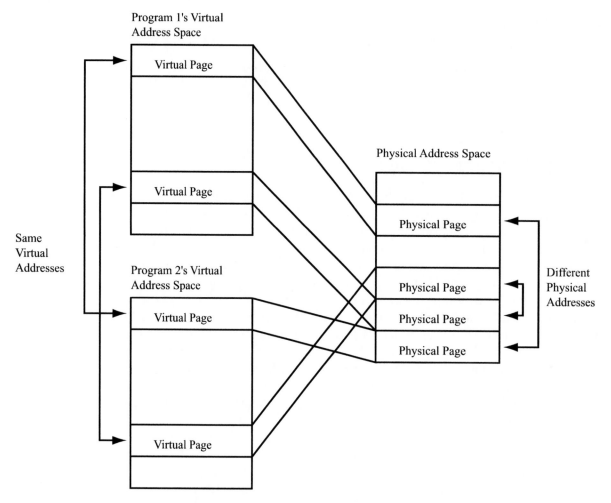

Fig. 10-11.   Protection through virtual memory.

data with each other, most operating systems allow them to specifically request that some of their virtual pages be mapped onto the same physical addresses.

The second benefit is that a program can create and use addresses in its own virtual address space without interference from other programs. Thus, programs don't have to know how many other programs are running on the system and/or how much memory those other programs use. Each program has its own virtual address space and can do address computations and memory operations in that address space, without worrying about any other programs that might be running on the machine.

The disadvantage of this approach is that the virtual-physical address mapping becomes part of the state of a program. When the system switches from executing one program to executing another, it needs to change the page table that it uses, and to invalidate any address translations in the TLB. Otherwise, the new program would use the old program's virtual-physical address mapping, and be able to access the old program's data. This increases the overhead of a context switch, because of the time required to invalidate the TLB and change the page table, and because the new program will take a large number of TLB misses as it starts executing with an empty TLB.

Some systems address this issue by adding process ID bits to each entry in the TLB that identify the program that the entry applies to. The hardware compares the process ID of the program making a memory reference to the process ID in the translation as part of determining whether a TLB hit has occurred, allowing translations from multiple programs to reside in the TLB at the same time. This eliminates the need to invalidate the TLB on each context switch but increases the amount of storage required for the TLB.

In modern systems, virtual memory is much more often a tool to support multiprogramming than a tool to allow programs to use more memory than is provided in the system's main memory. The cost of DRAM is low enough, and the time to resolve a page fault high enough, that most systems are configured with enough main memory that individual programs rarely, if ever, need to access the magnetic media level of the memory hierarchy. However, having virtual memory to provide protection between programs, and to allow automatic swapping of each program's data between the main memory and disk on a context switch, is extremely valuable, which explains why virtually all modern operating systems and hardware support virtual memory.

10.8   Caches and Virtual Memory

Many systems that use virtual memory also incorporate caches as the top level or levels of their memory hierarchy. In these systems, cache implementations vary in whether they use virtual addresses or physical addresses to select a set that might contain the address being referenced by an instruction and whether they use virtual or physical addresses to determine if a hit has occurred[2]. There are four possible combinations:

- *Virtually addressed, virtually tagged*—These caches use virtual addresses to both select a set and to determine if a hit has occurred. They have the advantage that it is only necessary to do an address translation if a cache miss occurs, but the disadvantage that all the data in the cache must be invalidated when a context switch occurs, to prevent the new program from accessing the old program's data. Adding process ID bits to each tag in the cache can eliminate this problem at the cost of increasing the amount of storage required for the tag array.

- *Physically addressed, physically tagged*—Caches that use physical addresses to select sets and to determine if a hit has occurred have no problems with virtual address aliasing between programs and can take advantage of the fact

---

[2] Since fully-associative caches only have one set, they don't use either the virtual or the physical address of a memory reference to select a set. Designers of fully associative caches do have to decide whether to use virtual or physical addresses to determine if a hit has occurred, and the arguments presented in this section apply to that decision.

that physical addresses are shorter than virtual addresses on many systems to reduce the size of their tag arrays. However, it is necessary to perform address translation before the cache is accessed, which increases the cache hit time.

- *Physically addressed, virtually tagged*—These systems combine the worst aspects of virtual and physical addressing and are pretty much never used. Using the physical address to select a set within the cache means that the cache access needs to wait for address translation to complete before it can begin, while the virtual tag means that the cache doesn't provide protection against the use of the same virtual address by multiple programs.

- *Virtually addressed, physically tagged*—Using virtual addresses to select a set within the cache and physical addresses to determine if a hit has occurred allows the cache lookup to begin in parallel with address translation but provides protection, unlike virtually addressed/virtually tagged systems. As long as address translation takes less time than accessing the tag array, this type of cache can be as fast as a virtually addressed/virtually tagged cache, since the physical address isn't needed for hit/miss determination until after the tag array lookup completes. TLBs tend to contain less data than a tag array, so address translation is generally faster than accessing the tag array unless a TLB miss occurs. This combination of speed and protection makes virtually addressed/virtually tagged caches the choice for most current systems. Figure 10-12 shows a diagram of cache accesses in this type of cache.

In systems with more than one level of cache memory, only the level 1 cache is typically implemented as virtually addressed/physically tagged, because each level

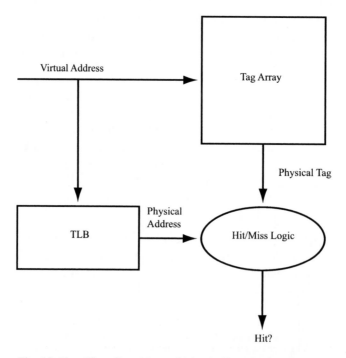

Fig. 10-12.   Virtually addressed/physically tagged cache access.

in the cache is accessed in sequence. Lower-level caches are usually physically addressed/physically tagged. Address translation is performed during the level 1 cache access, so the physical address is available by the time that the accesses to the level 2 and lower caches begin, making it simpler and equally fast to use physically addressed/physically tagged caches for these levels. Some systems check each level of the cache in parallel on a memory reference, to reduce the access time to lower levels of the cache. Such systems might use virtually addressed/physically tagged caches on all of their caches, to allow accesses to all levels of the cache to begin immediately.

10.9   Summary

Virtual memory is an essential component of modern memory systems, providing both large amounts of storage and protection. By allowing the bottom level of a memory hierarchy to be implemented out of hard disks or other magnetic media, virtual memory greatly increases the amount of storage available to programs, overcoming a significant limitation of early computer systems. As DRAM memory has become cheaper, this aspect of virtual memory has become less significant, but the ability to have multiple programs running on a single machine, each in its own address space, makes virtual memory a requirement for most modern operating systems.

In this chapter, we described the concept of address translation, the mapping from virtual to physical addresses in a virtual memory system. The mechanisms used to transfer pages of data between the main memory and the hard disk were described, and we discussed how address translation is used to provide protection. Page tables, the data structures used to store the address mappings for each program, were described, along with multilevel and inverted page tables, extensions to the page table concept that reduce the amount of main memory required for a program's page table.

Accessing a program's page table to perform address translation on each memory reference would greatly increase the latency of a memory reference, so virtual memory systems incorporate translation lookaside buffers to reduce translation time. TLBs act as caches for virtual-physical address mappings, greatly reducing translation time when the required translation is found in the TLB. TLBs are organized much like cache memories and are often implemented as set-associative structures.

Finally, we described how virtual memory systems interact with cache memories, in particular how the choice of when to perform address translation affects the cache. Systems that only perform address translation on cache misses (virtually addressed, virtually tagged) have low access times but must purge the cache on each context switch to prevent aliasing of data between programs or add bits to each tag array entry in the cache to identify the program that corresponds to the cache line. Physically addressed, physically tagged caches, which perform translation before the cache access starts, have no problems with aliasing, but are slower than other caches because the cache access cannot begin until address translation has been completed.

Virtually addressed, physically tagged caches provide the best aspects of each of the other approaches by using the virtual address to select a set in the cache, but the physical address to determine if a hit has occurred. This provides protection because physical addresses are used for hit determination, but allow fast access, because address translation can be done in parallel with accessing the tag array.

This chapter concludes our discussion of memory systems. In the next chapter, we will discuss I/O systems, and Chapter 12 will conclude this book by providing an introduction to multiprocessors, systems that use multiple processors to improve performance.

 Solved Problems

Virtual and Physical Addresses (I)

10.1 What is the difference between a virtual and a physical address?

Solution

Physical addresses directly reference locations in the system's memory. They are the addresses that the processor sends to the memory system. Virtual addresses are the addresses that programs use in their load and store operations. The virtual memory system is responsible for translating the virtual addresses used by a program into the physical addresses used by the memory system as part of executing each memory reference.

Virtual and Physical Addresses (II)

10.2 On a multiprogrammed computer, you notice that two programs are referencing the same virtual address but seem to be getting different results when they load from the address. Is this a problem?

Solution

In almost all cases, this is not a problem but the intended behavior of the system. By default, each program has its own virtual address space, and the virtual memory system manages the virtual-physical address translations so that no two program's virtual addresses map onto the same physical address, to prevent them from accessing each other's data. Thus, the most likely explanation for the observed behavior is that the two programs are accessing the same virtual address but different physical addresses. The only case where this would be a problem is if you knew that the two programs wanted to share data and had requested that the operating systems map their virtual addresses onto the same physical addresses.

Virtual and Physical Addresses (III)

10.3 If a processor has 32-bit virtual addresses, 28-bit physical addresses, and 2-KB pages, how many bits are required for the virtual and physical page numbers?

Solution

The base-2 logarithm of 2048 is 11, so 11 bits of each address are required to specify the offset within the page. Therefore, 21 bits (32 − 11) are required to specify the virtual page number, and 17 bits are required to specify the physical page number.

Virtual and Physical Addresses (IV)

10.4   A system has 48-bit virtual addresses, 36-bit physical addresses, and 128 MB of main memory. If the system uses 4096-byte pages, how many virtual and physical pages can the address spaces support? How many page frames of main memory are there?

Solution

$4096 = 2^{12}$, so 12 bits of the virtual and physical addresses are used for the offset within a page. Therefore, the VPN is (48 − 12) = 36 bits long, so the virtual address space can support 2^{36} virtual pages. The PPN is (36 − 12) = 24 bits long, so the physical address space can support 2^{24} physical pages.

To get the number of page frames in the system, we divide the amount of main memory by the size of each page to get the number of pages that can fit in the main memory at the same time. 128 MB/4 KB = 32,768 page frames. Thus, the amount of data that the operating system on this particular computer can map into the physical address space simultaneously is 32,768 pages, despite the fact that the physical address space would allow many more pages to be mapped, because there must be space in the main memory for every virtual page that is mapped onto a physical page.

Address Translation (I)

10.5   Why do the vast majority of systems use virtual and physical pages that are the same size?

Solution

Both virtual and physical addresses can be divided into a page number that identifies the page containing an address and an offset that identifies the location of the address within the page. If the virtual and physical pages on a system are the same size, then the offset from a virtual address can be concatenated onto the physical page number that corresponds to the virtual page containing the address to produce the physical address that corresponds to a virtual address. If a system's virtual and physical pages were different sizes, some more complicated means of generating the physical address from the physical page number and the offset field of the virtual address would be required.

Address Translation (II)

10.6   Given the following set of address mappings for an architecture in which virtual and physical addresses are 32 bits long and pages are 4 KB in size, what is the physical address that corresponds to each of the following virtual addresses?
   a.   0x22433007
   b.   0x13385abc
   c.   0xabc89011

Virtual Page Number	Physical Page Number
0xabc89	0x97887
0x13385	0x99910
0x22433	0x00001
0x54483	0x1a8c2

Fig. 10-13.   Example address mappings.

Solution

a.   In this system, the low 12 bits of the address (0x007, in this case) are the offset within the page, and the high 20 bits (0x22433) define the virtual page number. Looking in the table, we see that the physical page number corresponding to this virtual page number is 0x00001. Concatenating the offset within the page with the physical page number, we get the physical address that corresponds to the virtual address (0x00001007).

b.   0x99910abc

c.   0x97887011

Page Tables (I)

10.7   A system has 32-bit virtual addresses, 24-bit physical addresses, and 2 KB pages.

  a.   How big is each page table entry if a single-level page table is used? (Round up to the nearest byte.)

  b.   How many page table entries are required for this system?

  c.   How much storage is required for the page table (single-level page table)?

Solution

a.   A page size of 2 KB means that 11 bits are required for the offset field in the virtual and physical addresses. Therefore, 13 bits are required for the PPN. Each page table entry needs to hold the PPN for its page and the valid and dirty bits, for a total of 15 bits, which is rounded up to 16 bits, or 2 bytes.

b.   With a page size of 2 KB, the virtual address space can hold 2^{21} pages, requiring 2^{21} page table entries.

c.   Each page table entry requires 2 bytes of storage, so the page table takes up 2^{22} bytes, or 4 MB.

Page Tables (II)

10.8   For a system with 2-bit virtual and physical addresses and page sizes of 1 KB, how many levels would be required in a multilevel page table? How much additional storage would be required for the multilevel page table as compared to a single-level page table for the system? Round the size of a page table entry up to a power of 2 bytes to simplify address calculations, and assume that entries in all levels of the page table are the same size as entries in the bottom level of the page table.

Solution

With 1-KB pages, the system has 22-bit VPNs and PPNs. Since each page table entry must hold a PPN, a valid bit, and a dirty bit, the page table entry rounds up to 4 bytes. This means that 256 page table entries can be stored in a page, and the groups of address bits used to index each level in the page table are $\log_2(256) = 8$ bits long. Therefore, the VPN will be divided into 3 groups of bits, with lengths 8, 8, and 6 bits for a 3-level page table.

A single-level page table for this system would require 2^{22} entries, one for each page in the virtual address space, taking up 16 MB of memory, which is also the amount of storage required for the bottom level of the multilevel page table. Since there are 256 page table entries in a page of data, the level above the bottom is 1/256th of the size of the bottom level, or 64 KB. The next level up (the top level) would be 1/256th of that, or 256 bytes, except that it must take at least one 1-KB page. In a situation like this, where the number of levels in the page table has to be rounded up to the next integer, the top level of the page table would usually be the one that the uneven number of bits is used to address, to reduce wasted storage. Therefore, the total storage required for the multilevel page table is 1 KB + 64 KB + 16 MB, for a total overhead of 65 KB because a multilevel page table was used.

Page Tables (III)

10.9 A system has 4096-byte pages and uses a multilevel page table. If the system requires a 4-level page table, what are the minimum and maximum number of bits in its virtual addresses? Assume that page table entries take 64 bits of space at all levels in the page table, regardless of the number of bits in the virtual addresses, to simplify your calculations.

Solution

Remember from Fig. 10-7 that, in a system with a multilevel page table, the VPN is divided into "groups" of bits, each of which addresses one level in the page table. The total size of the virtual address is equal to the number of groups of bits times the size of each group, plus the number of bits required for the offset within the page. Because 4096 bytes per page = 2^{12} bytes per page, 12 bits of address are required for the offset within page field.

With 4096-byte pages and 64 bits per page table entry, a page of data can hold 512 entries. Because $512 = 2^9$, up to 9 bits of the VPN can be used to address each level in the page table. (Each "group" of bits is 9 bits long.) The maximum number of bits in the virtual address is therefore 4 groups × 9 bits per group + 12 bits of offset = 48 bits. The minimum-possible number of bits in the virtual address is simply 1 more than could fit in a 3-level page table, or (3 groups × 9 bits per group + 12 bits of offset) + 1 = 40 bits. Thus, virtual addresses in this system must be between 40 and 48 bits long.

Translation Lookaside Buffers

10.10 A given processor has 32-bit virtual and physical addresses. The page size is 1 KB, and the processor's TLB has 128 entries, and is 4-way set-associative. How much storage is required for the TLB? Assume that the TLB doesn't round TLB entries up to the next byte.

Solution

Since there are 128 entries in the TLB, the total storage is 128 × the size of each entry. Each entry needs to contain a valid bit, a dirty bit, the PPN of the page, and the VPN minus the number of bits used to select the set in the TLB.

With 32-bit addresses and 1 KB pages, the VPN and PPN are 22 bits each. With 128 entries and 4-way set-associativity, there are 32 sets in the TLB, so 5 bits of the VPN are used to select a set. Therefore, we only have to store 17 bits of the VPN in order to determine if a hit has occurred, but we need all 22 bits of the PPN to determine the physical address of a virtual address. This gives a total of 41 bits per TLB entry. 41 × 128 = 5.125 KB.

Translation Time with TLB

10.11 If a processor's TLB has a hit rate of 90 percent, and it takes 200 cycles to search the page table, what is the average address translation time? Assume that the cache is virtually tagged and physically addressed to hide the translation time if a TLB hit occurs.

Solution

Using our standard equation for average access time, the average translation time is $(T_{hit} \times P_{hit}) + (T_{miss} \times P_{miss})$. Since T_{hit} is 0 in this case, the equation simplifies to $T_{miss} \times P_{miss} = 200$ cycles × 0.1 = 20 cycles.

Interaction of TLB and Cache

10.12 A processor's TLB takes 2.2 ns to translate an address on a cache hit. The tag array of the cache takes 2.5 ns to access, the hit/miss logic takes 1.0 ns, the data array has an access time of 3.4 ns, and it takes 0.5 ns to return the data to the processor if a hit occurs. What is the cache hit latency of the cache when a TLB hit occurs if the cache is virtually addressed/virtually tagged? Virtually addressed/physically tagged? Physically addressed/physically tagged?

Solution

If the cache is virtually addressed/virtually tagged, we do not need to do an address translation at all when a cache hit occurs. Therefore, the cache hit latency is the longer of the time to determine if a hit has occurred and the data array access time, plus the time to return the data once the hit/miss decision is made. The tag array takes 2.5 ns to access, and the hit/miss logic takes an additional 1 ns, so it takes 3.5 ns to determine if a hit has occurred, longer than the data array access time. Therefore, the cache hit latency is 3.5 ns + 0.5 ns (time to return data) = 4.0 ns.

In the virtually addressed/physically tagged case, the time to determine if a hit has occurred is equal to the latency of the hit/miss logic plus the greater of the tag array lookup time and the TLB address translation time. Since the critical path of the cache is the hit or miss determination, we can neglect the data array access time. The tag array takes 2.5 ns to access while the TLB translation takes 2.2 ns, so the latency in this case will be 2.5 ns (tag array access) + 1 ns (hit/miss determination) + 0.5 ns (return data) = 4.0 ns.

In the physically addressed/physically tagged case, address translation must be completed before the tag array access can begin, so the access time is 2.2 ns (TLB) + 2.5 ns (tag array) + 1.0 ns (hit/miss logic) + 0.5 ns (return data) = 6.2 ns.

Protection (I)

10.13 How does the virtual memory system prevent programs from accessing each other's data?

Solution

Each program has its own virtual address space. The virtual memory system is responsible for ensuring that different programs' virtual addresses translate to different physical addresses, so no two programs have virtual addresses that map onto the same physical address at the same time. This means that memory references from one program cannot target the physical addresses containing another program's data, preventing programs from accessing each other's data.

Demand Paging versus Swapping

10.14 Why do systems that use demand paging generally deliver higher performance than those that use virtual memory?

Solution

Demand paging systems copy pages into the main memory as programs access them, while swapping systems copy all of the memory used by a program into the main memory when the system context switches to the program. When a program only references some of its data during its timeslice, the demand paging system will copy less data from the hard disk into main memory since it only copies data when it is used. This reduces the amount of time spent copying data off of the hard disks, improving performance.

Write-Through Virtual Memory?

10.15 All of the page table and TLB designs presented in this chapter have assumed a write-back virtual memory system, providing a dirty bit to record whether each page has been modified since being brought into the physical memory. Suggest an explanation for why write-through virtual memory systems are not used.

Solution

Virtual memory systems are not write-through because of the huge difference in speeds between a system's main memory and its hard disks. Hard disks have access times of several milliseconds, while main memory access times are typically in the hundreds of nanoseconds range. If every write to the main memory had to be sent to the disk, as would occur in a write-through virtual memory system, the disk would be unable to keep up, and the processor would have to stop and wait for writes to be handled by the hard disk. Collecting all of the writes to a page and writing the modified page back to disk once when it is evicted (a write-back scheme) greatly reduces the number of writes to the disk, making it more feasible for the disk to keep up.

CHAPTER 11

I/O

11.1 Objectives

Until now, we have concentrated on only two of the components of a computer system: the processor and the memory system. Input/output (I/O) devices are the third major component of computer systems and are responsible for both communicating with the outside world and storing data for later retrieval. In this chapter, we will discuss how I/O devices are interfaced to the processor and memory system, as well as discussing hard disks, one of the most common I/O devices.

After finishing this chapter, you should

1. Be familiar with I/O buses and their use in interfacing devices to the processor
2. Understand interrupts, and be able to compare interrupts and polling
3. Be able to discuss and think about memory-mapped I/O
4. Be familiar with hard disks, including their physical organization and the algorithms used to schedule requests on them

11.2 Introduction

Computer architects tend to focus their attention on the processor first, the memory system second, and the I/O system third, if at all. Partially, this is because the benchmarks and metrics that have been used to compare computer systems have generally focused on the execution times of computationally intensive programs that do not use the I/O system much, and partially it is because some of the techniques used to implement I/O systems make it difficult to improve their performance at the rate that processor performance has improved.

However, I/O systems, particularly storage devices, are critical to the performance of many of the most important (and lucrative) applications of computing today. Transaction-processing systems, such as those used for airline ticket reservations, credit card transactions, and banking, require a great deal of I/O performance, because these systems must write the results of each transaction out to some form of permanent storage, such as a hard disk, before the transaction can be considered complete. Leaving the results in memory makes the system vulnerable to power failures, system crashes, and other errors that can destroy the data in the main memory.

The performance of these systems is measured in terms of the number of transactions (such as credit card purchases) that the system can perform each second and commit to the disk. Often, the limiting factor in this is the rate at which data can be transferred to/from the hard disk, with the processor spending much of its time idle waiting for the I/O system. Thus, buyers of these database systems are willing to pay a great deal of money for improved I/O performance, but are generally less concerned about the speed of their system's processor.

I/O systems can be divided into two major components: the I/O devices themselves and the technologies used to interface the I/O devices to the rest of the system. This chapter begins with a discussion of interface technologies, including I/O buses, interrupts, polling, and memory-mapped I/O. Given the enormous variety of I/O devices in use today, a thorough discussion of I/O devices is beyond the scope of this book. However, we will present an overview of how hard disks, one of the most common data storage devices in computer systems today, are designed and accessed.

11.3 I/O Buses

In Chapter 3, we introduced the block diagram of a typical computer system that is reproduced in Fig. 11-1. Separate memory and I/O buses are used to communicate with the memory system and I/O system. These buses communicate with the processor through a switch module.

The I/O bus creates an interface abstraction that follows the processor to interface with a wide range of I/O devices using a very limited set of interface hardware. Each I/O bus, such as the PCI bus found in many PCs and workstations, provides a specification for how commands and data are transferred between the processor and the I/O devices, and how multiple devices compete for use of the bus. Any device that is compatible with a system's I/O bus can be added to the system (assuming an appropriate device driver program is available), and a device that is compatible with a particular I/O bus can be integrated into any system that uses that type of bus. This makes systems that use I/O buses, as opposed to direct connections between the processor and each I/O device, very flexible, allowing a system to support many different I/O devices depending on the needs of its users and allowing users to change the I/O devices that are attached to a system as their needs change.

The main disadvantage of an I/O bus (and buses in general) is that the bus has a fixed bandwidth that must be shared by all of the devices on the bus. Even worse, electrical constraints (wire length and transmission line effects) cause buses to have less bandwidth than using the same number of wires to connect just two devices. Essentially, there is a trade-off between interface simplicity and bandwidth.

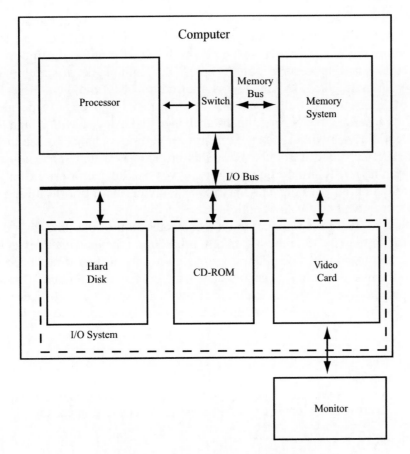

Fig. 11-1. Basic computer organization.

EXAMPLE
The original PCI bus operated at 33 MHz and transferred 32 bits of data at a time, for a total bandwidth of 132 MB/s. (More recent versions of PCI have increased both the clock rate and the width of the datapath.) If the hard disks attached to the bus could deliver a maximum of 40 MB/s, and the video card needed 128 MB/s of bandwidth to meet the demands of an application, it would not be possible to both access the disk at maximum bandwidth and transfer data to the video card at the required rate.

Early computers often accessed their main memory through the I/O bus rather than through a separate memory bus. This configuration reduced the number of signals going to the processor or switch, but it meant that main memory had to share the bandwidth available over the I/O bus. Over time, computers moved to separate connections for memory and the I/O bus to increase bandwidth.

11.3.1 ACCESSING THE I/O BUS

Each type of bus (PCI, SCSI, etc.) defines a protocol for how devices may access the bus, when data may be sent, and so on. One of the key elements of this is the *arbitration policy* that is used to decide which device may access the bus at a given time. Most buses allow any device on the bus to request the use of the bus and have a policy for deciding which device gets to use the bus if more than one device wants to access it at the same time. For example, in the SCSI protocol, each device has a *SCSI ID* that is used to identify it on the bus. When multiple devices request the bus, the one with the highest ID wins and is allowed to access the bus.

The SCSI arbitration policy has the advantage that it is easy to decide which device gets access to the bus, but the disadvantage that a device with a high SCSI ID can prevent a device with a lower ID from ever getting a chance to use the bus by making repeated requests for the bus. This problem is called *starvation* and can occur any time an arbitration policy always gives one device priority over another. Some arbitration policies prevent starvation by giving more priority to the devices that have been waiting for the bus longest.

The time to perform an operation on a bus is the sum of the time for a device to request use of the bus, the time to perform arbitration (decide which device can use the bus), and the time to complete the operation once a device has been granted access to the bus. Some bus protocols may place limits on the amount of time that a single operation can take to complete, to ensure that high-priority devices cannot be prevented from using the bus by long-latency operations initiated by low-priority devices.

EXAMPLE

If a bus requires 5 ns for requests, 5 ns for arbitration, and takes an average of 7.5 ns to complete an operation once access to the bus is granted, can the bus perform 50 million operations per second?

Solution

To achieve 50 million operations/s, each operation must complete in an average of 20 ns. Adding the request, arbitration, and average completion times for this bus gives an average time of 17.5 ns per operation. Thus, the bus will be able to complete more than 50 million operations per second on average.

11.4   Interrupts

Many I/O devices generate *asynchronous* events—events that occur at times that the processor cannot predict or control, but which the processor must respond to reasonably quickly to provide acceptable performance. An example of this is the keyboard on a workstation or PC. The processor cannot predict when the user will press a key but must react to the keypress in well under a second or the response time will be noticeable to the user. *Interrupts* are the mechanism used by most processors to handle this type of event. Essentially, interrupts allow devices to request that the processor stop what it is currently doing and execute software to process the device's request, much like a procedure call that is initiated by the external device rather than by the program running on the processor.

Interrupts are also used when the processor needs to perform a long-running operation on some I/O device and wants to be able to do other work while waiting for the operation to complete. For example, disk drives typically have access times of approximately 10 ms, which can be millions of processor cycles. Rather than waiting for the disk drive to complete a read or write request, the processor would like to execute some user program while the disk drive is handling the request. Using interrupts, the processor can send the request to the disk drive and then perform a context switch to begin executing the user program. When the disk is done with the operation, it signals an interrupt to inform the processor that the operation is complete and that any result data from the operation is available.

11.4.1   IMPLEMENTING INTERRUPTS

To implement interrupts, the processor assigns a signal, known as an *interrupt request line*, to each device that can issue an interrupt. Typically, each device is also assigned an *interrupt acknowledge* line that the processor uses to signal the device that it has received and begun to process the interrupt request. The processor also provides a set of memory locations, known as the *interrupt vector*, that contains the addresses of the routines, called *interrupt handlers*, that should be executed when an interrupt occurs.

Figure 11-2 shows how the interrupt vector for a processor with four interrupts might be laid out. The interrupt vector consists of four words of memory, one for each interrupt. When the processor is powered on, these memory locations contain undefined values. Software (generally the operating system, but sometimes user programs) must store the addresses of the interrupt handlers for each interrupt in the appropriate locations in the interrupt vector before the devices attached to each interrupt request line can be used.

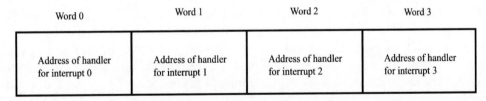

Word 0	Word 1	Word 2	Word 3
Address of handler for interrupt 0	Address of handler for interrupt 1	Address of handler for interrupt 2	Address of handler for interrupt 3

Fig. 11-2.   Example interrupt vector.

To interrupt the processor (assert an interrupt), a device sends a signal on its interrupt line. The device is typically required to continue to assert its interrupt until the processor acknowledges the interrupt. When the processor receives the interrupt signal, it sends a signal on the appropriate interrupt acknowledge line to tell the interrupting device that the interrupt has been received. It then looks up the appropriate location in the interrupt vector to find the address of the start of the interrupt handler for the device and performs a context switch to start execution of the interrupt handler. The context switch is necessary to ensure that the program running on the processor when the interrupt occurs is able to resume execution after the interrupt completes. After the interrupt handler completes, another context switch occurs and execution returns to some user program (not necessarily the one that was running when the interrupt occurred). In general, interrupts are invisible to user programs in the same way that timeslices allocated to other user programs are invisible. The only way that a program can tell that an interrupt has occurred is to access the system's real-time clock and determine that more time than usual has elapsed between two events.

11.4.2 INTERRUPT PRIORITIES

Since interrupts are asynchronous, it is possible that more than one device may assert an interrupt at the same time, or that multiple interrupts may build up while one is being handled. To decide which order interrupts should be handled in, most processors assign a priority to each interrupt, such as deciding that lower-numbered interrupts have priority over higher-numbered ones. When more than one interrupt is waiting for the processor, the processor picks the one with highest priority. Some processors allow high-priority interrupts to interrupt lower-priority interrupt handlers, while others always finish one interrupt handle before allowing another to begin.

Like other priority-based scheduling systems, interrupt priorities have the problem that a series of high-priority interrupts can prevent a low-priority interrupt from being handled. In cases where the system wants to give priority to some of the devices, this may be acceptable. In other cases, it isn't. To address this issue, some processors provide a mode in which an interrupt's priority drops every time it is handled or allow software to change the priorities of interrupts as needed.

11.4.3 POLLING VERSUS INTERRUPTS

One alternative to using interrupts for I/O devices is *polling*. In polling, the processor periodically checks each of its I/O devices to see if any of them have a request that it needs to handle. For example, instead of having the hard drive signal an interrupt when it has a block of data for the processor, the operating system could check every few milliseconds to see if the data was available. This would allow the processor to respond to asynchronous external events without the additional hardware required for interrupts.

Using polling instead of interrupts can provide performance advantages if the processor has no other work that it could be doing while I/O operations are proceeding. If the processor has nothing else to do, it can enter a tight loop where all it does is repeatedly poll (check) the I/O devices to see if anything needs to be done. If so, the processor can just branch to the routine to handle the request. In contrast, responding to an interrupt requires performing a context switch to save the current program state so it can be restored at the end of the interrupt, increasing the latency to begin handling the interrupt.

However, polling has two significant disadvantages that make interrupts the preferred choice except when response time to a given event is absolutely critical. First, polling consumes execution resources even when there are no I/O requests to handle, since the processor must check each device to determine that there are no waiting I/O requests. The average delay before responding to an event is based on the polling frequency, so the processor must poll frequently to ensure acceptable response time. This can consume a significant fraction of the processing cycles.

EXAMPLE

How often must a system poll an I/O device if it wants the average delay between when the device wants to make a request and the time it is polled to be at most 5 ms? If it takes 10,000 cycles to poll the I/O device, and the processor operates at 500 MHz, what fraction of the processor cycles are spent polling? What if the system wants to provide an average response delay of 1 ms?

Solution

Assuming that I/O requests are evenly distributed in time, the average time that a device will have to wait for the processor to poll is half the time between polling attempts. Therefore, to provide an average delay of 5 ms, the processor will have to poll every 10 ms, or 100 times/s. If each polling attempt takes 10,000 cycles, then the processor will spend 1,000,000 cycles polling each second, or 1/500th of the available processor cycles.

To provide an average delay of 1 ms, the processor will have to poll every 2 ms, or 500 times/s. This will consume 5,000,000 cycles/s, or 1/100th of the execution cycles.

The second disadvantage of polling is that systems that use polling require that the software running on the processor (either the operating system or the user program) schedule polling. This means that either the application programmer must know how often the system wants to poll and write programs such that they poll with that frequency, or that the operating system interrupt the execution of user programs to poll the I/O devices. This second option simplifies the task of writing applications for the system, but it raises the question of how the operating system knows when the right amount of time has elapsed to schedule a polling event. Unless the user program knows to turn the processor back over to the operating system every so often, it is very hard for the operating system to know when it should poll or even perform context switches in a system without interrupts.

These two disadvantages, overhead and programming complexity, make interrupts a better choice than polling for handling asynchronous events in most systems. In fact most operating systems implement multiprogramming through the use of a *timer interrupt* that periodically signals the operating system to perform a context switch to allow a different program to use the processor. Polling is generally only used when either there is only one program running on the system or when it is absolutely critical that the system respond to the completion of an I/O request as soon as possible.

11.5   Memory-Mapped I/O

To use the I/O system, the processor must be able to send commands to the I/O devices and read data from them. Most systems use a mechanism called *memory-mapped I/O* for this. In memory-mapped I/O, the command registers (also called control registers) for each I/O device appear to the programmer as memory locations. When the program reads or writes these memory locations, the hardware transforms the memory operation into a transaction over the I/O bus that reads or writes the appropriate register on the device. In the case of a read, the result of the operation is transferred back to the processor over the I/O bus and written into the destination register of the load.

Figure 11-3 illustrates how the command registers of a hard disk that uses 32-bit command registers might be handled by memory-mapped I/O. The command register is used to tell the device what the processor wants it to do. The platter, track, and sector registers encode the location of the data that the processor wants to read or write (these terms will be defined in Section 11.8). The start address field tells the disk where in the main memory the data for the request should be read from (in the case of a write to the disk) or written to (in the case of a read from the disk), and the size field tells the disk how much data to transfer. These registers are used for DMA memory transfers, which will be discussed in Section 11.6.

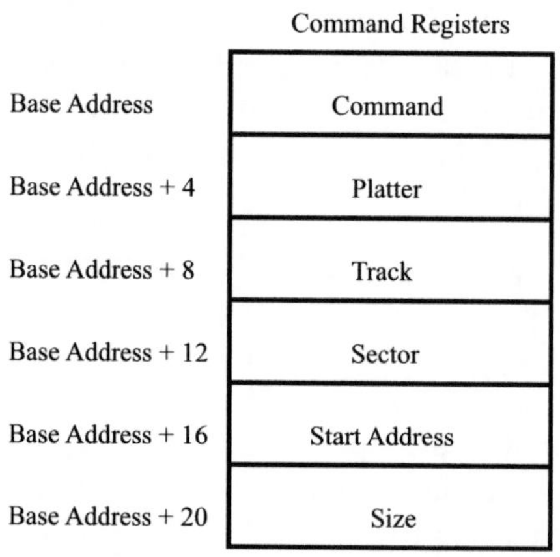

Fig. 11-3.   Memory-mapped I/O.

Because a variety of devices can be attached to an I/O bus, the architecture typically defines a block of memory addresses that contain the command registers of each potential I/O device, although the arrangement of these blocks varies from processor to processor. Figure 11-4 shows an example of how these memory blocks might be laid out on a processor that associates a region of memory with the device attached to each interrupt line. In this example, the architecture has defined 512 bytes of control registers for each device, not because most devices require this many control registers, but to ensure that there are no difficulties caused by devices that require more space for control registers than the architecture allows.

Address Space

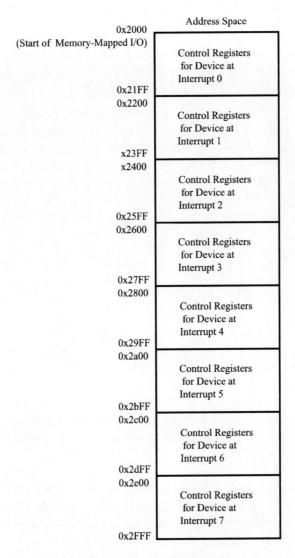

0x2000
(Start of Memory-Mapped I/O)

| Control Registers for Device at Interrupt 0 |
0x21FF
0x2200

| Control Registers for Device at Interrupt 1 |
x23FF
x2400

| Control Registers for Device at Interrupt 2 |
0x25FF
0x2600

| Control Registers for Device at Interrupt 3 |
0x27FF
0x2800

| Control Registers for Device at Interrupt 4 |
0x29FF
0x2a00

| Control Registers for Device at Interrupt 5 |
0x2bFF
0x2c00

| Control Registers for Device at Interrupt 6 |
0x2dFF
0x2e00

| Control Registers for Device at Interrupt 7 |
0x2FFF

Fig. 11-4.   Sample memory map.

In Fig. 11-3, we defined each control register on the disk drive in terms of an offset from the base address of the region of memory allocated to the device. If such a disk were attached to an interrupt on the system whose memory map is given in Fig. 11-4, the address of each control register would be computed by adding the offset of the control register to the base (lowest) address of the region of memory allocated to the hard disk's interrupt.

EXAMPLE
If the disk drive from Fig. 11-3 is attached to interrupt 4 of the computer whose I/O memory map is shown in Fig. 11-4, what is the address of the sector register?

Solution

The base address of the region allocated to interrupt 4 is 0x2800, and the offset to the sector register is 12 (0xc) bytes. Therefore, the address of the control register is 0x2800 + 0xc = 0x280c.

Memory-mapped I/O allows the processor to interface to a wide variety of devices without needing to know what types of devices the processor will interface to when it is designed. When a device is built, the designers can simply write a *device driver* that interfaces with the operating system and tells it how to control the device. Processors that do not use memory-mapped I/O often rely on special instructions to control I/O devices.

11.6   Direct Memory Access

Many I/O devices operate on large blocks of data, often several kilobytes in length, allowing the latency of a long operation such as a hard disk access to be amortized across the transfer of the entire block, rather than requiring a separate disk access for each byte or word of data. These devices typically contain a small memory buffer that holds the block of data being moved to/from the device. The memory-mapped command registers of the device allow the processor to read or write words to or from the buffer with load and store operations that the hardware turns into requests over the I/O bus.

Using this scheme, the processor must execute a load or store operation for each word of data that is sent to or from an I/O device to copy the data into or out of the device's buffer. While transactions over the I/O bus typically occur at a lower rate than the processor's clock speed, there is not enough time between I/O bus transactions to allow the processor to context-switch to some other task, meaning that the processor will be busy whenever data is being transferred over the I/O bus. As the utilization of the I/O bus approaches 100 percent, the processor will spend all of its time transferring data over the I/O bus, and none performing other computations.

Direct memory access (DMA) systems were developed to address this problem. In a DMA system, I/O devices can directly access the memory without intervention by the processor. Figure 11-5 illustrates the sequence of events involved in a DMA transfer to copy the results of an I/O operation into the main memory.

To start the DMA sequence, the I/O device signals an interrupt to request attention from the processor. The processor responds by checking the device's status via the memory-mapped control registers and issues a command telling the device to do a DMA transfer to move the result data into the memory. Once the DMA start command has been issued, the processor begins working on something else while the I/O device transfers the data into the memory. When the DMA transfer is complete, the I/O device signals another interrupt to let the processor know that the DMA is done and it may access the data.

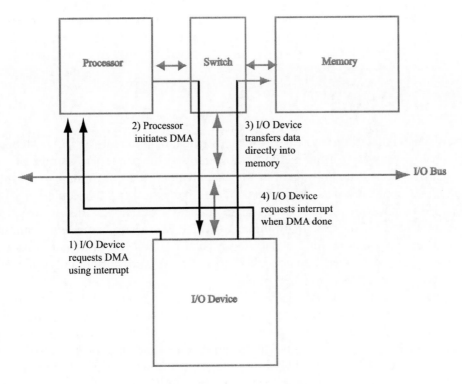

Fig. 11-5.   Direct memory access.

Using DMA transfers can substantially reduce the number of processor cycles spent handling I/O, freeing the processor for other computations. However, the I/O device and the processor do have to share the memory bandwidth, meaning that the available memory bandwidth for programs is reduced while DMA is occurring.

11.7   I/O Devices

There are an enormous number of different I/O devices for current computer systems, which can be divided into three loose categories: devices that receive input from humans, devices that display output to humans, and devices that interact with other machines. Devices that receive input directly from humans, such as keyboards and mice, tend to have relatively low bandwidth requirements, but require prompt response time. For example, a typist who types at 60 words per minute is only generating five characters per second of I/O, assuming an average word length of five letters. This is a trivial amount of I/O bandwidth, but the typist quickly notices the delay if the computer doesn't respond immediately to keystrokes.

Devices that display output to humans, such as video cards, printers, and sound cards, can require a substantial amount of output bandwidth, but little input bandwidth. Devices that interact with other machines, like disk drives, CD-ROMs, network interfaces, and so forth, often need high bandwidth in both directions and low response time from the processor in order to deliver peak performance. Understanding the needs of different I/O devices is critical to obtaining good overall performance from the system.

11.8   Disk Systems

Hard disks are one of the most performance-critical components of I/O systems. In addition to supporting virtual memory, they are used for permanent storage of data. As mentioned in the introduction to this chapter, the performance of many commercial applications is determined by the bandwidth of the computer's hard disks. Hard disks are named to distinguish them from floppy disks, which are commonly used to transfer small amounts of data from one computer to another. The typical data capacity for a 3.5-in floppy disk is 1.44 MB, while hard disks can have capacities of greater than 75 GB. Hard disks are also substantially quicker to access than floppy disks.

Figure 11-6 shows a typical hard disk subsystem in the context of a computer's I/O system. An adapter card is attached to the processor's I/O bus, and hard disks are attached to the adapter's bus rather than being directly connected to the I/O bus. Because the bandwidth available from a single disk drive is typically much lower than the bandwidth of an I/O bus, this arrangement allows several disks to share a single slot on the I/O bus without restricting their ability to transfer data, freeing up

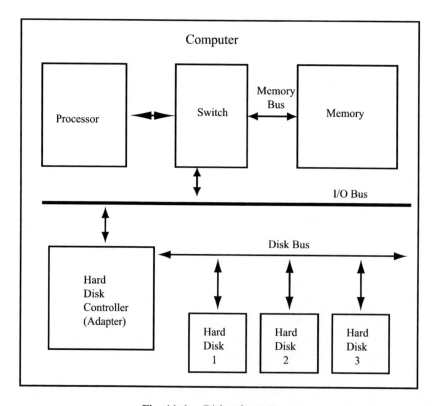

Fig. 11-6.   Disk subsystem.

space on the bus for other devices. It also allows a single model of hard disk to interface to a variety of I/O bus formats. For example, a hard disk that uses the SCSI protocol can interface to a PCI I/O bus through an adapter card that is compatible with the PCI format, or to a different bus by using a different adapter card.

11.8.1 HARD DISK ORGANIZATION

A typical hard disk is made up of several *platters*, flat plates that the data is stored on, as shown in Fig. 11-7. Each platter has its own read/write head, allowing accesses to data on different platters to proceed in parallel. Within each platter, data is organized into *tracks* (concentric rings) and *sectors* (fractions of a ring), as illustrated in Fig. 11-8. On a given hard disk, each sector contains the same amount of data, often 512 bytes.

Older hard disks were organized such that each track contained the same number of sectors. This made controlling the device easier, since each track contained the

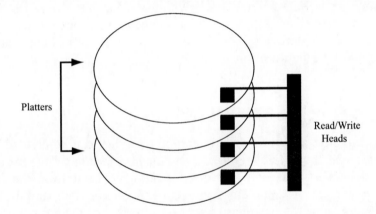

Fig. 11-7. Disk organization.

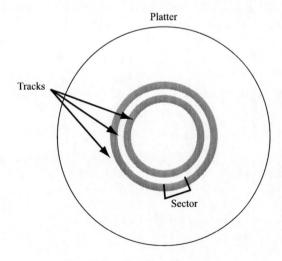

Fig. 11-8. Tracks and sectors.

same amount of data, but resulted in the disk containing much less data than it could otherwise have, because the real limiting factor on how much data can be stored on a track is the number of bits per inch that the disk head can read or write. On disks that have a constant number of sectors per track, the number of sectors per track is set based on the number of bits that the drive can fit on the innermost (smallest) track, which is a function of both the circumference of the innermost track and the technology used to construct the disk. The other tracks contain the same number of bits, but they are written less densely, so that each sector takes up the same fraction of the track's circumference as on the innermost track. This wastes a significant fraction of the potential storage capacity of the outermost tracks, as bits are written much less densely on those tracks than on the inner tracks.

More recent disks store data more densely by keeping the density at which bits are written closer to constant and varying the number of sectors stored on each track so that tracks further out from the center of the disk contain more data. In theory, each track could contain a different number of sectors to maximize the amount of data stored on the disk. In practice, disk manufacturers divide the disk into several zones of contiguous tracks. Each track within a zone has the same number of sectors, but the number of sectors per track increases as zones move out from the center of the disk. This provides a good compromise between storage capacity and the complexity of the hardware in the disk.

11.8.2 REQUEST SCHEDULING

The time to complete a read or write operation on a disk can be divided into three parts: the *seek time*, the *rotational latency*, and the *transfer time*. The seek time is the amount of time that it takes to move the read/write head from the track it is currently accessing to the track that contains the requested data, and the rotational latency is the time that the head has to wait once it reaches the correct track before the requested sector arrives under the read/write head. The transfer time is the amount of time that it takes to read or write the sector once it reaches the read/write head, which is basically the time that it takes the sector to pass under the read/write head. This neglects the time to transmit the data from the read/write head to the hard disk adapter, which is determined by the design of the interface logic on the disk, and is therefore hard to compute from the disk's other parameters. The rotational latency is a function of the rate at which the hard disk spins, while the transfer time is a function of the rotation rate and the number of sectors on the track.

EXAMPLE
If a disk spins at 10,000 r/min, what is the average rotational latency time of a request? If a given track on the disk has 1024 sectors, what is the transfer time for a sector?

Solution

At 10,000 r/min, it takes 6 ms for a complete rotation of the disk. On average, the read/write head will have to wait for half a rotation before the needed sector reaches it, so the average rotational latency will be 3 ms. Since there are 1024 sectors on the track, the transfer time will be equal to the rotation time of the disk divided by 1024, or approximately 6 microseconds.

One way the operating system or the hardware can influence the performance of the hard disk is by selecting the order in which requests are handled if there are multiple outstanding requests. There are three commonly used policies: first-come-first-serve (FCFS), shortest-seek-time-first (SSTF), and LOOK scheduling. In *first-come-first-serve*, the disk handles requests in the order that they were made, as shown in Fig. 11-9. FCFS scheduling has the advantage that it is easy to implement, but can require much more motion of the disk head than other scheduling policies. Since the seek time of a request is proportional to the number of tracks that the read/write head has to travel across to satisfy the request, this increase in disk motion leads to longer average seek times and lower performance.

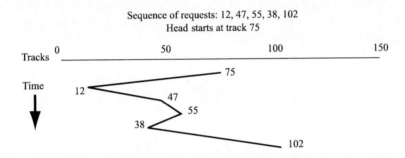

Fig. 11-9. First-come-first-serve disk scheduling.

Shortest-seek-time-first scheduling reduces seek time by always handling the request whose track is closest to the current position of the disk head. Figure 11-10 shows how this scheduling policy would handle the sequence of requests from Fig. 11-9. SSTF scheduling can significantly reduce the average seek time of a disk, but has the disadvantage that a sequence of requests to tracks near each other can prevent a request to a further-away track from ever being completed (starvation). As an example, consider a program that starts out by making requests to tracks 1, 2, and 100, and then makes a sequence of requests to tracks 1 and 2. If the request to track 1 is handled first, the request to track 2 will be handled second, followed by the next request to track 1, and so on. Until the sequence of requests to tracks 1 and 2 ends, the request to track 100 will never be satisfied.

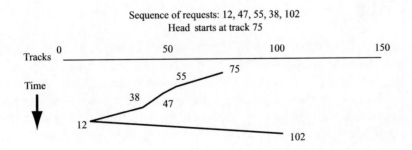

Fig. 11-10. Shortest-seek-time-first scheduling.

LOOK scheduling (also called elevator scheduling) is a compromise between FCFS and SSTF that generally delivers better performance than FCFS without the possibility of starvation. In LOOK scheduling, the head starts moving either inward or outward on the platter, satisfying all of the requests for tracks that it passes. When it reaches the track of the innermost or outermost request, it reverses direction, handling pending requests as it reaches their track. This is similar to the way that most elevators work. Once the elevator starts moving upward, it continues upward until it reaches the highest floor that anyone has requested. It then begins moving downward until it reaches the lowest requested floor.

Figure 11-11 illustrates LOOK scheduling, with the head starting out moving outward (toward higher-numbered tracks) on the disk. This algorithm prevents starvation by guaranteeing that once the head starts moving toward the track required by a given request, it keeps moving in that direction until it has satisfied the request. Since the disk has both inner and outer limits on the head's motion, it is guaranteed that the head can only move away from the track required by a request for a limited amount of time, and therefore that no sequence of requests can keep a given request from being completed.

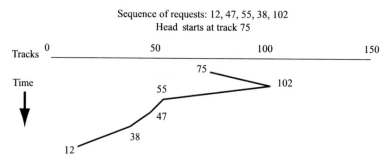

Fig. 11-11.   LOOK scheduling.

Actual systems tend to use either SSTF or LOOK scheduling, sometimes with slight variations on the algorithms presented here. In general, LOOK scheduling is better for systems that are expected to place heavy demands on the disk, because the chance of starvation in SSTF increases with the fraction of the time that the disk is busy.

11.9   Summary

A computer's I/O system generally contains data storage devices, devices that receive data from the outside world, and devices that transmit data to the outside world. I/O devices communicate with the processor through an I/O bus, which allows the computer to interface with a wide variety of devices without requiring a dedicated interface for each device. However, the I/O bus limits the bandwidth of the I/O system because all of the devices on the bus must share its available bandwidth.

I/O systems generally use either interrupts or polling to communicate with I/O devices. In polling, the processor repeatedly checks to determine whether any of the I/O devices require attention, creating a trade-off between the desire for rapid response to any I/O event and the desire to limit the amount of the processor's time spent polling. Interrupts provide a mechanism that allows the I/O devices to signal the processor when they need attention, allowing the processor to ignore the I/O devices except when they signal. Using interrupts can greatly reduce the amount of processor time spent interacting with I/O devices, although polling may be a better approach if the processor has no other work to do while waiting for some I/O request to complete.

Most processors use memory-mapped I/O to directly control I/O devices. In this technique, the control registers of an I/O device are mapped onto memory locations in the processor's address space. When the processor reads or writes one of these memory locations, it is really accessing one of the control registers. This technique allows the processor to support many different I/O devices, because all the hardware has to do is allocate sufficient address space to each device to handle its I/O registers. Software that interfaces with the device is responsible for understanding the mapping between memory locations and control registers and for performing the correct sequence of memory operations to control the device.

Direct memory access is a technique that allows the processor to instruct a device to copy a block of data directly to or from the memory system. This reduces the amount of processor effort required to transfer data between the I/O system and the memory system, improving performance.

The last section of this chapter described hard disks in more detail, as they are one of the most common I/O devices in use today, and one whose performance is most critical to application performance. We described the division of disks into platters, tracks, and sectors and showed how to compute the average latency of an I/O operation on the disk. Finally, several scheduling algorithms were described that attempt to reduce the time to complete a series of disk accesses, and the trade-offs between minimum completion time and fairness in each of these algorithms were presented.

Solved Problems

I/O Buses

11.1 What are the pros and cons of using a standard I/O bus in a design, as opposed to a direct connection between the processor and each I/O device?

Solution

The main advantage of using a standard I/O bus is that users can then interface a variety of different I/O devices to the computer without the system designer having to consider all the possible devices that might want to interface with the system. As long as the I/O device manufacturer provides an appropriate device driver, any device that is compatible with the standard bus can be used with the computer. Also, using a standard I/O bus is generally cheaper, because users do not have to pay for the ability to have a direct connection from the computer to I/O devices that they may not want to use.

The main disadvantage of using a standard I/O bus is that it will be slower than a direct connection between the processor and each I/O device. All of the devices have to share the bandwidth of the I/O bus, which is typically significantly less than the bandwidth that can be achieved by a direct connection between the processor and an I/O device. This is why bandwidth-critical devices such as the memory system do have direct connections to the processor.

Bus Bandwidth

11.2 Suppose a given bus protocol requires 10 ns for devices to make requests, 15 ns for arbitration, and 25 ns to complete each operation. How many operations can be completed per second?

Solution

The total time for an operation is the sum of the request, arbitration, and completion times, which is 50 ns. Therefore, the bus can complete 20 million operations/s.

SCSI Bus Usage

11.3 A SCSI bus has four devices attached to it, with IDs 1, 2, 3, and 4. If each device wants to use 30 MB/s of bus bandwidth, and the total bandwidth of the SCSI bus is 80 MB/s, how much bandwidth will each device be able to use? Assume that whenever a device is denied access to the bus, it tries again as soon as the bus is free and keeps trying until it gets access.

Solution

Device 4 has the highest priority, so it gets access to the bus whenever it tries and is able to use its full 30 MB/s. Of the 50 MB/s remaining, device 3 is able to use 30 MB/s, because it only loses arbitration when device 4 wants to use the bus. Device 2 uses all of the remaining 20 MB/s, because it always beats device 1, which gets no bandwidth, Here, we're ignoring startup issues—device 1 might get one chance to access the bus if its first request was made before any of the other devices wanted to use the bus.

Fair Bus Arbitration

11.4 Suppose that the bus from Problem 11.3 used a fair arbitration policy, in which the device that had been waiting for the bus the longest had the highest priority. How much bandwidth would each device be able to use then?

Solution

In the fair arbitration policy, each device will get an equal number of chances to use the bus, because any device that loses an arbitration will have higher priority to use the bus than the device it lost to until it gets a chance to use the bus. Therefore, the 80-MB/s bandwidth of the bus will be evenly divided between the devices, each of which will get 20 MB/s.

Interrupt Priorities

11.5 A given processor has eight interrupt lines (numbered 0–7), and a policy that low-numbered interrupts have priority over higher-numbered ones. The processor starts with no interrupts pending, and the following sequence of interrupts occurs: 4, 7, 1, 3, 0, 5, 6, 4, 2, 1. Assume that handling any interrupt takes enough time that two more interrupts arrive while the first interrupt is being handled, until all of the interrupts have arrived, and that interrupts cannot interrupt each other. (Many processors allow high-priority interrupts to interrupt low-priority interrupt handlers, but assuming that interrupts can't interrupt each other simplifies the problem of thinking about priorities.) What order are the interrupts handled in?

Solution

A good way to approach this sort of problem is to create a list of pending events (such as interrupts). Whenever the processor is free, it handles the highest-priority pending event, removing it from the list. Thus, interrupt 4 is handled first, because it arrives first. When the processor is done with interrupt 4, interrupts 7 and 1 are pending, so interrupt 1 gets handled. Repeating this process gives the following order of interrupt handling: 4, 1, 0, 3, 2, 1, 4, 5, 6, 7.

Interrupts versus Polling

11.6 A given processor requires 1000 cycles to perform a context switch and start an interrupt handler (and the same number of cycles to context-switch back to the program that was running when the interrupt occurred), or 500 cycles to poll an I/O device. An I/O device attached to that processor makes 150 requests per second, each of which take 10,000 cycles to resolve once the handler has been started. By default, the processor polls every 0.5 ms if it is not using interrupts.

a. How many cycles per second does the processor spend handling I/O from the device if interrupts are used?

b. How many cycles per second are spent on I/O if polling is used (include all polling attempts)? Assume that the processor only polls during timeslices when user programs are not running, so do not include any context-switch time in your calculation of polling costs.

c. How often would the processor have to poll for polling to take as many cycles per second as interrupts?

Solution

a. The device makes 150 requests, each of which require one interrupt. Each interrupt takes a total of 12,000 cycles to handle (1000 to start the handler, 10,000 for the handler, 1000 to switch back to the original program), for a total of 1,800,000 cycles spent handling this device each second.

b. The processor polls every 0.5 ms, or 2000 times/s. Each polling attempt takes 500 cycles, so it spends 1,000,000 cycles per second polling. In 150 of the polling attempts, a request is waiting from the I/O device, each of which takes 10,000 cycles to complete, for another 1,500,000 cycles total. Therefore the total time spent on I/O each second is 2,500,000 cycles with polling.

c. The processor spends 1,800,000 cycles/s handling I/O with interrupts, of which 1,500,000 are spent processing the I/O requests. This leaves 300,000 cycles/s available for polling if the processor is to spend the same total amount of time handling I/O with polling and interrupts. Each polling attempt takes 500 cycles, so the processor can do 600 polls/s and spend the same fraction of its time handling I/O via polling as with interrupts.

Direct Memory Access

11.7 An I/O device transfers 10 MB/s of data into the memory of a processor over the I/O bus, which has a total bandwidth of 100 MB/s. The 10 MB/s of data is transferred as 2500 independent pages, each of which are 4 KB in length. If the processor operates at 200 MHz, it takes 1000 cycles to initiate a DMA transaction and 1500 cycles to respond to the device's interrupt when the DMA transfer completes, what fraction of the CPU's time is spent handling the data transfer with and without DMA?

Solution

Without DMA, the processor must copy the data into the memory as the I/O device sends it over the bus. Since the device sends 10 MB/s over the I/O bus, which has a total bandwidth of 100 MB/s, 10 percent of each second is spent transferring data over the bus. Assuming the processor is busy handling data during the time that each page is being transferred over the bus (which is a reasonable assumption because the time between bus transfers is too short to be worth doing a context switch), then 10 percent of the processor's time is spent copying data into memory.

With DMA, the processor is free to work on other tasks, except when initiating each DMA and responding to the interrupt at the end of each transfer. This takes 2500 cycles/transfer, or a total of 6,250,000 cycles spent handling DMAs each second. Since the processor operates at 200 MHz, this means that 3.125 percent of each second, or 3.125 percent of the processor's time, is spent handling DMAs, less than one-third of the overhead without DMA.

Disk Capacity (I)

11.8 A hard disk with 5 platters has 2048 tracks/platter, 1024 sectors/track (fixed number of sectors per track), and 512 byte sectors. What is its total capacity?

Solution

512 bytes×1024 sectors = 0.5 MB/track. Multiplying by 2048 tracks/platter gives 1 GB/plat-platter, or 5 GB capacity in the drive. (In this problem, we use the standard computer architecture definitions of MB = 2^{20} bytes and GB = 2^{30} bytes. Many hard disk manufacturers use MB = 1,000,000 bytes and GB = 1,000,000,000 bytes. These definitions are close, but not equivalent.)

Disk Capacity (II)

11.9 A manufacturer wishes to design a hard disk with a capacity of 30 GB or more (using the standard definition of 1 GB = 2^{30} bytes). If the technology used to manufacture the disks allows 1024-byte sectors, 2048 sectors/track, and 4096 tracks/platter, how many platters are required? (Assume a fixed number of sectors per track.)

Solution

Multiplying bytes per sector times sectors per track times tracks per platter gives a capacity of 8 GB (8×2^{30} bytes) per platter. Therefore, 4 platters will be required to give a total capacity of ≥ 30 GB.

Fixed versus Variable Number of Tracks/Sector

11.10 The innermost track on a hard disk platter has a radius of 0.25 in (i.e., is located at 0.25 in from the center of the spindle). The outermost track has a radius of 1.75 in. What is the ratio of the capacity of the disk if a variable number of tracks per sector is used compared to the capacity if a fixed number of tracks/sector is used? Assume that each track has as many sectors as it can hold, neglect issues related to the fact that the number of sectors on a track has to be an integer, and assume that there are many tracks on the disk. (Yes, this can be done without knowing the number of tracks or number of sectors on any one track.)

Solution

In both schemes, the number of tracks on the platter is the same, so the ratio of capacities will be the same as the ratio of the number of sectors in an average track. In the fixed number of sectors/track scheme, the number of sectors on each track is determined by the number that can be fit on the innermost track, and all tracks have the same capacity. Using a variable number of sectors per track, the amount of space a sector takes up on a track will be the same for all tracks, so the ratio of the capacity of the average track to that of the innermost track is equal to the ratio of the length of the average track to the length of the innermost track. Since the capacity of each track in the fixed number of sectors scheme is the same as the capacity of the innermost track, this ratio will be the ratio of the total capacities of the two schemes.

Circumference is linear with radius, so the average-length track will be the one halfway between the innermost and outermost tracks. The innermost track has a radius of 0.25 in, and the outermost has a ratio of 1.75 in, for a difference of 1.5 in. Half of that is 0.75 in, which when added to the radius of the innermost track gives a radius of 1.0 in for the average track. The ratio of the circumferences of two tracks is the same as the ratio of their radii, so the average track will have 4 times the capacity of the innermost track, and the variable-number-of-sectors scheme will give 4 times as much capacity on the disk as the fixed-number-of-sectors scheme.

Disk Access Times (I)

11.11 A hard disk with one platter rotates at 15,000 r/min and has 1024 tracks, each with 2048 sectors. The disk head starts at track 0 (tracks are numbered from 0 to 1023). The disk then receives a request to access a random sector on a random track. If the seek time of the disk head is 1 ms for every 100 tracks it must cross:

a. What is the average seek time?

b. What is the average rotational latency?

c. What is the transfer time for a sector?

d. What is the total average time to resolve a request?

Solution

a. Since the disk head starts at track 0, it will have to travel 0 tracks to handle a request to track 0, 1 track to handle a request to track 1, and so on, up to 1023 tracks to a request to track 1023. On average, the head will have to travel half of the way to the outermost track, or 511.5 tracks. At 100 tracks/ms, this gives an average seek time of 5.115 ms.

b. At 15,000 r/min, each rotation takes 4 ms. The average rotational latency is half the rotation time, or 2 ms.

c. Each rotation takes 4 ms. There are 2048 sectors per track, so each sector takes $4 ms/2048 = 1.95$ microseconds to pass under the read/write head. Therefore, the transfer time is 1.95 microseconds.

d. The average access time is just the sum of the three components, or 7.117 ms (rounding to four significant digits). As stated in the text, this neglects the time to transmit the data to the processor.

Disk Access Times (II)

11.12 Researchers have been investigating systems in which the operating system deliberately places the most-frequently-used files on the outer tracks of a system's hard disk to improve performance.

a. Why would this improve performance?

b. Would this approach give better performance on a system that had a variable or a fixed number of tracks per sector?

c. In a system that used a fixed number of sectors per track, does it matter whether the operating system places the most-frequently-used files on the inner or outer tracks, or is it just important that they be placed close together?

d. How does your answer to c change on a system that uses a variable number of sectors per track?

Solution

a. If files are randomly assigned to tracks, the most-frequently-used files will tend to be spread evenly across the disk and I/O requests will also tend to be evenly spread across the disk. Placing the most-frequently-used files on the outer tracks means that most I/O requests will be to those tracks. This reduces the average number of tracks that the disk head has to cross to satisfy a memory request, reducing the average seek time.

b. In a fixed-sectors-per-track system, all tracks contain the same number of sectors, and that number is determined by the number of sectors that fit on the innermost track of the disk. In a variable-sectors-per-track system, the innermost track generally has the same number of sectors as in a fixed-sectors-per-track system, but the outermost tracks contain many more sectors and thus much more data. This means that the most-frequently-used files can be placed on fewer tracks on a disk that has a variable number of sectors per track than on a disk that has a fixed number of sectors per track, since the most-frequently-used files are placed on the outermost tracks. Thus, the average number of tracks that the disk head has to cover will be smaller when this approach is used on a disk that has a variable number of tracks per sector, leading to lower seek times and better performance.

c. On a disk that has a fixed number of sectors per track, all of the tracks on a disk contain the same amount of storage, making them equivalent. It doesn't matter which set of adjacent tracks are used to hold the most-frequently-used files on such a system, because all tracks are the same. The performance benefit comes from placing the most-frequently-used files close together, reducing average seek time.

d. On disks that have a variable number of sectors per track, the outermost tracks contain more data than the innermost tracks. Thus, placing the most-frequently-used files on the outermost tracks allows them to be compacted onto fewer tracks than placing them on the innermost tracks, so placing the most-frequently-used files on the outermost tracks will give better performance.

Disk Scheduling Policy (I)

11.13 Which of the three disk scheduling policies discussed in this chapter would be best in each of the following situations:

a. A general-purpose system where bandwidth is important but any given I/O request must be completed in a reasonable amount of time

b. A system where it is known that the program will only make one I/O request at a time

c. A system where bandwidth is absolutely critical but there is no limit on how long a given request may take to complete

Solution

a. In this case, LOOK scheduling is probably best. LOOK generally delivers better bandwidth than FCFS, and it can also guarantee that any given request will be handled relatively quickly.

b. Here, there really isn't a scheduling policy, since there's only one outstanding I/O request at any time. With only one request outstanding, all three policies will handle requests in the order that they are made. Given that, a FCFS policy should be used, since it is simplest.

c. SSTF should be used here. It generally has the highest bandwidth of the three policies, but it does have the problem that any given request can be arbitrarily delayed by other requests for tracks closer to the disk head. In this case, that is acceptable, making SSTF the best choice.

Disk Scheduling Policy (II)

11.14 If the read/write head of a disk starts at track 100, and the disk has requests pending to tracks 43, 158, 44, 203, and 175 (in that order of arrival), what is the total number of tracks that the read/write head will cross to satisfy these requests under the FCFS, SSTF, and LOOK policies? (For LOOK scheduling, assume that the head starts out moving outward from track 100, toward higher track numbers.) Include the destination track, but not the starting track, in the number of tracks crossed, so moving from track 100 to track 90 would cross 10 tracks.

Solution

FCFS: Requests are handled in order of arrival, so the head goes to track 43 first, crossing 57 tracks, 158 second, crossing 115 tracks, and so on, for a total of 473 tracks.

SSTF: Track 44 is closest to the read/write head, so its request gets handled first, followed by track 43. The sequence in which the requests get handled is 44, 43, 158, 175, and 203, for a total of 217 tracks crossed.

LOOK: The disk head starts by sweeping outward, handling all of the requests to outward tracks, then it turns around and comes inward. The order that requests get handled in is: 158, 175, 203, 44, and 43, for a total of 263 tracks crossed.

CHAPTER 12

Multiprocessors

12.1   Objectives

This chapter concludes our discussion of computer architecture and organization by providing an introduction to multiprocessor systems. After completing this chapter, you should

1. Be familiar with basic multiprocessor architectures, including centralized-memory and distributed-memory systems
2. Be able to discuss speedup in multiprocessor systems, including common causes of less-than-linear and superlinear speedup
3. Understand the difference between shared-memory and message-passing systems, and be able to compare these two approaches
4. Understand the MESI cache-coherence protocol and the requirements of strong memory consistency

12.2   Introduction

As their name suggests, multiprocessor systems utilize more than one processor to improve performance. Early multiprocessor systems used multiple processors to improve throughput by executing independent jobs on different processors. Since then, there has been a great deal of research on using multiprocessors to reduce the execution times of individual applications by dividing a single program's work across multiple processors.

Multiprocessors are attractive because of the technological and practical limitations on improving processor performance at any given time. As we discussed, techniques such as instruction-level parallelism, caches, and pipelining deliver diminishing performance improvements as the amount of chip area devoted to them increases, limiting the maximum performance that can be achieved with a single processor. By dividing a single program's work among multiple processors, multiprocessors can achieve greater performance than is possible with a single processor in any given fabrication technology.

12.3 Speedup and Performance

Like designers of uniprocessor systems, multiprocessor architects often measure performance in terms of *speedup*. In the context of multiprocessors, speedup generally refers to how much faster a program runs on a system with *n* processors than it does on a system with one processor of the same type. Figure 12-1 shows an example speedup graph. The vertical axis plots the speedup over the uniprocessor system, while the horizontal axis is the number of processors in the system. Note that the origin for these graphs is often at $(1, 1)$, rather than $(0, 0)$, because speedup is measured relative to a one-processor machine, not a zero-processor machine.

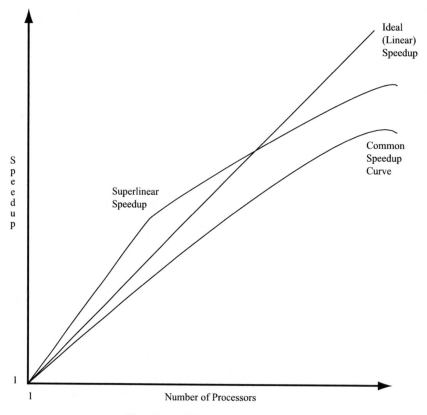

Fig. 12-1. Example speedup graph.

12.3.1 LIMITATIONS ON SPEEDUP

An ideal multiprocessor system would have *linear speedup*—the execution time of a program on an *n*-processor system would be $1/n$th of the execution time on a one-processor system. This speedup rate is represented by the Ideal (Linear) Speedup line on the example graph. In practice, systems generally display speedup curves similar to the Common Speedup Curve shown in the graph. When the number of processors is small, the system achieves near-linear speedup. As the number of processors increases, the speedup curve diverges from the ideal, eventually flattening out or even decreasing.

There are many reasons why systems generally display less-than-linear speedup. The three most common reasons are as follows:

1. *Interprocessor communication*—In a multiprocessor system, whenever one processor generates (computes) a value that is needed by the fraction of the program running on another processor, that value must be communicated to the processor(s) that need it, which takes time. On a uniprocessor system, the entire program runs on one processor, so there is no time lost to interprocessor communication.

2. *Synchronization*—Another complication introduced by multiprocessors is that it is often necessary to synchronize the processors to ensure that they have all completed some phase of the program before any processor begins working on the next phase of the program. For example, programs that simulate physical phenomena, such as airflow over an object, generally divide time into steps of fixed duration and require that all processors have completed their simulation of a given timestep before any processor can proceed to the next, so that the simulation of the next timestep can be based on the results of the simulation of the current timestep. This synchronization requires interprocessor communication, introducing overhead that is not found in uniprocessor systems.

3. *Load balancing*—In many parallel applications, it is difficult to divide the program across the processors such that each processor's chunk of the work takes the same amount of time. When this is not possible, some of the processors complete their tasks early and are then idle waiting for the others to finish. This uneven distribution of tasks across the processors increases the overall execution time, because all of the processors are not in use at all times.

In general, the greater the amount of time required to communicate between processors, the lower the speedup that programs running on the system will achieve. Inter-processor communication latency obviously affects the amount of time required to communicate data between the parts of the program running on each processor. It also affects the amount of time required for synchronization, because synchronization is typically implemented out of a sequence of inter-processor communications. Load balance is not generally affected by interprocessor communication time, but systems with low communication latencies can take advantage of algorithms that dynamically balance an application's load by moving work from processors that are taking longer to complete their part of the program to other processors so that no processors are ever idle. Systems with longer communication latencies benefit less from these algorithms because communication latency determines how long it takes to move a unit of work from one processor to another.

12.3.2 SUPERLINEAR SPEEDUP

In the last section, we stated that the ideal speedup on a multiprocessor system was equal to the number of processors in the system. In general this is true, but some programs exhibit *superlinear speedup*, achieving speedup of greater than n on n-processor systems. Superlinear speedups occur because programs are sometimes more efficient on multiprocessor systems than on uniprocessor systems, allowing each of the processors in an n-processor multiprocessor to complete its fraction of the program in less than $1/n$th of the program's execution time on a uniprocessor.

There are two common reasons why programs achieve superlinear speedup:

1. *Increased cache size*—In a multiprocessor, each processor often has as much cache memory associated with it as the single processor in a uniprocessor. Thus, the total amount of cache memory in the multiprocessor is often greater than the total amount of cache in a uniprocessor. When a program whose data does not fit in the cache of a uniprocessor is run on a multiprocessor, the data required by the portion of the program that runs on each processor may fit in that processor's cache, reducing the average memory latency and improving performance. If the uniprocessor that the multiprocessor was being compared to had as much cache memory as the total cache memory in the multiprocessor, the program would not display superlinear speedup.

2. *Better structure*—Some programs perform less work when executed on a multiprocessor than they do when executed on a uniprocessor, allowing them to achieve superlinear speedups. For example, programs that search for the best answer to a problem by examining all of the possibilities sometimes exhibit superlinear speedup because the multiprocessor version examines the possibilities in a different order, one that allows it to rule out more possibilities without examining them. Because the multiprocessor version has to examine fewer total possibilities than the uniprocessor program, it can complete the search with greater than linear speedup. Rewriting the uniprocessor program to examine possibilities in the same order as the multiprocessor program would improve its performance, bringing the speedup back down to linear or less.

12.4 Multiprocessor Systems

Multiprocessors consist of a set of processors connected by a communications network, as shown in Fig. 12-2. Early multiprocessors often used processors that had been specifically designed for use in a multiprocessor to improve efficiency. In recent years this has changed, and most current multiprocessors use the same processors that are found in contemporary uniprocessor systems, taking advantage of the large sales volumes of uniprocessors to lower prices. As the number of transistors that can be placed on a chip increases, features to support multiprocessor systems are being integrated into processors intended primarily for the uniprocessor

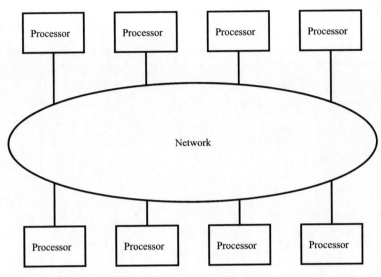

Fig. 12-2. Basic multiprocessor.

market, leading to more efficient multiprocessor systems built around these processors.

The design of networks for multiprocessors is a complex topic that is beyond the scope of this book. For this chapter, we will treat the network as a "black box" that allows any processor to communicate with any other processor, ignoring the details of how this is done.

Multiprocessors can have either centralized or distributed memory systems. In a centralized memory system, as shown in Fig. 12-3, there is one memory system for the entire multiprocessor, and the memory references from all of the processors go to that memory system. In a distributed memory system, as shown in Fig. 12-4, each processor has its own memory system, which it can access directly. To obtain data that is stored in some other processor's memory, a processor must communicate with it to request the data.

Centralized memory systems have the advantage that all of the data in the memory is accessible to any processor, and that there is never a problem with multiple copies of a given datum existing. However, the bandwidth of the centralized memory system does not grow as the number of processors in the machine increases and the latency of the network is added to the latency of each memory reference. To address these limitations, many centralized-memory multiprocessors provide a local cache for each processor and only send requests that miss in the processor's cache over the network to the main memory. Requests that hit in the cache are handled quickly and do not travel over the network, reducing the amount of data that the network must carry and allowing the main memory to support more processors. However, more than one cache may have a copy of a given memory location, creating the same coherence problem that occurs in distributed memory systems.

Distributed memory systems offer the advantage that each processor has its own local memory system. This means that there is more total bandwidth in the memory system than in a centralized memory system, and that the latency to complete a

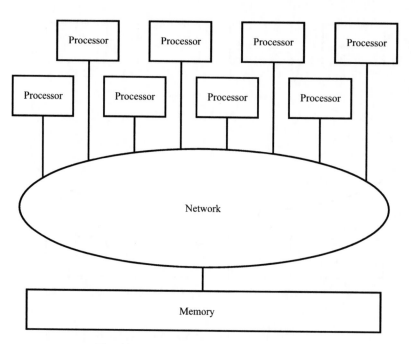

Fig. 12-3. Centralized-memory multiprocessor.

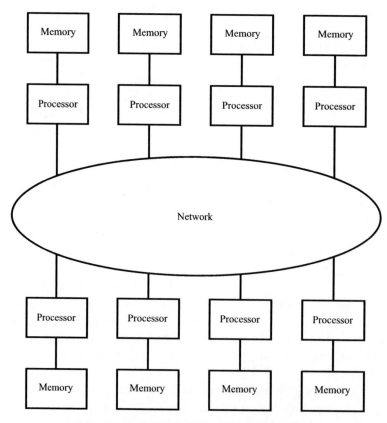

Fig. 12-4. Distributed-memory multiprocessor.

memory request is lower, because each processor's memory is located physically close to it. However, these systems have the disadvantage that only some of the data in the memory is directly accessible by each processor, since a processor can only read and write its local memory system. Accessing data in another processor's memory requires communication through the network. Also, there is the possibility that two or more copies of a given datum could exist in different processors' memories, leading to different processors having different values for the same variable. This is called the *coherence* problem and is a major source of complexity in shared-memory systems, which are discussed in Section 12.6. Message-passing systems, which are covered in Section 12.5, do not have as much of a problem with coherence as shared-memory systems, because they do not allow processors to read and write data contained in other processors' memories.

Centralized memory systems are often the better design when the number of processors in the system is small. For these systems, a single memory system may be able to meet the bandwidth demands of the processors, particularly if each processor has a local cache memory. When a centralized memory system is able to meet the bandwidth demands of the processors, the reduction in design and programming complexity that comes from not having to manage multiple independent memories is a strong argument in favor of this type of memory system. As the number of processors grows, it becomes impossible for a centralized memory system to meet the bandwidth needs of the processors, and it becomes necessary to use a distributed memory system. Distributed memory systems are also used when the latency of the network is long enough that using a centralized memory system would make memory latencies unacceptably long, even if a centralized memory system could meet the bandwidth needs of the processors.

12.5   Message-Passing Systems

There are two major programming models for multiprocessor systems: shared-memory and message-passing. In shared-memory systems, the memory system handles inter-processor communication by allowing all processors to see data written by any processor. In contrast, message-passing systems communicate through explicit messages. To send a message, a processor executes an explicit SEND(data, destination) operation (generally a procedure call) that instructs the hardware to send the specified data to the destination processor. Later, the destination processor executes a RECEIVE(buffer) operation to copy the sent data into the specified buffer, making it available for use. If the processor responsible for sending the data has not executed its SEND operation before the RECEIVE is executed, the RECEIVE operation waits for the SEND to complete, enforcing the order of SEND and RECEIVE operations. This process is illustrated in Fig. 12-5.

In message-passing systems, each processor has its own address space, and processors cannot read or write data contained in another processor's address space. Because of this, many message-passing systems are implemented as distributed-memory machines, since they can reap the latency benefits of associating a memory

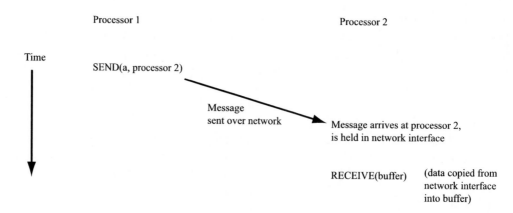

Fig. 12-5. Message-passing.

with each processor without the complexity of having to allow processors to access each other's memories.

12.6 Shared-Memory Systems

In shared-memory systems, communication is implicit, rather than explicit. Shared-memory systems provide a single address space that all of the processors can read and write. When a processor writes a location in the address space, any subsequent reads of that location by any processor see the result of the write, as illustrated in Fig. 12-6. The system performs any interprocessor communication required to make memory operations visible on all of the processors.

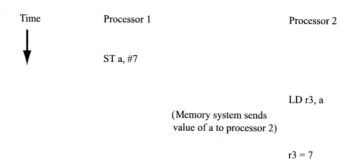

Fig. 12-6. Shared-memory example.

12.6.1 MEMORY CONSISTENCY MODELS

Much of the complexity involved in designing a shared-memory system comes from the fact that the multiprocessor must present the illusion that there is a single memory system despite the fact that there are multiple physical memories in the machine. Shared-memory multiprocessors can be implemented as either centralized-memory or distributed-memory systems, but either of these designs will have cache memories associated with each processor to reduce memory latency, creating the possibility that multiple copies of a given datum will exist in different caches. The shared-memory system is responsible for specifying the conditions under which multiple copies of a datum can exist, and for enforcing those conditions so that programmers can write programs that execute correctly.

The *memory consistency model* of a multiprocessor defines when memory operations executed on one processor become visible on other processors. The most commonly used memory consistency model is *strong consistency*, which dictates that the memory system act exactly as if there were only one memory in the computer that different processors take turns using. Other consistency models exist, most of which implement various forms of *relaxed consistency* by allowing different processors to have different values for a given datum until the program requests that all memories be made consistent.

12.6.2 STRONG CONSISTENCY

In systems that provide strong consistency (also called sequential consistency), the memory system may execute multiple memory operations in parallel, but these parallel operations must generate the same result as if they were executed on a system that had a single memory system that was shared by all the processors, as illustrated in Fig. 12-7. Providing strong consistency in a shared-memory multiprocessor generally makes the system easier to program, because data written by any memory operation becomes immediately visible to all of the processors in the system. In contrast, systems with relaxed consistency may require more programmer effort, but they often achieve better performance than systems with strong consistency because the relaxed consistency model allows more memory operations to be performed in parallel.

To implement strong consistency, the memory system must meet two requirements:

1. On any processor, the results of a program must be the same as if the memory operations in the program occurred in the order that they appear in the program. Out-of-order superscalar processors generally require this of any program they execute, so it is possible to implement strong consistency on an out-of-order processor.

2. On all of the processors, the results of all memory operations must be the same as if they had occurred in some sequential order. Essentially, this means that if one processor sees two memory operations happening in a particular order, all processors must see those operations happen in the same order.

Strong consistency allows references to different addresses to proceed in parallel, because executing references to different addresses in parallel gives the same results as if they were executed sequentially. Multiple reads to the same address can also proceed in parallel, because they will return the same result regardless of whether they are executed in parallel or sequentially. However, reads and writes to an address or multiple writes to an address have to be serialized so that each write can be seen to have executed at a specific time.

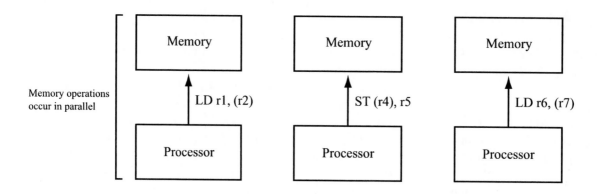

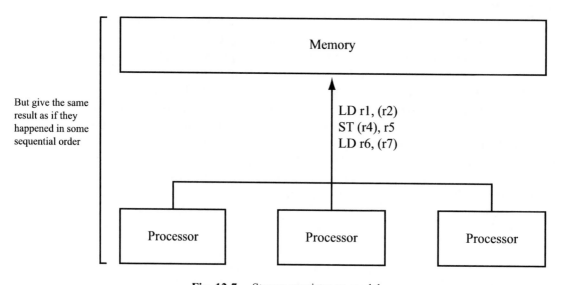

Fig. 12-7.   Strong consistency model.

12.6.3 CACHE COHERENCE

The *cache-coherence protocol* of a shared-memory multiprocessor defines how data may be shared and replicated across processors. While the memory consistency model defines when programs running on the processors will see operations executed on other processors, the cache-coherence protocol defines the specific set of actions that are executed to keep each processor's view of the memory system consistent. Generally, cache-coherence protocols operate on cache lines of data at a time, communicating an entire line between processors when necessary, rather than just sending a single word.

Cache-coherence protocols can be divided into two categories: invalidation-based and update-based. In an invalidation-based protocol, as illustrated in Fig. 12-8, multiple processors are allowed to have read-only copies of a cache line if no

Events	Processor 1	Processor 2	Processor 3
Start	No Copy	No Copy	No Copy
Processor 1 reads line	Read-Only Copy	No Copy	No Copy
Processor 2 reads line	Read-Only Copy	Read-Only Copy	No Copy
Processor 3 writes line (other copies invalidated)	No Copy	No Copy	Writable Copy
Processor 2 reads line	No Copy	Read-Only Copy	Read-Only Copy

Fig. 12-8. Invalidation-based cache-coherence protocol.

processor has a writable copy of the line. Only one processor can have a writable copy of a given line at any time, and no processors may have a read-only copy if any processor has a writable copy. When a processor wants to write a line that one or more other processors have copies of (either read-only or writable), the line is *invalidated*, forcing all processors that currently have copies of the line to give up their copies so that the requesting processor can get a copy in the appropriate state.

Update-based protocols, as illustrated in Fig. 12-9, allow multiple processors to have writable copies of a line. When a processor writes a line that one or more other processors have copies of, an *update* occurs, transmitting the new value of the data in the line to all of the sharing processors. Depending on the application, either an invalidation-based or update-based protocol may deliver better performance.

Events	Processor 1	Processor 2	Processor 3
Start	No Copy	No Copy	No Copy
Processor 1 reads line	Writable Copy	No Copy	No Copy
Processor 2 reads line	Writable Copy	Writable Copy	No Copy
Processor 3 writes line (updates sent to processors 1 and 2)	Writable Copy	Writable Copy	Writable Copy
Processor 2 reads line (sees value written by Processor 3)	Writable Copy	Writable Copy	Writable Copy

Fig. 12-9. Update-based cache-coherence protocol.

Invalidation-based protocols generally deliver better performance on applications with substantial data locality, because update-based protocols require a communication each time a shared line is written. Invalidation-based protocols only incur communication when a processor that does not have a copy of a line needs to access the line or a processor with a read-only copy of a line needs to write the line, which can result in much lower communication costs if processors perform many memory operations between the time they first access a line and the time some other processor accesses the line.

In contrast, update-based protocols can achieve better performance on programs where one processor repeatedly updates a datum that is read by many other processors. In this case, it can be more efficient to send each new value of the datum to all of the processors that need it than to invalidate all of the copies of the line containing the datum each time it is written.

12.6.4　MESI PROTOCOL

The MESI protocol is a commonly used invalidation-based cache-coherence protocol. In MESI, each line in a processor's cache is assigned one of four states to track which caches have copies of the line: modified, exclusive, shared, or invalid. The invalid state means that the processor does not have a copy of the line. Any access to the line will require that the shared-memory system send a request message to the memory that contains the line to get a copy of the line. The shared state means that the processor has a copy of the line, and that one or more other processors also have copies. The processor may read from the line, but any attempt to write the line requires that the other copies of the line be invalidated. If a line is in the exclusive state, the processor is the only one that has a copy of the line, but it has not written the line since it acquired the copy. The modified state means that the processor is the only one with a copy of the line, and it has written the line since it acquired the copy. In both the exclusive and modified states, the processor may read and write the line freely.

MESI distinguishes between the exclusive and modified states so that the system can figure out where the most recent value of a line is stored. If a line is exclusive in a processor's cache, the copy of the line in the main memory is up-to-date, and the processor can just discard the line if it needs to invalidate the line. If it is modified, the processor has the most recent value of the line, and it must write the line back to the main memory when it is invalidated. Figure 12-10 shows the state transitions in the MESI protocol.

12.6.5　BUS-BASED SHARED-MEMORY SYSTEMS

A common design for shared-memory systems is the bus-based system shown in Fig. 12-11. In these systems, a bus is used as the communications network that connects the processors to each other and the centralized memory system. Bus-based shared-memory systems are used because the bus allows a variable number of processors to communicate with each other without changing the hardware and because the bus makes it easy to implement cache coherence. The primary

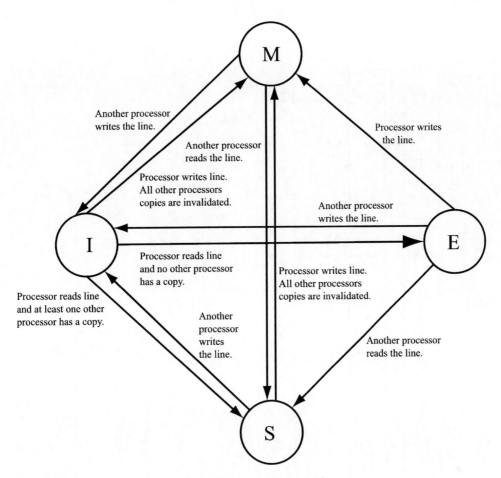

Fig. 12-10. MESI protocol.

disadvantage of bus-based shared-memory systems is that the bandwidth available over the bus does not grow as the number of processors in the system increases, making them unsuitable for multiprocessors with more than a few processors.

Maintaining cache coherence in a bus-based multiprocessor is easy because each processor in the system can observe the state of the memory bus, allowing it to see any requests that other processors make to the main memory. This is called *cache snooping*, because all of the caches spy on the actions of the other processors. When one processor makes a memory reference to an address that is contained in another processor's cache, the other processor can see the request, respond with the required data, and modify the state of its copy appropriately without ever involving the main memory. Thus, memory references on a bus-based shared-memory system can actually complete faster if some other processor has a copy of the required line than if the line has to be read from the main memory.

12.6.6 SYNCHRONIZATION

One problem with shared-memory systems is that there is little ordering of operations between processors. In message-passing systems, a processor that

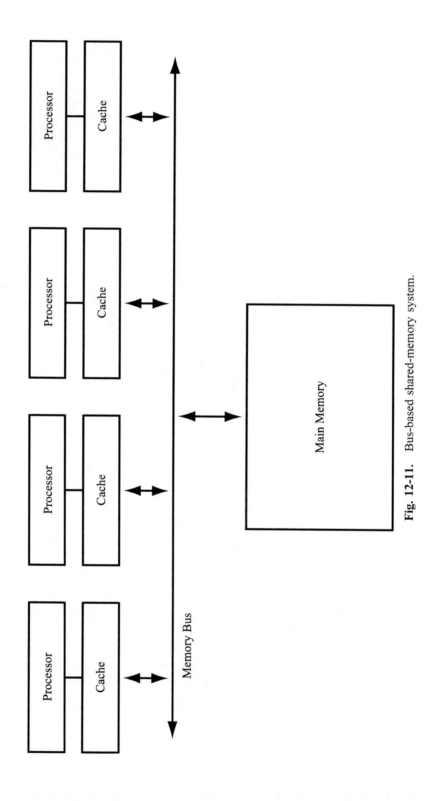

Fig. 12-11. Bus-based shared-memory system.

executes a RECEIVE operation knows that the sending processor has executed its matching SEND before the RECEIVE completes, because the RECEIVE cannot complete until the SEND is done. In shared-memory systems, memory references can occur at any time, so programs must perform explicit synchronization operations when it is necessary that operations occur in a particular order.

There are two common synchronization operations: *barriers* and *locks*. Barriers require that each processor in the multiprocessor reach the start of the barrier operation before any processor can complete the barrier. They are useful when a program executes in phases that need to complete before the next phase can begin. For example, a parallel weather simulation might use barriers to ensure that all processors had finished simulating a given hour's weather before allowing any of them to start simulating the next hour.

Locks ensure that only one processor at a time accesses a given variable or executes a given procedure. When a processor executes a lock operation, it stalls until it has been granted access to the lock, at which point it may proceed. When the processor is done with the variable or procedure, it executes an unlock operation to allow another processor access.

There are a number of different implementations of barriers and locks, with different implementations being best suited to different networks, processor architectures, and numbers of processors. A programmer's choice of how to implement synchronization operations and where synchronization operations should be placed in a program has a great deal of impact on the performance of a program, and this is one of the more significant challenges to learning to program multiprocessors effectively.

12.7 Comparing Message-Passing and Shared Memory

It is likely that message-passing and shared memory will continue to be the dominant multiprocessor communication paradigms for the foreseeable future. Each approach has its advantages and disadvantages that keep one method from being dominant over the other. The most significant advantage of shared-memory systems is that the computer handles communication, making it possible to write a parallel program without considering when data must be communicated from one processor to another. However, to achieve good performance, the programmer must consider how data is used by the processors to minimize inter-processor communication (requests, invalidations, and updates). This is particularly true on shared-memory systems with distributed memories, because the programmer must also think about which processor's memory should have the main copy of a piece of data.

The downside of shared-memory systems is that the programmer's ability to control inter-processor communication is limited, since all communication is handled by the system. On many systems, transferring a large block of data between processors is more efficient if it is done as one communication, which is not possible on shared-memory systems, since the hardware controls the amount of data transferred at one time. The system also controls when communication happens, making it difficult to send data to a processor that will need it later in order to keep the processor from having to request the data and then wait for it.

Message-passing systems can achieve greater efficiency than shared-memory systems by allowing the programmer to control inter-processor communication, but this comes at the cost of requiring that the programmer explicitly specify all communication in the program. Controlling communication can improve efficiency by allowing data to be communicated at the time it becomes available, instead of when it is needed, and by matching the amount of data communicated in each message to the needs of the application instead of the line size of the system that the application runs on. In addition, message-passing systems require fewer synchronization operations than shared-memory systems, because SEND and RECEIVE operations provide a great deal of the required synchronization by themselves.

In general, message-passing systems are very attractive for many scientific computations, because the regular structure of these applications makes it easier to determine what data must be communicated between processors. Shared-memory systems are more attractive for irregular applications, because of the difficulty of determining what communication is required at the time the program is written. Because each programming model is best suited to a different set of applications, many multiprocessors are starting to provide support for both message-passing and shared-memory on the same system. This allows programmers to choose the programming model that best suits their application. It also allows *incremental parallelization*, in which a program is first written in a shared-memory style to reduce implementation time. Once the program is working correctly, time-critical communications are rewritten in message-passing to optimize performance, allowing the programmer to trade off additional implementation effort against improved performance at a fine grain.

12.8 Summary

This chapter has provided an introduction to multiprocessors, systems that combine multiple processors to improve performance. The performance of a single processor is limited by the underlying fabrication technology, and multiprocessors offer a technique to boost speed beyond this limit, albeit at significantly increased hardware cost. Multiprocessor performance is usually measured by the speedup of the multiprocessor over a single-processor system. The ideal speedup of a multiprocessor is equal to the number of processors in the system, although most programs achieve lower speedups than this due to communication, synchronization, and load-balancing costs. Some programs achieve superlinear speedups by being more efficient on multiprocessors than they are on uniprocessors.

The two main programming models for multiprocessors are message-passing and shared-memory. Message-passing systems require that the programmer insert explicit SEND and RECEIVE operations into the program to communicate data between processors, while shared-memory systems maintain a shared address space that allows any processor to see data written by any other processor. Message-passing systems are often more efficient than shared-memory systems, but shared-memory programs generally require less effort to implement than message-passing programs.

Multiprocessor systems are an area of active research. Research efforts focus on reducing communication and synchronization costs to improve performance, and on developing programming techniques that reduce the amount of effort required to achieve good speedups.

 Solved Problems

Communication and Synchronization Costs

12.1. Explain why communication and synchronization costs cause many programs to achieve lower than linear speedups on multiprocessors.

Solution

One way to look at this is that synchronization and communication costs are additional work that the parallel version of the program has to do that the sequential (one processor) version did not have to do. Thus, the total work that the multiprocessor version of a program has to do is the sum of the work that the sequential program had to do plus the synchronization and communication times. When this total work is divided among the n processors in a multi-processor, each processor has more work to do than $1/n$th of the original program, so the total speedup is less than n.

Load Balancing

12.2. Explain why poor load balancing leads to less-than-linear speedup.

Solution

In a multiprocessor, a program isn't done until each processor has completed its fraction of the overall program. If a program is poorly load-balanced, some of the processors have more than their share of work to do, so they take longer to complete their portion of the program than they would if the work were evenly divided, meaning that the overall execution time of the program is longer than it would be with an even work division.

Synchronization Cost

12.3. A program repeatedly executes a loop that has 120 iterations. Each iteration takes 10,000 cycles. On multiprocessor systems, 50,000 cycles are required to synchronize the processors once all iterations of the loop have completed.

    a.   What is the execution time of each loop on a uniprocessor system?

    b.   What is the execution time of each loop on a 2-processor system, and what is the speedup over the uniprocessor system?

    c.   What is the execution time of each loop on a 4-processor system, and what is the speedup over the uniprocessor system?

Solution

a. 120 iterations × 10,000 cycles = 1,200,000 cycles.

b. On a two-processor system, each processor would handle 60 iterations, for a base execution time of 600,000 cycles. Adding the communication time gives an execution time of 650,000 cycles and a speedup of 1.85.

c. Each processor executes 30 iterations, for an execution time of 350,000 cycles and a speedup of 3.43.

Communication Time

12.4. Assume the same parameters for the program as in Problem 12.3, but ignore synchronization time. Instead, assume that each iteration has a flat communication cost of 500 cycles per processor in the system (i.e., 1000 cycles/iteration on a two-processor system plus 500 cycles/iteration for each additional processor). What would the speedup be if the program was executed on a system with two, four, or eight processors?

Solution

With two processors, each processor executes 60 iterations. Each iteration has a base execution time of 10,000 cycles, plus 1000 cycles, for a total execution time of 660,000 cycles and a speedup of 1.82. With four processors, each processor executes 30 iterations, and the communication cost per iteration is 2000 cycles, so the execution time is 360,000 cycles and the speedup is 3.33. With eight processors, the communication time is 4000 cycles per iteration, there are 15 iterations per processor, and the execution time is 210,000 cycles. This gives a speedup of 5.71.

Load Balancing

12.5. A program consists of five tasks, which have execution times of 2000, 4000, 6000, 8000, and 10,000 cycles. It is not possible to divide the execution of one task among multiple processors, but there are no communication or synchronization costs. If the tasks are distributed across the processors to achieve the shortest execution time, what is the speedup for executing the program on:

a. Two processors

b. Four processors

c. Eight processors

Solution

On one processor, the program's execution time is 30,000 cycles, the sum of the execution times of the tasks.

a. The most even division of tasks among the processors gives 16,000 cycles of work to one processor and 14,000 to the other, so the execution time on two processors is 16,000 cycles, which gives a speedup of 1.875.

b. On four processors, the most even task distribution assigns 10,000 cycles of work to one processor, 8000 to the second, and 6000 to each of the other two. This gives an execution time of 10,000 cycles, for a speedup of 3.

c. On an eight-processor machine, the best division is to assign one task to each processor (leaving three with no work to do), which gives an execution time of 10,000 cycles (limited by the longest task) and a speedup of 3.

Superlinear Speedup

12.6. A program references 280 KB of data. When run on a multiprocessor, it displays less-than-linear speedup on two or four processors, but superlinear speedup on eight. What is the the most likely explanation for the superlinear speedup if each processor has 64 KB of cache?

Solution

The increased amount of cache in the multiprocessor system is the most likely explanation. With one, two, or four processors, the total amount of cache is less than the amount of data referenced. With eight processors, there is a total of 512 KB of cache in the system, which is greater than the 280 KB of data referenced by the program. Therefore, the entire data set can fit in the cache on eight processors, improving performance and allowing superlinear speedup.

Message-Passing Systems (I)

12.7. A message-passing program executes on two processors. In this system, the delay from when a message is sent until when it is available to be received on the destination processor is 1000 cycles, and it takes 500 cycles to complete a RECEIVE operation if the message being received is available.

a. What is the shortest-possible delay between when a message is sent and when the contents of the message are available for use by the program on the destination processor?

b. On cycle 100, the program running on processor 0 sends a message to processor 1. On cycle 200, the program running on processor 1 executes a RECEIVE operation to receive the message. When does the RECEIVE complete?

c. When would the RECEIVE operation from part **b** of this exercise complete if the program running on processor 1 executed the RECEIVE on cycle 2000 instead of cycle 200?

Solution

a. 1500 cycles. It takes 1000 cycles for the message to arrive at the destination processor, and another 500 for it to be received by the program running on the destination processor.

b. The way to approach this problem is to realize that the RECEIVE operation blocks until the message arrives at processor 1, then takes 500 cycles to complete. Since the message was sent on cycle 100, it arrives at processor 1 on cycle 1100, and the RECEIVE completes on cycle 1600.

c. In this case, the message still arrives at processor 1 on cycle 1100, since it was sent on cycle 100. However, the program running on processor 1 waits until cycle 2000 to execute the RECEIVE operation. Since the message that is being received has already arrived at processor 1 when the RECEIVE is executed, the RECEIVE completes in 500 cycles, on cycle 2500.

Message-Passing (II)

12.8. A message-passing program running on two processors executes the following sequence of tasks:

Processor 0	**Processor 1**
Compute for 1000 cycles	Compute for 500 cycles
Receive message 1	Send message 1 to processor 0
Compute for 2000 cycles	Compute for 500 cycles
Send message 2 to processor 1	Receive message 2
Compute for 5000 cycles	Compute for 7000 cycles

What is the total execution time of this program (i.e., when does the last task complete on the processor that takes longer)? Use the message timing parameters from Problem 12.7. For this problem, assume that a processor that sends a message is busy for the entire 1000-cycle time that it takes for the message to reach the destination processor.

Solution

The best approach to this problem is to track how events proceed on each processor. Both processors start at the same time. On cycle 500, processor 1 sends message 1 to processor 2, which arrives at cycle 1500. Processor 1 then computes for 500 cycles and tries to receive message 2 on cycle 2000. Processor 0 tries to start receiving message 1 on cycle 1000, but it doesn't arrive until cycle 1500, so the RECEIVE completes on cycle 2000. Processor 1 then computes for 2000 cycles and sends message 2 starting on cycle 4000, which arrives on cycle 5000. Processor 0 then computes for 5000 cycles, completing its task on cycle 10,000. Meanwhile, processor 1 has been waiting for message 2 since cycle 2000, and the RECEIVE finally completes on cycle 5500. Processor 1 then computes for 7000 cycles, finishing on cycle 12,500.

The total execution time for the program is the longer of the execution times on the two processors, so the execution time is 12,500 cycles.

MESI Protocol (I)

12.9. A four-processor shared-memory system implements the MESI protocol for cache coherence. For the following sequence of memory references, show the state of the line containing the variable a in each processor's cache after each reference is resolved. All processors start out with the line containing a invalid in their cache.

Operations:
read a (processor 0)
read a (processor 1)
read a (processor 2)
write a (processor 3)
read a (processor 0)

Solution

Operation	Processor 0	Processor 1	Processor 2	Processor 3
P0 reads a	E	I	I	I
P1 reads a	S	S	I	I
P2 reads a	S	S	S	I
P3 writes a	I	I	I	M
P0 reads a	S	I	I	S

MESI Protocol (II)

12.10. Suppose the protocol used on the system from Problem 12.9 returned a shared copy instead of an exclusive copy when a location that is not cached by any processor is read. What would the state of the memory location containing a be after each operation from that exercise then?

Solution

Operation	Processor 0	Processor 1	Processor 2	Processor 3
P0 reads a	S	I	I	I
P1 reads a	S	S	I	I
P2 reads a	S	S	S	I
P3 writes a	I	I	I	M
P0 reads a	S	I	I	S

Update-Based Protocols (I)

12.11. For the sequence of operations in Problem 12.9, show the state of the line on each processor if an update-based shared-memory protocol is used. Assume that the shared-memory protocol has three states: invalid, for when the node has no copy of the line; exclusive, when the node is the only node that has a copy of the line; and shared, when multiple nodes have copies of the line.

Solution

Operation	Processor 0	Processor 1	Processor 2	Processor 3
P0 reads a	E	I	I	I
P1 reads a	S	S	I	I
P2 reads a	S	S	S	I
P3 writes a	S	S	S	S
P0 reads a	S	S	S	S

Update-Based Protocols (II)

12.12. In the sequence of operations from Problem 12.11, how many update messages are required? Count one update message for each node that has to be told about the new value of a location. (This models the execution of an update-based protocol on a system with a network that only allows point-to-point communication. Systems that provide support for broadcasting data to all nodes, such as bus-based multiprocessors, may require fewer update messages.)

Solution

Update messages only occur when a location is written, and there is only one write in the sequence of operations (the write to *a* by processor 3). At the time the write occurs, three other processors have copies of *a*, so update messages have to be sent to each of them. Therefore, three update messages are required.

Consistency Models

12.13. a. Suggest some explanations for why relaxed consistency models might allow higher performance than strong consistency models.

    b. Why are relaxed consistency models more difficult to program for than strong consistency models?

(*Note*: This a more open-ended question than most of those found in this text, and not one for which a concrete answer can be found in the chapter.)

Solution

a. Strong consistency models require that all processors see the same view of the memory at all times, requiring that any change to the memory be made visible everywhere in the multiprocessor at once. This can require a large number of messages if changes to a given location are frequent. In contrast, relaxed consistency models generally only require that different processors' views of memory be made consistent at specific times, such as when requested by the program. This means that memory operations executed on one processor only need to be made visible to the other processors when the program requests, which can reduce the amount of communication required. For example, if a given processor performed 10 writes to a particular location between times that the program requested that the memory be made consistent, only the final value of the location would have to be transmitted to the other processors through update messages or cache line invalidations. In a strong memory consistency model, all 10 of the writes would have to be made visible to other processors, which would take more communication.

b. The main additional complexity involved in programming for a strong consistency model is that the programmer must decide when the memory should be made consistent and place requests that the memory be made consistent into the program. In addition, it is possible for different processors to have different values for a memory location that has been written since the last request that the memory be made consistent. This can lead to errors if the programmer is not careful.

Shared-Memory versus Message-Passing

12.14. For programs with each of the following sets of characteristics, would a shared-memory multiprocessor or a message-passing multiprocessor be a better choice, all other factors being the same?

a. Values tend to be computed well before they are used.
b. The control structure is very complicated, making it difficult to predict which data will be needed by each processor.

Solution

a. In this case, a message-passing system would be likely to deliver better performance because a message-passing system could send values to the processors that will need them when the values are computed, so that the values reach their destinations before they are needed. This hides the communication delay from the processors that need the values, improving performance. In contrast, a shared-memory system only communicates data when it is requested by a processor, so the requesting program must wait for the data to be sent before it can proceed.

b. A shared-memory system would likely be better for this program, because it implicitly communicates data to processors as they reference it. The programmer does not have to be able to predict all of the communication required by the program, which can be very hard in irregular applications.

To implement a program like this on a message-passing system, the programmer would have to either send all data values to any processor that might need them or have programs request data from the processors that have it when they need the data. Sending data to any processor that might need it results in unnecessary communication, while having programs request the data that they need effectively turns the message-passing system into a shared-memory system, except that programs must explicitly handle requests instead of relying on the hardware to handle them.

INDEX